Pound/Ford

Ezra Pound and Ford Madox Ford at Rapallo.
Courtesy of the Cornell University Library

Pound/Ford

The Story of a Literary Friendship

THE CORRESPONDENCE BETWEEN EZRA POUND
AND FORD MADOX FORD
AND THEIR WRITINGS ABOUT EACH OTHER

Edited and with an Introduction and Narrative
Commentary and Notes by
Brita Lindberg-Seyersted

A NEW DIRECTIONS BOOK

Manufactured in the United States of America
First published clothbound in 1982
Published simultaneously in Canada by George J. McLeod, Ltd., Toronto

Library of Congress Cataloging in Publication Data

Pound, Ezra, 1885-1972.
    Pound/Ford, the story of a literary friend-
ship.
    (A New Directions Book)
    Bibliography: p. 201
    Includes index.
    1. Pound, Ezra, 1885-1972—Correspondence.
2. Ford, Ford Madox, 1873-1939—Correspondence.
3. Poets, American—20th century—Correspondence.
4. Novelists, English—20th century—Correspondence.
I. Ford, Ford Madox, 1873-1939.   II. Lindberg-
Seyersted, Brita.   III. Title.
PS3531.082Z487   1982   826'.912'08 [B]   82-2255

ISBN 0-8112-0833-8   AACR2

New Directions Books are published for James Laughlin
by New Directions Publishing Corporation
80 Eighth Avenue, New York 10011

Contents

Introduction

The friendship between Ezra Pound and Ford Madox Ford lasted for thirty years. It began in London and continued in Paris; it was maintained by steady but irregular contacts throughout the years when the vicissitudes of life placed them in different regions and circumstances. After his death Ford was still present in Pound's memory as a living force and as a touchstone for critical standards. In the early London years they saw a great deal of each other; during certain periods there were probably daily contacts, highlighted with stimulating discussion and lively conspiracy. Later, when new interests and preoccupations entered their lives, they naturally met less often, but their support of each other—in writing and through other kinds of actions—as well as their joint efforts to promote good literature created strong and lasting bonds. Pound very actively supported Ford's founding of the *Transatlantic Review* in Paris; they strove to keep up the artistic standards of the various literary magazines to which they contributed: *Poetry, The Little Review, The Dial, The New Review.* During Pound's first months in London it was Ford's *English Review* that supplied him with badly needed funds; decades later it was Pound who helped Ford out with personal short-term loans. They were on the lookout for jobs for each other—not always finding a grateful response at the receiving end; Pound was especially recalcitrant in later years about accepting offers or suggestions of lecturing or teaching jobs in the United States. Even after Pound had settled permanently in Rapallo, they met now and then: in Paris where Pound came fairly regularly in the 1920s and early 1930s, or, less often, in Italy. Their last meeting took place in New York City, under rather inauspicious circumstances: Ford was ill, and Pound was depressed.

Throughout these years their friendship was without ruptures, quarrels, or serious disagreements. True, they sometimes disagreed and showed their irritation, be it at an incomprehensible way of writing or at a stubborn unwillingness to take no for an answer, and there were whole aspects of their lives they never discussed, if we are to judge from their correspondence and their writings about each other: family, love, politics. It was indeed a *literary* relationship. What strikes one above all about their long friendship, as it is reflected in letters and other writings and in contacts and conversations which are recorded, are the ties of warm affection and unfailing loyalty that held them together through thick and thin, right through their final voluntary exiles.

In spite of different sociocultural backgrounds Pound and Ford had much in common. With varying emphases they drew on the same literary traditions: Pre-Raphaelitism, Browning, the Nineties; Flaubert, James, Conrad, and Hardy were figures rated highly by both of them. They shared other more specific and random likes and dislikes: Milton was rejected for his inversions and his rhetoric; Landor was appreciated; Joyce's early work found favor with them as being successfully experimental, whereas his "Work in Progress"—eventually published as *Finnegans Wake*—seemed a dead end; their response to Wordsworth was mixed and, at any rate, lukewarm. They united in an aversion to traditional (read: pedantic and one-sided) academicism, which they saw epitomized in a dehumanized form of German philology. This same academicism also existed in the land of Shakespeare and Keats (neither of whom was an undisputable hero); here it took the form of scholarship devoted to studying the proverbial laundry lists of deceased writers and letters from their illiterate mistresses. Sharing a cosmopolitan outlook Pound and Ford desired a nonparochial standard in art, "a Weltlitteratur standard," as Pound said. They professed to dislike didactic writing, although much of Pound's prose is just that. He admitted he was guilty of "the missionary sperrit."[1] However, to work for the reader's personal improvement was alien to both of them.

Although young Pound was said to imitate Ford's behavior down to the Fordian "whisper," he never adopted the patronizing pose, the "Olympian manner," as Ford himself euphemistically termed it.[2] Stephen Crane defended Ford: since Ford patronized everybody, he would be sure to patronize Almighty God, too, when that day came, but God would get used to it, "for Hueffer is all right." One of Ford's favorite poses was that of the English Gentleman; he was willy-nilly attracted to the image of the English Tory, "with his horse-sense, his scepticism, his individual honesty."[3] Pound's prewar persona was that of the Eccentric Artist; less given to posing than Ford, he usually turned out, on personal acquaintance, to be gentle and rather shy, not at all the cocksure, blustering loudmouth that rumor made him out to be.

Less exalted aspects of daily life, such as eating and dancing, were also interests common to the two friends. It is no coincidence—in fact it could almost be taken as proof that Ford *is* the model for the Stylist of section X of *Mauberley*—that Pound lets him offer "succulent cooking"; Ford took a semiprofessional interest in food, and Pound was known for his *gourmandise*.

The main areas where Pound and Ford meet can be summarized thus: their love for and knowledge of Mediterranean culture; their dedication to literature; and their unselfish and tireless promotion of writers and writing. As a culmination of his career Ford put his love of his preferred culture into two books; the Mediterranean culture dominates Pound's entire production. Ford believed that man is explicable only by his imaginative literature, and as one of his Olivet students said, to "write honestly and well" was the most important thing in the world for him.[4] Pound's ambition went beyond himself and aimed at purifying a whole civilization. He linked the health of a country's literature to that nation's power to survive. There was an impersonal quality to Pound's commitment: "As a writer," he said, "I am given to no one and to all men."[5] This devotion to literature exacted personal sacrifices, from them and from those close to them: the egotism of "an old man mad about writing"[6] and the paranoiac obsession of the crusader were the negative aspects of this passion.

With little regard for personal likes and dislikes they assisted and promoted other writers: Lawrence, Lewis, Joyce, Eliot, Hemingway, and countless others. At Ford's death there lay waiting for him great numbers of manuscripts from young authors seeking advice and help. Pound's tutoring stretches from frank criticism of his friend William Carlos Williams' early efforts to advice dispensed to the international pilgrims who flocked around him on the lawn of St. Elizabeths Hospital in Washington, D.C. The best critic, Pound thought, was the one who did "the next job."[7] It was natural that he should give so much time and energy to promoting other artists and writers, in an almost impersonal manner. To him the proven quality was perhaps less important than the promised possibility. One suspects that he did not actually *read* the works of his contemporaries very closely, at least not their prose (or novels), with a few notable exceptions, such as *The Waste Land.*

Though generous and fair as private critics, there was one thing neither could endure: stupidity. Needless to say, they made enemies in several camps.

The inevitable lacunae in the association between Pound and Ford resulted, on the one hand, from Ford's problematic attitude to English upper-class culture, and on the other hand, Pound's absorption in economics and his attempts to locate the sociopolitical ills that, in his view, threatened to destroy our civilization. Pound felt that his friend's hanging on to outmoded ideas limited his outlook and creativity; Ford declined to review Pound's *ABC of Economics,* ostensibly for lack of competence on the subject. While Pound was moving toward Fascism, Ford publicly declared his disgust with this ideology. Their replies to a questionnaire sent to various intellectuals concerning Franco and Spanish Fascism (*Authors Take Sides on the Spanish War*) indicate the divergent ways they were heading. Pound refused to take sides, while Ford came out strongly against Fascism.

Any discussion of Pound and Ford set in a biographical context must confront two stumbling blocks: Pound's anti-Semitism and Ford's distortion of facts, his "lies." Pound's anti-Semitism, whether we regard it as "metaphorical" or not, is echoed in his later letters to Ford in the' form of abuse and invectives directed at his "enemies." Perhaps because he knew of Ford's interest in Zionism and the Jewish cause, he avoided discussion of these matters. As part of a shrill and monotonously aggressive rhetoric, however, his abuse makes many letters, or portions of them, distasteful reading. One needs to return to the unsurpassed beauty of some of his poetry in order to redress the balance. What went wrong with Pound in the 1930s? It seems no satisfactory answer has been offered as yet.

Ford's great flaw, his "mythomania," does not mar his letters to Pound; they are open and straightforward. There was perhaps no need to "lie" or pose when addressing his friend. His cavalier handling of facts, which so exasperated numerous listeners and readers, is of course the very backbone of the storytelling technique of his reminiscences; and so much of his writing is reminiscence. Much to the despair of the biographer (even Pound was irritated by this habit of his) Ford did not care about factual truth; he did not intend his anecdotes to be taken as serious contributions to history. "Truth is relative," was his defense.[8] Many of his stories are obviously "yarns"; they are so incredible that only the humorless will fall into the trap of taking them at face value. Some of these yarns are worthy of a Faulkner; for instance, the one which tells of how, after the war, he opened the portmanteau he had used as a soldier and the locked-in poison gas poured out and entered his lungs! To Ford there was evidently no clear-cut distinction between "anecdotes," "lies," and "romancing." To "romance" a little when talking of himself is a necessary escape for a poet. The romance then becomes a part of himself and is "the true truth."[9] Faulkner, another unreliable witness, distinguished between "the fact of a thing" and "the truth of a thing."[10] (He does not seem to have shared Ford's fate of being morally condemned for his "lies.") The best way to come to terms with Ford's "lies," his self-praise and his self-dramatization, is no doubt to regard them as part of a conscious *style;* the speaker's tone of voice is often one of teasing humor and exaggeration. The "lying" was of course also a kind of entertainment.

No, Ford's "lies" can probably be condoned by most of us; what constitutes a real stumbling block in our appreciation of Ford the writer is the fact that he too often admitted into his books careless and trivial passages which are not worthy of the Stylist.

Ford's influence on Pound's literary theory has been generally recognized; some commentators also see Ford's impact on Pound's poetry.

Ford's general influence may be more profound than one can actually *prove* by a chronological sorting out of statements and examples and by bringing in the testimony of Pound himself. The reason for this is most certainly that so much of Ford's "preaching" took place in conversation, during walks and over the dinner table. Pound would probably not have objected to the view that he was the recipient of ideas and formulations. He recognized how important it was for the beginning poet to educate himself and learn his subject. From there on every man is on his own. "What a good man gets from another man's work," he told a young writer, "is: precisely the knowledge that the other man has done a job, and that he, the first man, *need not* do that same job or an imitation of it, but is free to do his own job."[11]

Throughout the years Pound was eager to acknowledge Ford's seniority in advocating certain literary "doctrines." We find him doing so in essays, for example, in "The Prose Tradition in Verse," in books, such as *ABC of Reading,* in his obituary of Ford, and in later statements. Pound had a problematic relation to the demands of the "prose quality" of verse; craftsman as he was, he also felt that *technique* could be overemphasized at the expense of *subject.* This internal and open debate is reflected in the correspondence between Pound and Ford.

Quite some time before the Imagist group gathered at the feet of T. E. Hulme and before the New Poetry of the Chicago School had found its way into *Poetry* magazine, Ford had—in one of his "Literary Portraits"— promoted the view that modern literature should deal with "modern English life as it is lived."[12] Both in his early theoretical writing and in his verse Ford stressed the living language, the language of speech, even dialect and slang, as being the right medium for poetry. As he wrote to a friend with literary ambitions: "Your poetry should be your workaday life. [. . .] for what the poet ought to do is to write his own mind in the language of his day." His own aim, he insisted elsewhere, was "to register my own times in terms of my own time [. . .] ."[13] There is no doubt that Pound was duly impressed by these exhortations and that for several years after meeting Ford he strove in the direction of realism, toward the contemporary and the colloquial. He was emphatic in his comments on one point in F. S. Flint's chronicling of the history of Imagism: it was Ford who had started the drive for "current" speech as the mode of modern poetry.

In his own writings Pound echoed Ford's doctrines of contemporary language and subject matter. In an article on prewar French poets he praised "the presentative method"; this is "what is called 'rendering one's own time in the terms of one's own time.' " In his preface to *Poetical Works of Lionel Johnson,* editor Pound criticized Johnson's bookish language. The aim of his own group of younger poets, he declared, was "natural speech, the language as spoken. [. . .] We would write nothing that we might not say actually in life—under emotion."[14] At about the same time he impressed these ideas upon Harriet Monroe, in similar terms. About twenty years later, in her *A Poet's Life,* he footnoted these statements with the acknowledgment that Ford "had been hammering this point of view" into him from the very start of their acquaintance.[15] Pound may also have picked up certain clichés from Ford, such as the more-power-to-your-elbow greeting by which Ford rounded off many of his letters.

Ford was aware of his influence on Pound; he once told one of Pound's protégées, the fledgling writer Iris Barry, of his pleasure at finding in her "an indirect product" of his own "preachings." He reminded her that he had "always been preaching to people not to write 'about' things but to write *things* [. . .] ."[16] *Res non verba,* this phrase was to express Ford's distinctive mark in one of Pound's late summings-up of his significance as a theorist.

With Pound's growing self-assurance and independence came a recognition of his identity as a poet, and he was able to work out his own compromise between the two who had influenced him during his early years in London, Ford and Yeats.

Graham Greene may have been the first to point to similarities in the methods of Ford's writings and the *Cantos.* He suggested that it is in their handling of time that a work like Ford's *Provence* and the *Cantos* are similar; simultaneity is essential here. Hugh Kenner has also drawn parallels between Ford's time-shift technique and the handling of time in the *Cantos.* Pound's ideogrammic method can be linked to Ford's recommendation that in dialogue the speeches of the characters should be juxtaposed, rather than follow each other as answers to the previous speech.

Reminiscence is fundamental to the method and matter of both writers. (Pound is unquestionably the more trustworthy as regards dates, places, and other details!) Dependence on anecdote characterizes both of them, Ford almost obsessively so throughout his career, Pound especially in the later cantos. To Ford as reader and literary historian all books were contemporaneous, and this view of the past, with an even wider application, is essential to Pound's ideogrammic method.

The disagreements and dissimilarities between the two as writers and theorists are especially visible in the issue of Impressionism vs. Imagism. Pound's early, slightly hesitant interest in Impressionism as a mode of writing did not last long. As Ford understood Impressionism, this "Englished" form of Flaubertian theory and practice sought a higher kind of realism; its main method was to let a sensitive observer or participant *render,* as exactly as possible, impressions of life that force themselves upon the witness's attention. Impressionism could render states of mind, but it did not attempt to order the external world. It was informal and digressive; in Ford's practice it often became chatty and loose. In the Impressionist novel everything should combine toward the rendering of an Affair, while ordinary "nuvvles" focused on the Strong Situation. The writer must make himself invisible or absent; direct presentation was preferred at the expense of mediation.

Pound could not rest satisfied with this way of looking at the aim and method of rendering reality. He soon began to argue with Ford about the, as he thought, exaggerated emphasis on technique. The stress on visual and oral perceptions was limiting to the artist. After all they are only the material out of which you build the sane ideogram.

This same criticism was of course often leveled at the movement that Pound named and made famous. To begin with he was absorbed by the idea of the Image with its qualities of intensity and condensation, but when he saw that it tended to be *stationary,* he abandoned it and moved on to the Vortex, which combined hardness and concentration with energy. Pound had fairly early come to insist on the distinction between Impressionism and Imagism. By the early 1920s a select few deserved the name of Imagist—neither Ford nor F. S. Flint qualified. By the 1930s the term had in fact undergone a sea change in his critical vocabulary. At times it seemed to imply a *standard,* rather than a particular *kind* of poetry; at other times it stood for the total poem.

Ford was flattered to be counted among the Imagists; and indeed if Imagism meant relying on visual and oral perceptions to render states of mind, he had certainly been an Imagist years before the movement was even heard of. Only one of his poems, "In the Little Old Market-Place," was published under this label. More than a dozen years after Ford's poem was included in *Des Imagistes,* Pound offered the view that Ford and a few others should by rights have been "catalogued" in another group, but, as he admitted, "in those far days there weren't enough non-symmetricals to have each a farm to themselves."[17]

The correspondence between Pound and Ford necessarily captures only parts of their relationship, for one thing because Pound kept few letters during his London years. It manages, however, to reflect some of the firmest bonds between them: the commitment to writing and the promotion of each other and of other writers. It also illustrates—somewhat sadly—their enforced preoccupation with money, or more correctly, the lack of it. The human interest of their letters lies primarily in the mutual feelings of affection and loyalty that withstood even the stresses of Pound's growing Fascist sympathies and his various obsessions in the late 1930s, as well as of Ford's increasing isolation in ill health and poverty. While the letters on the whole are friendly and open about financial and professional problems, they are reticent or next to silent about intimately personal matters. It is above all a *literary* friendship that they document.

Ford disliked letter writing, and his celebrated conversation is no doubt weakly reflected in his letters to Pound. He probably missed the stimulation of an immediate response. It was quite literally true that it was Ford's *talk* that was so important to Pound. Although the letters, then, are no substitutes for leisurely conversation, one can at least get some idea from them of the Ford-Pound verbal interplay.

Pound was of course one of the really great letter writers. Among American correspondences perhaps only Emily Dickinson's letters can compete with his in originality. He took letter writing seriously. In one of his Rome Radio broadcasts he said that he had come to the conclusion that "A letter PROVES what the bloke who wrote it wanted the receiver to believe ON the day he wrote it."[18] Contrary to Ford, Pound *composed* his letters, not in tranquillity with a view to posterity, but in the haste and impatience of the urgent, direct message. By these verbal compositions he wished to make himself understood and above all to persuade, to move to action.

At times Ford ran out of patience with his friend's epistolary eccentricities, and Pound sometimes complained of apparent breaks in the lines of communication. But although the signals at the end were sparse and rather faint, the lines between them were never broken.

While the correspondence between Pound and Ford gives only a partial view of their relationship, their writings and comments about each other significantly fill in the picture. Through them we learn about Pound's reverence for Ford the editor and the literary conversationalist, as well as about his muted interest in the novelist, poet, and author of reminiscences. Ford expresses his amused and bemused pleasure in this wild young man from the West, his belief in the *Cantos*—it did not perhaps amount to an absorption in them—and above all his delight in an independent and fertile mind.

So we can observe Pound and Ford joining forces, one contributing his "apostolic fury"[19] and the other the world-weary fervor of "an old man mad about writing," and their Poundings and Hoofings echo through the letters and other writings which are rendered in the story of their friendship told in the following chapters.

The letters[20] extant today are held by a few American university libraries. The originals of all but five of the letters from Pound to Ford are at the Olin Library, Cornell University. One letter (*P 2*) is at the Joseph Regenstein Library, University of Chicago. Two letters for which originals are missing (*P 1* and *P 21*) have been copied from carbons of D. D. Paige's transcripts of Pound's letters. These carbons are at the Yale University Library. (Yale also holds Pound's own carbons of a few of his letters to Ford.) Two others (*P 54* and *P 55*) have been transcribed from Pound's retained carbons.

Ford's letters to Pound are, with a very few exceptions, in the Ezra Pound Archive of the Collection of American Literature, Bejnecke Rare Book and Manuscript Library, Yale University. Three letters (*F 14, F 16,* and *F 17*) have found their way to the Lilly Library, Indiana University, Bloomington, Indiana, through the acquisition of part of the William Bird Papers. (*F 16* and *F 17* might have been separate parts of *one* letter, but in the present volume they are regarded as two items.) One letter from Ford (*F 15*) is at Cornell. It is an unsigned, one-sentence message written on the reverse of a piece of music (with the text of a song in French), and it may never have been sent off. One of his letters (*F 35*) has been transcribed for inclusion here from Ford's carbon, which is at Cornell.

Most of the letters are published here for the first time. Seventeen to Pound were printed in *Letters of Ford Madox Ford,* edited by Richard M. Ludwig. They correspond to the following letters as rendered in the present volume: Nos. 3–6, 10, 12, 18, 22, 30, 31, 37, 38, 40, 45, 47–49. They appear here with occasional, minor differences in wording, punctuation, etc. Two letters (*F 5* and *F 47*) have been assigned other dates than in Ludwig's edition. Only a portion of one of Pound's letters (*P 58*) was included in *The Selected Letters of Ezra Pound,* edited by D. D. Paige. In his *Ford Madox Ford and the Transatlantic Review,* Bernard J. Poli quotes from two letters from Ford (*F 16* and *F 17*), which Poli regards as one letter. Working with the recently uncovered originals, instead of the carbons of Paige's transcripts which were available to Poli, I have attributed the authorship of a minor part of this material to Pound. His other handwritten notes scribbled in the margins and elsewhere of these two letters are also rendered here. In his biography of Ford, Arthur Mizener quotes from several letters by Pound; he quotes very fully from a letter in which Pound answers his friend's criticism of "Eighth Canto" (*P 18*). The letter containing Ford's remarks on this canto (*F 14*) has only recently come to light, in response to a circular letter by the present editor. Until the Lilly Library acquired its part of the William Bird Papers, this important letter was hidden in the famous "Bird trunk." It is thus printed here for the first time.

Most of the reviews and essays included here have been published previously, usually in English or American periodicals. A few of Ford's pieces on Pound have been reprinted after their first appearance. His review of *Personae: The Collected Poems of Ezra Pound,* entitled "Ezra," was included in his *New York Essays.* Eric Homberger included this piece as well as Ford's review of *Cathay,* entitled "From China to Peru," in *Ezra Pound: The Critical Heritage.* Some of Pound's writings on Ford have likewise been reprinted one or more times. His review of the 1913

Collected Poems, originally titled "Mr Hueffer and the Prose Tradition in Verse," reappeared as "The Prose Tradition in Verse" in *Polite Essays* and in *Literary Essays,* edited by T. S. Eliot, and his obituary of Ford was collected in *Selected Prose 1909–1965,* edited by William Cookson. The obituary was included in "Homage to Ford Madox Ford," *New Directions No. 7; Ford Madox Ford: Modern Judgments,* edited by Richard A. Cassell; and *Ford Madox Ford: The Critical Heritage,* edited by Frank Mac-Shane. A shorter review of Ford's *Collected Poems,* entitled "Ford Madox Hueffer," was reprinted in *Ford Madox Ford: The Critical Heritage.* An English version of his "interview" with Ford, "Madox Ford at Rapallo," was reprinted in *Pavannes and Divagations.* This was Olga Rudge's retranslation of a piece which had first appeared in Italian in the Rapallo paper *Il Mare.*

Hitherto unpublished are three essays—or notes for essays—by Pound; the notes were written in (presumably) 1924 and 1926, respectively, and dealt with the series of books printed in Paris and named by him "The Inquest" (only the sections on Ford are included here). The typescripts of these notes are in the Ezra Pound Archive at the Beinecke Library, Yale University, which also contains the typescript of a complete essay on Ford, written in Italian and entitled "Appunti: 'Return to Yesterday.' Memorie di Ford Madox (Hueffer) Ford." This essay appears here for the first time in an English translation by the present editor. Excerpts from an essay by Ford, entitled "Some Expatriates," are printed here for the first time. The essay was presumably written in 1926. The typescript is privately owned (by Donald Gallup).

Throughout Ford's published reminiscences and other nonfiction works there are frequent references of varying lengths to his friend. One passage in his *Return to Yesterday* which describes Pound's entrance into the literary society of prewar London was reprinted with the title "Enter Ezra Pound" in Volume One of *The Bodley Head Ford Madox Ford,* edited by Graham Greene; it was also included in Michael Killigrew's selection of Ford's reminiscences and other writings, *Your Mirror to My Times.*

Pound, too, referred now and then to his friend in his published writings: in editorial comments, such as the "Status Rerum" statement in *Poetry,* in reviews and articles, some of them reprinted in *Polite Essays,* and in books, such as *Gaudier-Brzeska.* After Ford's death, Pound often mentioned him in interviews and elsewhere. The memory of Ford is vivid in letters written during the St. Elizabeths years, and a permanent place was created for him in the *Cantos.*

Still another kind of primary material which is drawn on to illuminate the relationship between Pound and Ford is their references to each other in letters to other correspondents. Some of this material has not been published before. Pound's letters to his parents make up a significant category of such supportive evidence.

The majority of Ford's letters were typed; this is a boon to the transcriber, for his handwriting is at times almost illegible. As a rule he included a rather full address in the letterhead. In the late twenties he sometimes used stationery with his Paris address printed on it. (For a brief period there were two addresses: 84 Rue Notre-Dame-des-Champs and 32 Rue de Vaugirard.) In the early thirties he had stationery with a printed heading giving name and address (VILLA PAUL. CHEMIN DE LA CALADE. CAP-BRUN. TOULON. VAR). As editor and teacher he used official paper (the *Transatlantic Review* and Olivet College). He seems to have retained carbons of his letters, at least in the 1930s. A few have survived.

Apart from the difficult handwriting, Ford's letters present no particular problems for the transcriber-editor. In his handwritten letters he used abbreviations such as "w^d." One idiosyncracy of punctuation which occurs often in his published writings appears also in his letters. This is the use of a varying number of dots. (No doubt more than one reader was exasperated by "those damned dots."[21])

Pound's letters are a great challenge to transcriber and editor with their eccentricities of spelling, punctuation, line arrangement, indentation, etc. They were part of a highly individual style which seems to have developed gradually during his London years and which may be identified as a conscious way of composing around 1920 or a little later. Most of his letters are typed; the handwritten messages are usually either postcards or letters written during travels. He evidently began to use a typewriter quite early. At least in the 1930s (from 1933?) he retained carbons of his letters; those that have survived of his letters to Ford are from the late 1930s.

Pound's stationery is of particular interest, for its occasional artistic quality, but even more importantly for the light it can shed on the conjectural dating of some of his letters. After he had found permanent housing in London he had stationery printed with his address at the top (5, Holland Place Chambers, Kensington, W.). His Paris stay was not sufficiently settled for this sort of fixing his whereabouts. It was after he had spent a few years in Rapallo that the permanence of his residence was reflected in his stationery. What may be the earliest variant of his Rapallo writing paper, represented in the Pound-Ford correspondence, is documented from 1931 on. It is fairly plain, with his name in capitals in the top lefthand corner vis à vis the address (RAPALLO VIA MARSALA, 12 INT. 5). This text is in blue print. By June 1932 the letterhead has got an addition in small italics at the top center: *"res publica, the public convenience."* Postcards written in these years (the early 1930s) bear his name and address in red. By September 1932 he has a new kind of stationery: in addition to his name and address—in green—there is a profile of the author, reproduced from a portrait by Gaudier-Brzeska and placed in the middle of the letterhead. His next letter to Ford, dated 5 March [1933], is written on similar paper; the only difference is that profile and printed text are in red. In April another kind of stationery is introduced: the profile is gone, and the name and address, in smaller, red print, appear at the top. It was perhaps used alternately with the sort which bears the profile in red. By the spring of 1934 he had switched to paper which features, in the upper lefthand corner, a head of Pound, reproduced from a drawing by Wyndham Lewis, and name, address, and date (year) according to the Fascist calendar (ANNO XII) at the top right. Drawing and text are in green. Owing to a lacuna in the correspondence one cannot from these letters tell when Pound introduced the stationery that he used for a greeting written in December 1936. His name and address appear here in the top righthand corner, the year both according to standard and Fascist dating is placed in the middle, and in the lefthand corner there is a motto: "A tax is not a share[.] A nation need not and should not pay rent for its own credit." In the bottom lefthand corner there is a picture of a griffin. Design and text are in blue. By the fall of 1937 the Gaudier profile is back again, with name and address on either side. Text and profile are in blue. What distinguishes this batch from the earlier one is the addition—in the top righthand corner—of the year supplied according to the Fascist calendar (ANNO XVI). This kind of paper, updated, is also used in the final year of the Pound-Ford correspondence. In the year 1938 postcards bear Pound's name and address in light red print (not the brownish red of earlier years).

Pound seems to have begun to date his letters according to the Fascist calendar about December 1931. This is Noel Stock's surmise, and it is corroborated by the present correspondence. The earliest letter which bears the Fascist calendar date is that of 27 December 1931, or, as Pound wrote it out, 27 Dec. anno X. The Fascist system of dating has proved a trap even for the experts. Since this calendar commemorates Mussolini's March on Rome, which culminated on 28 October 1922, the *new* year begins approximately two months before our standard New Year. This means that letters written in the months of November and December should be assigned to the year preceding the one indicated by the Fascist calendar dating. 27 December anno X is thus 27 December *1931,* while 27 January anno X is 27 January *1932*.

Sometimes Pound took care to correct the dating of the letterhead, for example, changing (the printed) "1937" to "1936" in a letter dated December anno XV (*P 45*); or adding by hand a digit to the roman number—XVI > XVII—in a letter written in December 1938 (*P 56*).

Among Pound's idiosyncracies as letter writer his "typography" is one of the most striking and problematic. His unorthodox paragraphing and indentation were no doubt part of a rhythmic and intonational pattern of composition. Letter writing was related to poetic composition in this respect, and Pound's explanation (given in a February 1939 letter to another correspondent) of this aspect of the *Cantos* may serve to illuminate this feature of his letters: "ALL typographic disposition, placings of words *on the page*, is intended to facilitate the reader's intonation [. . .] ." In the same letter he also comments on his use of abbreviations. They "save *eye* effort," he explains. "Also show speed in mind of original character supposed to be uttering or various colourings and degrees of importance or emphasis attributed by the protagonist of the moment."[22]

Pound's punctuation is also highly idiosyncratic. Single or double slashes often replace periods; double or triple horizontal lines are used as dividers or marks of pauses. Nonstandard capitalization of words or letters are again signs of intonation. They are sometimes part of an "Old Hickory" dialect that is presumably meant to express a humorous, down-to-earth folk wisdom. His unorthodox spelling sometimes serves the same purpose; often it helps give voice to the author's feelings and attitudes.

In this unusual mixture of conscious composition and hasty improvisation both Pound's carefulness and his eagerness are seen in his corrections, deletions, and additions. When typing he often used capitals as marks of deletion, most frequently series of £s or Hs. He was not above correcting slips and errors, either by hand or by typing, and many remaining slips and errors are clearly a result of a compromise between urgency and care.

It has been my aim to reproduce Pound's and Ford's letters as faithfully as possible. Thus the rule has been to retain the authors' *spelling, punctuation, word division, underlining,* and *capitalization.* Certain modifications have, however, been necessary or desirable. In order to stay within the bounds of conventional typography Pound's idiosyncratic typing and writing habits have had to be rendered in a somewhat tamed fashion. Furthermore, the reader's legitimate concerns about a legible and pleasing text have been considered.

Only *misspellings* which are clearly inadvertent and which may create ambiguity or arrest the reader's attention unduly have been corrected. Clearly accidentally transposed letters and errors—mostly typographical slips—on the order of "tye" (for "the"), "ignorsnt," and "formard" (for "forward") have been silently corrected. *Repetitions* that are clear instances of dittography have also been silently corrected.

Dashes have been standardized to two types: one-em and one-en dashes. They are usually printed with intervening spaces, in accordance with the custom of both authors. *Ellipses* are printed as Pound and Ford wrote them; Ford in particular made frequent and deliberate use of unorthodox ellipses, to suggest a pause or the trailing off of a thought. A Poundian mark for a break or pause: an elongated *double dash* (=), has been retained in a standardized form.

Underlining in the letters is reproduced as such, whether it is single, double, or triple. In some instances I have interpreted certain lines, single, double, or triple, which appear in Pound's letters, as being dividers between paragraphs.

In his handwritten manuscripts, Ford uses *superscripts* in certain words, such as "c^d.," "sh^d.," "w^d.," and "y^r." All such superior letters have been lowered without comment. Similar superscripts in, e.g., dates, used by both authors, have likewise been lowered.

Pound's idiosyncratic *line divisions, indentations, spacing of lines,* and *paragraphing* do not easily submit to typographical conventions and conveniences. In order to transmit to the reader at least a faint picture of Pound's creative spacing and his rhythmical placing of words and lines on the page, a compromise has been arrived at: where Pound uses indentation of various sizes, a standardized indentation has been applied; wherever he begins a new paragraph without indicating it by indenting, and with or without larger than normal space between lines, this is shown by wider spacing between paragraphs (standardized to double space). In all other cases single space between lines is used. The varying degrees of spacing between words, lines, paragraphs, and sections have had to be ignored. When Pound uses spacing to indicate the beginning of a new sentence, a period has been supplied within brackets. Pound's device of expressing strong emotions by ending questions or exclamations by a series of identical punctuation marks, preceded by greater than normal spacing, has seemed important enough to retain in a standardized form. In many instances it has seemed impossible to know or even guess Pound's intentions, if any, with the unorthodox spacing, and normalization has appeared to be a convenient solution.

Ford shows no idiosyncracies in these respects, and in the printing of his letters these features have been normalized, without comment.

The authors' *insertions* are incorporated in the text within angle brackets (⟨ ⟩)—with the exception of such trivial insertions as "a," "the," etc. Only significant *deletions* are restored as editorial insertions within square brackets.

With a view to presenting a text which is pleasing to the eye, editorial emendations have been kept to a minimum: in a few cases *missing words* or *letters* have been supplied within square brackets. In order to clarify an ambiguous or confusing syntax I have, in a few instances, added, within brackets, a *missing period* to end a sentence. Other editorial insertions occasionally *identify names* and *titles* to ease the reader's task. *Missing quotation marks* and *parentheses* have been supplied without comment in cases where there can be no doubt.

The *position* of the *place of writing* and the *date* has been standardized. Addresses printed on the stationery used are reduced to the name of the town, etc., from which the letter was sent, and are supplied within brackets. In other cases, when the place of writing is known or conjectured, it is also supplied within brackets. Lines which are seemingly intended to set off the place and date from the letter proper are ignored.

The *date* appears as set out in the manuscript (except for its position). Missing information is given in square brackets; conjectural dates are discussed in notes accompanying individual letters.

The position of the *salutation* and the *complimentary close* has also been standardized. Where the complimentary close is a single word or phrase—as it most often is—it appears in the edited form on the same line as the signature (contrary to the practice of the authors). Unless otherwise specified, signatures represent autograph names or initials. Complimentary closes vary in typed letters: they may be typed or, frequently, written by hand. Such variations are not reported by the editor.

In editing Pound's two *unpublished* prose writings (in English) which deal with Ford, I have aimed at a readable text while at the same time keeping their character of *notes* or *drafts*. Obvious slips of typing, spelling, etc., have been silently corrected when readability required this procedure. My English translation of Pound's essay in Italian is based on my transcription of the original typescript. In this typescript there are several corrections, some of which are made in another hand than Pound's, presumably by Francesco Monotti, who had helped him with translations into Italian of other prose pieces. (I owe this suggestion to Donald Gallup and Mary de Rachewiltz.) The excerpts from Ford's unpublished essay "Some Expatriates" are rendered without any editorial alterations.

Pound's and Ford's previously published writings about each other are reprinted here with a few typographical errors and misspellings (mostly of names) silently corrected.

Many institutions and individuals have advised and helped me in preparing this book. My deep gratitude goes to all the research librarians who have served me. Donald Eddy, Curator of Rare Books at the Cornell University Library, and Donald Gallup, former Curator of the Collection of American Literature at the Beinecke Rare Book and Manuscript Library, have given me invaluable assistance. The Oslo University Library has efficiently provided me with material from near and far. The Lilly Library at Indiana University, the Joseph Regenstein Library at the University of Chicago, Olivet College Library, and the Humanities Research Center at the University of Texas at Austin responded graciously to my request for material and information. The libraries at Harvard, Princeton, and Hamilton extended great hospitality to the scholar. The private collection of Edward Naumburg, Jr., New York, was an early introduction to Ford's writings. James Laughlin, Mary de Rachewiltz, and Janice Biala kindly answered questions about the whereabouts of letters and other matters.

Among the numerous friends and colleagues who have helped me in the demanding job of annotating the Pound-Ford correspondence I thank in particular Oddrun Ohren, Oslo University Library, and my friend Gösta Forsström, Uppsala. I have benefited from my husband Per Seyersted's experience in reading and editing difficult manuscripts. My polyglot colleague Bjørn Braaten could be appealed to for quotations from many languages. Two other colleagues at the University of Oslo, Roy Tommy Eriksen and Roy J. Wigzell, corrected some of the errors in the original draft of my translation of Pound's Italian essay. Roy Tommy Eriksen was especially helpful in suggesting alternative readings and in sharing his knowledge of Dante with me. Faith Ann Johansson kindly read my manuscript and suggested stylistic and other improvements in my English text. Lissa Fougner, Else Bjerke Westre, and Aagot Winter-Hjelm typed various versions of this difficult manuscript.

I owe a particular debt to Mary de Rachewiltz and Donald Gallup for reading my entire manuscript; by their suggestions and corrections they helped fill in lacunae and weed out errors in my commentary and notes. Joan Winterkorn, formerly of the Rare Book Room at Cornell University Library, did me a similar service with the Ford material. Helen Vendler and B. Bernard Cohen kindly read parts of an earlier version of the manuscript.

It is obvious that I could not have undertaken to tell this story of the friendship between Pound and Ford without having had recourse to four indispensable books: Donald Gallup's *A Bibliography of Ezra Pound;* David Dow Harvey's *Ford Madox Ford 1873–1939: A Bibliography of Works and Criticism;* Noel Stock's *The Life of Ezra Pound;* and Arthur Mizener's *The Saddest Story: A Biography of Ford Madox Ford.* I owe a very particular debt to Arthur Mizener for providing me with additional information and leads beyond those given in his splendidly documented biography.

Of the several scholars who have dealt with the relationship between Pound and Ford, Herbert N. Schneidau, Eric Homberger, and, most recently, Violet Cameron Skorina may be the ones who have most strongly emphasized Ford's importance to Pound. So far the scholarly interest has largely been directed at the London years. Bernard J. Poli gave us glimpses of the Pound-Ford collaboration during the Paris years, while Arthur Mizener added information on their later association. The present volume surveys the entire span of the friendship between the two and attempts a full picture of the most significant features of this friendship.

Finally my thanks go to the American Council of Learned Societies, the Norwegian Research Council for Science and the Humanities, the University of Oslo, and the Telluride Association at Cornell University, which in their various ways have made it possible for me to complete this book.

Acknowledgments

Letters and writings by Ezra Pound are quoted here, in full or in part, with the kind permission of the Ezra Pound Literary Property Trust. I am indebted to the Cornell University Library for permission to print, in full or in part, manuscript letters from Pound to Ford Madox Ford, Stella Bowen, and Wyndham Lewis. The Yale University Library allowed me to print letters from Pound to Ford which exist only as retained carbons or as copies of transcripts made by D. D. Paige, as well as excerpts from letters from Pound to his parents (Paige transcripts), one letter to Violet Hunt (carbon), and letters to William Carlos Williams, which are all in the Collection of American Literature, Beinecke Rare Book and Manuscript Library. Pound's hitherto unpublished notes and essay on Ford, which are also in the Collection of American Literature, appear here with the permission of the Yale University Library. The Joseph Regenstein Library, University of Chicago, permitted me to publish one letter from Pound to Ford which is among the *Poetry* Magazine Papers, 1912–1936, Department of Special Collections. Letters from Pound to E. E. Cummings are excerpted by permission of the Houghton Library, Harvard University. The Burke Library, Hamilton College, allowed me to quote from letters in their Pound Collection. The quote from a letter from Dorothy Pound (Copyright © 1982, the Estate of Dorothy Pound) is printed by permission. I was granted permission to quote from a letter from Pound to Arnold Gingrich which is in the Henry W. and Albert A. Berg Collection, The New York Public Library, Astor, Lenox, and Tilden Foundations.

I gratefully acknowledge permission from New Directions, New York, and Faber and Faber, London, to reprint or quote from previously published material by Ezra Pound: *ABC of Reading* (Copyright 1934 by Ezra Pound); *The Cantos of Ezra Pound* (Copyright 1934, 1937, 1940, 1948, © 1956, 1959, 1962, 1963, 1966, 1968 by Ezra Pound; Copyright © 1972 by the Estate of Ezra Pound); *Literary Essays of Ezra Pound*, edited by T. S. Eliot (Copyright 1918, 1920, 1935 by Ezra Pound); *Pavannes and Divagations* (Copyright © 1958 by Ezra Pound); *Personæ* (Copyright 1926 by Ezra Pound); *Pound/Joyce: Letters and Essays*, edited by Forrest Read (Copyright © 1967 by Ezra Pound); *The Selected Letters of Ezra Pound 1907–1941*, edited by D. D. Paige (Copyright 1950 by Ezra Pound); *Selected Prose 1909–1965*, edited by William Cookson (Copyright © 1973 by the Estate of Ezra Pound).

Articles by Ezra Pound reprinted here in full first appeared in *Poetry Review* (London), *New Freewoman* (London), *Poetry* (Chicago), *Future* (London), *Transatlantic Review* (Paris), *Il Mare* (Rapallo), and *Nineteenth Century and After* (London).

Letters and writings by Ford Madox Ford are quoted in full or in part with

The Convergence of the Twain
1909-1914

LONDON

When the unknown American poet Ezra Pound first swam into Ford Madox Ford's ken, Ford was an established figure in literary London. By 1909 he had reached one of the peaks of his career: as founder and editor of the *English Review* he was for a short time at the center of the literary and cultural life of the metropolis. The *Review* was one of his most important achievements. It earned him great, though brief, fame and many admirers, but it also brought him as many enemies—and financial ruin.

After acting out the role of the country gentleman, Ford (or Hueffer, as he was then called) had been more and more drawn to London. He needed now and then to be in the midst of the literary world, and he was ambitious enough to want to play a central part in shaping the cultural atmosphere. By the fall of 1908—when Pound arrived in London—Ford had been settled for about a year in a flat at 84 Holland Park Avenue in Kensington. As editor he always left the door of his office-home open for budding geniuses to enter. And they did come: D. H. Lawrence—discovered by Ford; mysterious-looking Wyndham Lewis, who, so the story went, when not finding the editor in the office proper sought him out in the bathtub; and Ezra Pound. Ford's knack of spotting quality in a manuscript was legendary. He thought that "if you are an editor" and you hit upon what you want, "you can pitch the story straight away into your wicker tray with the few accepted manuscripts [. . .]."[1] One glance at Lawrence's "Odour of Chrysanthemums" was enough to convince him that the story was excellent.

The birth of the *English Review* has come to be surrounded by myths. Ford claimed that he had wanted to create a forum for a poem by Thomas Hardy which no other magazine in England was willing to print because of its shocking subject matter. The first issue of the *Review* accordingly featured Hardy's "A Sunday Morning Tragedy," which deals with a death as a result of illegal abortion. At times Ford preferred other myths, such as the one that he had wished to help Joseph Conrad to some money by printing his "A Personal Record" and other writings.

Arthur Mizener, in his comprehensive and detailed biography of Ford, sorts out the facts of the founding of the *English Review*. During 1908 a group of writers—Ford, Conrad, H. G. Wells, and others—had been discussing the establishment of a new literary magazine which would give "imaginative literature a chance in England," as Ford put it.[2] By the fall of 1908 the enterprise had advanced far enough for Ford to hire a young journalist, Douglas Goldring, as his secretary and start looking for influential authors who would be willing to support the magazine by contributions or by general goodwill. Ford, Wells, Conrad, and Ford's friend Arthur Marwood (Ford's model for the Tietjens figure of *Parade's End*) threw together their forces, trying to find financial backing, sending out a circular stating the policy of the new review, and soliciting literary contributions. The circular expressed Ford's editorial policy:

> The only qualification for admission to the pages of the Review will be— in the view of the Editors—either distinction of individuality or force of conviction, either literary gifts or earnestness of purpose, whatever the purpose may be—the criterion of inclusion being the clarity of diction, the force or the illuminative value of the views expressed. What will be avoided will be the superficiality of the specially modern kind which is the inevitable consequence when nothing but brevity of statement is aimed at. [. . .][3]

The *English Review* was registered as a company on 22 January 1909. The first issue, which appeared in December 1908, was excellent, and to this day it bears witness to Ford's great gifts as an editor: it included, in addition to Hardy's poem, Henry James's story "The Jolly Corner" and contributions by Conrad, Wells, Galsworthy, and W. H. Hudson.

The *Review* and its editor were splendidly launched into the literary world. This is how the editor looked in the eyes of his "sub," Douglas Goldring:

> My first impressions of Ford are of a tall thin man with fair hair and a blonde moustache which imperfectly concealed defective front teeth. He wore a grey-blue swallow-tail coat of uncertain cut, carried a leather despatch case of the kind the French call a *serviette* and had an "important" manner which in some ways suggested an Under-Secretary of State.[4]

To a less favorably disposed viewer Ford's most striking features were a complexion "the colour of raw veal, [. . .] prominent blue eyes and rabbit teeth [. . .]."[5] Ford loved to be in the midst of things. He could be seen lunching on Fridays at the Mont Blanc restaurant in Gerrard Street in Soho; once a month he dined at a restaurant in Fleet Street with members of the Square Club. He also dined at the Pall Mall restaurant, often in the company of H. G. Wells. It was there that Wells loudly announced: "Hurray, Fordie's discovered another genius! Called D. H. Lawrence!"[6]

Meanwhile Ford's private life was becoming exciting but very complicated. A literary woman had captivated his heart. Violet Hunt, daughter of artistic parents and author of several novels and other writings, was a charming and celebrated figure in literary circles. Her social background and literary interests created a *lien* between her and Ford; her very active involvement with the suffragette cause seems to have been an added attraction to Ford, who later wrote on suffragette and feminist subjects. Her novel *White Rose of Weary Leaf,* published in 1908, earned her general recognition. Henry James admired her; so did Wells and Lawrence (although the latter found her too intellectual). She had high ambitions to play a leading role in a fashionable and artistic milieu. To a certain extent she managed to create a literary and artistic *salon* in her house, South Lodge, at 80 Campden Hill, Kensington. It became a place where a bright newcomer would wish to be introduced.

However, problems were piling up. The finances of the *English Review* worsened, and Sir Alfred Mond, one of Violet Hunt's rich acquaintances, was persuaded to buy the enterprise, whereupon he promptly fired Ford from the editorship. Ford's wife Elsie refused to divorce him, and because of hurt pride Ford allowed himself to be sent to prison for ten days for contempt of court. Ford's domestic imbroglio estranged some of his old associates, and both he and Violet Hunt had to look to new friends for intellectual exchange and moral support.

From 1909 on, the name of Ezra Pound appears with increasing frequency in connection with the Ford-Hunt circle. We do not know when Ford and Pound met for the first time; we do not even know just exactly when Pound arrived in London. He came from Venice where he had published his first book of poems, *A Lume Spento,* in a small private edition. He had made his way to Europe on a cattleship with comparatively light baggage: an M.A. in Romance Languages, an abortive experience as a teacher of French and Spanish at a small college in Indiana, some vague plans for advanced studies in Romance Languages, and $80 to back up his plans. He had landed at Gibraltar and from there walked through Spain and southern France to Venice.

By September 1908 Pound had reached London on his educational journey. Ezra Pound definitely represented something new on the London scene. Intellectually precocious and having already acquired the stamp of "the latin Quarter type,"[7] he was beginning to reveal his personality. His college friend William Carlos Williams said about him (in 1904) that "not one person in a thousand likes him," adding that "there is some quality in him which makes him too proud to try to please people."[8] Fellow students at Hamilton College were puzzled by this rather eccentric transfer student. Women were attracted to the lively young man with the curly shock of reddish hair. To Hilda Doolittle, who met him when he was attending the University of Pennsylvania, he dedicated some of his earliest poems, collected into a hand-bound manuscript, "Hilda's Book."[9]

When Pound arrived in 1908, probably in the second half of September, he first took lodgings in a comfortable boardinghouse at 8 Duchess Street, Portland Place; he knew this place from an earlier stay in London. It did not seem like an auspicious start, however. "I came to London with £3 knowing no one," he reminisced in 1913.[10] On 27 September, in a letter to his father, Homer Loomis Pound, he expressed relief: "Revered Parent: 4£. Thank Gawd it has come."[11] He had had to move to a less expensive place in Islington in north London. Islington evidently marked a low point: "only pawn-broking venture was in Islington," he told Patricia Hutchins in 1953.[12] Shortly afterward he was able to move back into the respectable neighborhood where he had stayed before. When on 8 October he was admitted to the British Museum Reading Room he gave his address as 48 Langham Street.

In the letters which Pound wrote to his parents from London in 1908, he makes no mention of Ford or Violet Hunt. In a note written about twenty years later, he stated that he first met Ford in 1908 or 1909.[13] Early 1909 is the likely point in time when the twain converged. It was most probably Violet Hunt's feminist friend, the novelist May Sinclair, who introduced him to Ford. In a letter to his wife—postmarked 10 April 1909—Ford mentions, among the people he frequents in his bachelor's existence in London, "Ezra Pound (an American poet)." Pound's name occurs together with those of Violet Hunt and May Sinclair as having been present at a social event on 4 April.[14]

It might be possible to narrow down further the date when Ford and Pound first met. In her diary for these years, Violet Hunt refers to one of Ford's famous *bouts-rimés* parties as having taken place on 4 March 1909. Mizener conjectures that David Garnett may be describing the same party in his *The Golden Echo*. Garnett includes Ezra Pound among the poets competing for a crown of bay leaves. May Sinclair was also present. She told her host afterward that she "enjoyed the competition immensely, though I did do so badly."[15]

It was the bookseller Elkin Mathews in Vigo Street who first provided Pound with his entrance ticket to literary London. Through Mathews he made the acquaintance of Ernest Rhys, editor of Everyman's Library. Rhys in his turn introduced him to May Sinclair. In a February 1909 letter to his father Pound is anxious to show his parents that he is doing fine and is being appreciated in his new milieu. He tells them how May Sinclair "carted" him off from Ernest Rhys's place, where they had had tea, to the Lyceum Club for dinner.

In January 1909 Pound's circle of contacts had been extended to include two Australian writers, and it was through them that he met Mrs. Olivia Shakespear, novelist and friend of W. B. Yeats, and her daughter Dorothy. Mother and daughter attended a lecture course he gave the spring term of 1909 at the Regent Street Polytechnic. On 22 April he met a new set of poets. This was the group led by philosopher and poet T. E. Hulme. Pound felt that London was a fine place to be. "Am by way of falling into the crowd that does things here. London, deah old Lundon, is the place for poesy," he told his friend Bill Williams.[16]

In the spring Pound wrote to his father: "Have just received proofs of my 'Sestina: Altaforte' from the *English Review,* so I presume they intend to use it. The *Review* is probably the best magazine in the country and if the page numbers I and II on the proof mean anything, I am evidently going to have the place d'honneur in the June number." When the "Sestina" appeared in the June number of the *English Review,* it was the first time a poem by Pound was published in a recognized English magazine.

So we know that Ford and Pound had met by the first quarter of 1909 at the latest. Ford must have been quick to recognize Pound's talent. Altogether he printed nine of his poems in the *Review.* The magazine did more than serve as an outlet for a young poet seeking to establish himself in a new literary milieu; it enabled him to renew his wardrobe. "Have ordered a 5 £ suit at the expense of the *Eng. Rev.,*" he writes to his father. On 19 October he cashed a check for £2-0-0, made out to "Ezra Pound Esq." three days earlier and signed by Ford.[17] Very likely this was payment for poems printed in the October issue of the *Review.*

By the fall of 1909 Pound evidently was making frequent appearances at Violet Hunt's social events and private gatherings. She notes in her diary for 18 October 1909: "Ezra Pound." And for 14 November, more familiarly: "Ezra here."[18] No doubt he wished to be closer to the important centers; his new friends lived more or less within walking distance of each other in Kensington. In September he left his room in Langham Street, and after having stayed for a short time in Hammersmith—perhaps at the recommendation of Ford, whose mother lived in that neighborhood—he found his permanent bachelor's quarters at 10 Church Walk, Kensington. This was close to Campden Hill, where Violet Hunt lived, and Holland Park Avenue, where Ford resided in his office-home until he moved in at South Lodge, officially as the paying guest of Violet Hunt's mother. The district, Pound told Patricia Hutchins, was "SWARming" with writers and intellectuals.[19] Violet Hunt lent him some water colors by William Henry Hunt, and later pieces of sculpture by Henri Gaudier-Brzeska contributed to the simple charm of Pound's lodgings.[20] The only thing about the place he did not like was the noise made by the bells of a nearby church, St. Mary Abbots.

Now began Pound's beneficial climbs up Campden Hill Road to attend Violet Hunt's parties and to play tennis on the court adjoining South Lodge. Above all began the edifying and stimulating talks about literature with Ford which, as Pound insisted later in life, taught him so much about the theory and practice of poetry.

The earliest letter extant in the correspondence between Pound and Ford is a brief note from Pound written in the late fall of 1909. The fairly formal tone of this message was probably resulting from his addressing the editor of a prominent literary magazine. Ford printed the poem recommended by Pound, "Persephone" by the Australian poet Frederic Manning, in the December issue of the *English Review*. Pound's own "Canzon: The Yearly Slain," which was a "reply" to Manning's poem, appeared in the issue for January 1910.

P 1. Paige 133 (copy). Yale.

[London, November   1909]

Dear Mr. Hueffer:
   Manning has just written this quite beautiful "Persephone" which I can praise without reservation.
   I think you will thank me for getting it sent to you.

Pound.[21]

From the fall of 1909 on Pound and Ford saw more and more of each other. Master and disciple used each other as sounding boards for unpublished material. Pound, always eager to recommend enjoyable and worthwhile books to his mother, Isabel W. Pound, alerted her to Ford's novel *The Simple Life Limited;* he had had the proofs of the beginning of this work "in private audition."[22] By the following spring Pound and Ford were actually beginning to look like a team. Pound imparted to his parents, in exhilarated and hurried sentences, the full program of his activities: "Lunched with the distinguished novelist who is writing 'The Simple Life.' [. . .] He took me on to Lady Low's for tea, which was quite endurable. [. . .] I now go to walk with Hueffer. [. . .] Tomorrow I lunch with Violet Hunt, tea with the Shakespears, and depart at 8:45 P.M. for Paris."[23]
   A contemporary, the editor and critic R. A. Scott-James, paints a picture of the two from the perspective of the late 1950s, as they appeared to him in the years immediately before the First World War: "Ezra Pound seemed then to be following him [Ford] round wherever he went, playing like a mischievous urchin, letting off his gaminesque little jokes. Ford enjoyed the playfulness of Pound. He certainly liked the feeling of having as a disciple and playfellow one whom so serious a novelist as May Sinclair had 'discovered' and presented to the world as among the most promising of poets."[24] Pound's discipleship, it was said, extended to his way of speaking. They frequented the same clubs: The Square Club and The Poets' Club; they lunched and dined at the same cafés and restaurants: the Vienna Café, the Mont Blanc, Bellotti's, and the Tour Eiffel;

they went to the same night club: Madame Strindberg's The Cave of the Golden Calf.

Pound was in the thick of it, and it did not take long before he had made himself noticed and known, enough to be spoofed in *Punch.* "A new poet," it was announced, "is about to swim into our ken in the person of Boaz Bobb, a son of the Arkansas soil, who has long been resident in London studying Icelandic literature for the purposes of a new saga of the Wild West." The author remarked on Mr. Bobb's "delightful lack of re-straint and false shame."[25] Ford also figured in disguise in the "Book Chat" column, as Pound noted in a letter to his mother: "He [Hueffer] and I are in *Punch* together [. . .] ."[26] The paragraph on Ford, "Mr. WILLIAM LE QUEUX," aimed its gentle satire at revelations of low-life psychology.

During Pound's first two years in London a series of books had come from his hands: *A Quinzaine for This Yule, Personae, Exultations, The Spirit of Romance,* and *Provença.* In the first couple of years after the *English Review* venture, Ford turned to gathering together or bringing to completion several volumes of prose, some of the material having been previously serialized. There were novels: *A Call, The Portrait, The Simple Life Limited,* and *Ladies Whose Bright Eyes;* a book of reminiscences, *Ancient Lights;* and a volume of essays, *The Critical Attitude.* One slight book of poems appeared, *Songs from London.*

There was a lacuna in the Pound-Ford relationship, partly due to Pound's visit to the United States, from the summer of 1910 to February 1911. Almost immediately upon his return to London he left for the Continent, where he remained till August. In the spring he wrote to his mother from Paris: "Hueffer wants me in Giessen for some work but I don't know whether it's worth while." His reluctance was weakened by July, when he informed his mother, in a letter from his Italian *paradiso,* Sirmione, that "I may go up to see Hueffer after all, and from him over to London in the autumn."

What was Ford doing in this provincial little German town? In a des-perate attempt to straighten out his harassing domestic difficulties, he had voluntarily exiled himself to this town—for the time being. His plan was, so he stated, to obtain a divorce, against his wife's wishes, by a legal device of changed citizenship. We shall probably never know how genu-inely Ford himself believed in this transformation and the liberty he was to achieve as a result of it. Nor are all the important steps and stages of this liberating process known to us. (Elsie Martindale Hueffer, who died in 1949, never granted Ford the divorce he desired.)

Ford's behavior was no doubt both fantastic and foolish. The stuffy atmosphere of Giessen, the unaccustomed isolation—Violet Hunt, whom he planned to marry, could not permanently share his exile—and ill health added to his misery. He certainly needed a lively and witty companion to brighten his day with literary discussion. The ostensible reason for Pound's going up there was, as we have seen, to do some secretarial work for Ford. There is indeed evidence that he acted as secretary to Ford while at Giessen: there is a letter to Ford's literary agent, James B. Pinker, in Pound's hand, no doubt written under Ford's dictation. It bears the double signature "Ford Maddox [sic] Hueffer" and "E. P." The letterhead contains Ford's German address—15 Friedrichstrasse Giessen—printed in the top righthand corner.[27]

Ford did get his diversion! Rolling on the floor, if we may trust eyewitness and victim Pound in his obituary of Ford, his friend and master told him, better than in words, what he thought of Pound's latest volume of verse, *Canzoni*. He had brought it along, piping hot, to Ford's lair, but the British lion—who, by the way, looked more like a circus seal, at least to sarcastic Wyndham Lewis' eyes—did not approve. The *Canzoni* were just too sweetly artificial in diction and subject matter. Ford's laugh or groan worked as a brutal but salutary cleansing; Pound never tired of thanking him or his memory for the remedial surgery. Already in 1916, in a letter to Elkin Mathews, Pound tries to put his finger on what went wrong in *Canzoni*. For one thing, he suggests, in that volume he neglected to make the book into a whole—as he is doing, in 1916, with *Lustra*. "It is *not* so good as the others," he concludes. But this may be hedging; he more truly reflects Ford's reaction in this piece of self-criticism: "I was affected by hyper-aesthesia or over-squeamishness and cut out the rougher poems. I don't know that I regret it in that case for the poems weren't good enough, but even so the book would have been better if they had been left in, or if something like them had been put in their place."[28]

Pound later dated this decisive "lecture" to August 7th. (That very day a postcard from the two of them was sent to Ford's daughter Christina.[29]) Pound had arrived in Giessen a few days earlier. At the time, Ford's critical paroxysms soured the atmosphere somewhat. Back in London, Pound reports on his Giessen visit to his mother: "I had very little time to myself while with Hueffer. Not that there was much work done, but we disagree diametrically on art, religion, politics and all therein implied; and besides he's being married this afternoon or else this A.M. and going to the dentists in the P.M. I was dragged about to a number of castles, etc., which were interesting and about which I persistently refused to enthuse." He rounds off his morose remarks by recommending to his mother some recent prose works by Ford. In his next letter (29 August) he is more outspoken: "Hueffer and I kept the peace, but it can't be said that either of us got much work done. [. . .] also Hueffer dragged me about to Neuheim, which is a springs and baths hell, and to several castles in the vain hope of broadening my mind." Pound could not know that he had been visiting the scene of some of the crucial action in Ford's brilliant novel, *The Good Soldier!*

But Pound's grumblings did not last long; when Violet Hunt, and later Ford, returned to London, ostensibly joined in a marriage *à l'allemande,* Pound was very pleased; "there's one more pleasant room open again," he tells his mother (21 October). And from then on Pound and Ford and Violet Hunt were close companions: Ford introduced Pound to the eminent novelist-naturalist W. H. Hudson, who was something of a legend in literary circles; to the Master of Rye, who "glared" back at Pound at their first meeting, but who turned out, on closer acquaintance, to be "quite delightful."[30] He could proudly write to Harriet Monroe: " [. . .] I *do* see nearly everyone that matters [. . .] ."[31] He was engaged in a positive swirl of dinner parties and tennis games, always, it seems, with Ford as a hectic *primus motor*. With a Rossettian flourish, Pound dedicated his book of translations, *Sonnets and Ballate of Guido Cavalcanti*—somebody slipping up on the spelling—to his friends: "As much of this book as is mine I send to my friends Violet and Ford Maddox Hueffer."

It was about this time that Pound and Ford began to promote each other in print, however tentatively to start with. Pound, the poet, was observing how Ford, the prose writer, was experimenting with verse, with the aim of introducing contemporary speech and contemporary subject matter into a literary genre that was only just beginning to free itself of its nineteenth-century bonds. In some literary remarks, dated December 1911, Pound notes: "Ford Hueffer is making some sort of experiments in modernity." He praises a sort of poetic language that Ford in particular advocated at the time; there was to be no "rhetorical din, and luxurious riot." At least for himself, Pound says, he wants the poetry of "the next decade or so" to be "austere, direct, free from emotional slither." Reviewing these early remarks for inclusion in his *Pavannes and Divisions* with the overall heading "A Retrospect," he comments on this point: "What is there now, in 1917, to be added?"[32]

In the March 1912 issue of the *Poetry Review,* Pound published his earliest review of a work by Ford; this was Ford's volume of verse, *High Germany,* which was just out.

THE BOOK OF THE MONTH

High Germany. By Ford Madox Hueffer.

"MR HUEFFER is making some sort of experiment in modernity." The results will displease most readers. They are nevertheless interesting. They are more readable than the works of most of his contemporaries, because Mr Hueffer fills in the lacunæ between his occasional passages of poetry with doggerel instead of with dullness, rhetorical, heavy, ornate. The poems would be less significant if the author had not behind him a past of Pre-

Raphaelite practices. The experiment is, that is to say, serious.

Three poems, "The Starling," "In the Little Old Market-Place," "To All the Dead," succeed. In them, the author, so over-susceptible to influence, shakes himself free; he does what he set out to do; he is like only himself. The faults, if they be faults, are faults of intention, not of performance.

Mr Hueffer is so obsessed with the idea that the language of poetry should not be a dead language, that he forgets it must be the speech of to-day, dignified, more intense, more dynamic, than to-day's speech as spoken.

Mr Hueffer's cadence is good because it fits the mood of his work.

His flaw is the flaw of impressionism, impressionism, that is, carried out of its due medium. Impressionism belongs in paint, it is of the eye. The cinematograph records, for instance, the "impression" of any given action or place, far more exactly than the finest writing, it transmits the impression to its "audience" with less work on their part. A ball of gold and a gilded ball give the same "impression" to the painter. Poetry is in some odd way concerned with the specific gravity of things, with their nature.

Their nature *and* show, if you like; with the relation between them, but not with show alone.

The *conception* of poetry is a process more intense than the *reception* of an impression. And no impression, however carefully articulated, can, re-corded, convey that feeling of sudden light which the works of art should and must convey. Poetry is not much a matter of explications.

Thus in Mr Hueffer there is a fecundity of poetic idea and of impression, but the rendering, as in "All the Dead," first offends a little, then, as we see the relation of the conversational passages to those more intense, it impresses us. Here, we say, is life articulated; things in relation. It is Browning's method brought up to date. Yet on the third or fourth reading, the jokes are stale. We believe that which is really poetic in the poem could have been—with much more labour, to be sure, on the author's part—conveyed without them. Yet this poem, very strongly, and "The Starling," and "In the Little Old Market-Place," do convey the author's mood, a mood grown of his own life, his own belief, not second-hand, or culled from books. They are true music. They are rare music. And the book is interesting, let us say to me personally, because Mr Hueffer is searching—perhaps a little nonchalantly, but no matter—for a vital something which has in too great a degree slipped out of modern poetry.

EZRA POUND.

One of the slightly elegiac poems in *High Germany,* "Canzone À La Sonata," was dedicated to "E. P." It may have been composed at Giessen.

CANZONE À LA SONATA

To E.P.[33]

What do you find to boast of in our age,
To boast of now, my friendly sonneteer,
And not to blush for, later? By what line

Do you entrain from Mainz to Regions saner?
Count our achievements and uplift my heart;
Blazon our fineness, Optimist, I toil
Whilst you crow cocklike. But I cannot see

What's left behind us for a heritage
For our young children? What but nameless fear?
What creeds have we to teach, legends to twine
Saner than spun our dams? Or what's there saner
That we've devised to comfort those who part,
One for some years to walk the stone-clad soil,
One to his fathom-deep bed? What coin have we

For ransom when He grimly lays his siege
Whose dart is sharpened for our final hurt?
I think we do not think; we deem more fair
Earth with unthought on death; we deem him gainer
Whose brow unshadowed shows no wrinkled trail
Of the remembrance of the countless slain;
Who sets the world to fitful melody—

To fitful minstrelsy that's summer's liege
When all the summer's sun-kissed fountains spurt
Kisses of bubbling sound about our hair.
I think we think that singing soul the gainer
Who disremembers that spent youth must fail,
That after autumn comes, few leaves remain
And all the well-heads freeze, and melody

O'er frozen waters grows too hoarse with age
To keep us from extremity of fear.
When agèd poets pen another line
And agèd maidens coif their locks in saner
And staider snoods; when winter of the heart
Comes on and beds beneath the frozen soil
Gape open—where's your grinning melody?

Pound's praise of Ford's poetry may have had its reservations; for *discussions* of poetry, however, Ford is in Pound's estimate unequaled. In an editorial for *Poetry,* dated by Pound "December 10, 1912" and published in the issue for January 1913, he assesses the "Status Rerum" in London. He settles the balance between his two mentors, Yeats and Ford: "The state of things here in London is, as I see it, as follows: I find Mr. Yeats the only poet worthy of serious study. Mr. Yeats' work is already a recognized classic and is part of the required reading in the Sorbonne. There is no need of proclaiming him to the American public." Among

Yeats's English contemporaries Pound finds "a number of men who have written a poem, or several poems, worth knowing and remembering, but they do not much concern the young artist studying the art of poetry." The important work, in Pound's view, is being done in Paris. Ford's merits are above all as a theorist and critic: "I would rather talk about poetry with Ford Madox Hueffer than with any man in London. Mr. Hueffer's beliefs about the art may be best explained by saying that they are in diametric opposition to those of Mr. Yeats. Mr. Yeats has been subjective; believes in the glamour and associations which hang near the words. [. . .] He has much in common with the French symbolists. Mr. Hueffer believes in an exact rendering of things. He would strip words of all 'association' for the sake of getting a precise meaning. He professes to prefer prose to verse. You would find his origins in Gautier or in Flaubert. He is objective. This school tends to lapse into description. The other tends to lapse into sentiment."

Here Pound has actually formulated the dilemma of choice that was to plague him as a poet for some time to come: objectivity vs. subjectivity; precision vs. "association"; prose quality and realistic description vs. "glamour." For although Yeats may be "the only poet worthy of serious study," his method, Pound warns, is "very dangerous," and his gifts to English art are "mostly negative." Yeats's own poetry has not broadened in scope, and his followers "have come to nothing."

Ford's Giessen lesson has been doing its work, but Pound finds that Ford, in his own poetry, "has rarely 'come off.' His touch is so light and his attitude so easy that there seems little likelihood of his ever being taken seriously by anyone save a few specialists and a few of his intimates. His last leaflet, *High Germany,* contains, however, three poems from which one may learn his quality. They are not Victorian. I do not expect many people to understand why I praise them. They are *The Starling, In the Little Old Market-Place* and *To All the Dead.*" The youngest school, the *Imagistes,* Pound notes, share Ford's insistence on Precision, which is one of their "watchwords."[34]

We recognize the "objectivist" attitude in Pound's comments on some H. D. poems he had sent to the editor of *Poetry* a couple of months earlier; his praise is on the side of the Fordian ideal, which was, of course, all in tune with the credo of the *Imagistes:* "Objective—no slither; direct—no excessive use of adjectives, no metaphors that won't permit examination. It's straight talk, straight as the Greek!"[35] As for himself, Pound soon felt very much part of the *avant-garde* as a practicing poet. "It's absolutely the *last* obsequies of the Victorian period," he writes about his new work.[36]

Pound gave his unqualified approval of Ford's views on the kind of poetry a contemporary poet should aim at—"direct speech" and "vivid impression" being the watchwords—in his review of Ford's *Collected*

Poems (published November 1913, postdated 1914). It was Ford's Preface that especially interested him. It drew heavily on an essay that Ford had published in *Poetry,* "Impressionism—Some Speculations" (August and September 1913), with Pound as an enthusiastic purveyor. This was, Pound wrote to Harriet Monroe, "the best prose we've had or are likely to get." "F. M. H.," he emphasized, "happens to be a serious artist. The unspeakable vulgo will I suppose hear of him after our deaths. In the meantime they whore after their Bennetts and their Galsworthys and their unspeakable canaille. He and Yeats are the two men in London. And Yeats is already a sort of great dim figure with its associations set in the past."[37]

Pound's review of *Collected Poems* appeared in the *New Freewoman* for 15 December 1913.

FORD MADOX HUEFFER

Mr. FORD MADOX HUEFFER is presented to us as the father or at least the shepherd of English Impressionist writers—not that Mr. Hueffer is an institution. Mr. Hueffer is younger by a decade than most of the English Institutions. Mr. Hueffer has preached "Prose" in this Island ever since I can remember. He has cried with a high and solitary voice and with all the fervours of a new convert. "Prose" is his own importation. There is no one else with whom one can discuss it. One is thankful for Mr. Hueffer in [a] land full of indigenous institutions like Gosse, and Saintsbury, and the "Daily Mail" professor at Cambridge for the reluctance of Abraham to take these three upholders of obsolete British taste to his once commodious bosom is a recurring irritation to nearly every young artist.

Mr. Hueffer having set himself against them and their numerous spiritual progeny, it is but natural that he is "not taken seriously" in Institutional quarters.

Mr. Hueffer has written some forty books, very good, quite bad, and indifferent. He can and, sometimes, does write prose. I mean Prose with a very big capital letter. Prose that really delights one by its limpidity.

And now they have collected his Poems. And he has written a charmingly intelligent and more or less inconsequent preface. He has written a preface that one can take seriously as criticism because he declines to lie. He frankly says what he likes—a paradigm for all would-be critics. And for the most part the things he likes are good and the things he dislikes abominable.

It is true that he invents a class of German lyricists, and endows them with qualities more easy to find among the French writers. He supposes a whole tribe of Heines, but no matter. The thing that he praises is good; it is direct speech and vivid impression.

As for the poems themselves one does not need to be a devotee of letters to be amused by "Süssmund's Address to an Unknown God." It is a "conversation" such as one might have heard from the author in any drawing-room at any one of his more exasperated moments this five years. We feel that that author has expressed himself and has mirrored the world of his day. *His* world that is, London, a circle of diners and writers. And his refrain

"God, fill my purse and let me go away."

is its soul cry and its sum of all wisdom.

The acme of intelligence is again reached in "The Three-Ten."

"When in the prime of May-Day time dead lovers went a-walking,
How bright the grass in lads' eyes was, how easy poets talking.
Here were green hills," etc.

The stanza is rather obscure, but we learn that he is comparing the past and present, the fields of Bayswater with the present pavement, and implying the difference in custom. He ends,

"But see, but see! The clock marks three above the Kilburn Station,
Those maids, thank God! are 'neath the sod and all their generation."

It is a light song, but one has only to open the pages of Cowper to return and sing it with fervour.

Of course Mr. Hueffer is obscure, but after knowing his poems for three or four years one finds oneself repeating his phrases with an ever-increasing passion.

When Mr. Hueffer is not reactive; when he is not "getting things off his chest" and off all our chests altogether, he shows himself capable of simple, quite normally poetic poetry, as in "Finchley Road."

. . . . . .
"You should be a queen or a duchess rather,"

In some very ancient day and place as follows:

"Lost in a great land, sitting alone

. . . . . .
And you'd say to your shipmen: 'Now take your ease,
To-morrow is time enough for the seas.'
And you'd set your bondmen a milder rule
And let the children loose from school.
No wrongs to right and no sores to fester.
In your small, great hall 'neath a firelit daïs,
You'd sit, with me at your feet, your jester,
Stroking your shoes where the seed pearls glisten,
And talking my fancies. And you, as your way is,
Would sometimes heed and at times not listen,
But sit at your sewing and look at the brands."

Mr. Hueffer has in his poems the two faces that one has long known in his novels—the keen modern satires as in that flail of pomposities "Mr. Fleight" and the pleasant post-pre-Raphaelite tapestry as we find is in such chapters as that on the young knight of Edgerton in his bath,[38] or in "The Young Lovell."

His emotions make war on his will, but his perception of objects is excellent. From a technical point of view the first poems in the book are worthy of serious study. Because of his long prose training Mr. Hueffer has brought into English verse certain qualities which younger writers would do well to consider. I say younger writers for the old ones are mostly past hope.

I do not mean that one should swallow the impressionist manner whole or without due discrimination.

In "The Starling" the naturalness of the language and the suavity with which the rhyme-sounds lose themselves in the flow of the reading, are worthy of emulation.

Naturalness of speech can of course be learned from Francis Jammes and other French writers, but it is new and refreshing in contemporary English.

As Mr. Hueffer in his opening bow declares himself to be, not a poet but merely a very distinguished amateur stepping into verse from the sister art, one need not carp at his occasional lapses. And there is no doubt whatever that this is the most important book of verse of the season, and that it, moreover, marks a phase in the change which is—or at least which one hopes is coming over English verse. (I refer to the first three sections of the book, the reprints of earlier work need not come into discussion.) Mr. Hueffer has also the gift for making lyrics that will sing, as for example the "Tandaradei" more or less after Von der Vogelweide, and "The Three-Ten" which I have mentioned. This is no despicable gift and there is no man now living in England who is possessed of it in more notable degree.

Hang it all, if "a lyric" means a song calculated to be sung to music such as we know it, we would not be far wrong in calling Mr. Hueffer the best lyrist in England. This métier he certainly knows and he calculates for both composer and vocalist. The "Tandaradei" is one of the few things in modern English that Brahms might have set without being wholly disgusted.

EZRA POUND.

Pound did a second, longer, review of *Collected Poems* for *Poetry,* where it appeared in June 1914. He called it "Mr Hueffer and the Prose Tradition in Verse." It was reprinted as "The Prose Tradition in Verse." It is again clear that with a few exceptions, Ford's *poems* interested Pound less than his *ideas* about poetry. Great praise went to a new poem that Ford published in the same issue of *Poetry,* "On Heaven." This poem, Ford said, had been written at the request of Violet Hunt, who asked for a description of a "working Heaven." By the use of colloquial language and ordinary incidents Ford tries to give his idea of a graspable heaven. Pound had himself arranged for the publication of this poem, and had been quite emphatic in his comments to Harriet Monroe: "The Hueffer good? Rather! It is the most important poem in the modern manner. The most important single poem that is."[39] He consequently nominated Ford for the *Poetry* award for 1913–14.

THE PROSE TRADITION IN VERSE[40]

In a country in love with amateurs, in a country where the incompetent have such beautiful manners, and personalities so fragile and charming, that one cannot bear to injure their feelings by the introduction of competent criticism, it is well that one man should have a vision of perfection and that he should be sick to the death and disconsolate because he cannot attain it.

Mr Yeats wrote years ago that the highest poetry is so precious that one should be willing to search many a dull tome to find and gather the fragments. As touching poetry this was, perhaps, no new feeling. Yet where nearly everyone else is still dominated by an eighteenth-century verbalism, Mr Hueffer has had this instinct for prose. It is he who has insisted, in the face of a still Victorian press, upon the importance of good writing as opposed to the opalescent word, the rhetorical tradition. Stendhal had said, and Flaubert, de Maupassant and Turgenev had proved, that 'prose was the higher art'—at least their prose.

Of course it is impossible to talk about perfection without getting yourself very much disliked. It is even more difficult in a capital where everybody's Aunt Lucy or Uncle George has written something or other, and where the victory of any standard save that of mediocrity would at once banish so many nice people from the temple of immortality. So it comes about that Mr Hueffer is the best critic in England, one might say the only critic of any importance. What he says to-day the press, the reviewers, who hate him and who disparage his books, will say in about nine years' time, or possibly sooner. Shelley, Yeats, Swinburne, with their 'unacknowledged legislators,' with 'Nothing affects these people except our conversation,' with 'The rest live under us'; Remy de Gourmont, when he says that most men think only husks and shells of the thoughts that have been already lived over by others, have shown their very just appreciation of the system of echoes, of the general vacuity of public opinion. America is like England, America is very much what England would be with the two hundred most interesting people removed. One's life is the score of this two hundred with whom one happens to have made friends. I do not see that we need to say the rest live under them, but it is certain that what these people say comes to pass. They live in their mutual credence, and thus they live things over and fashion them before the rest of the world is aware. I dare say it is a Cassandra-like and useless faculty, at least from the world's point of view. Mr Hueffer has possessed the peculiar faculty of 'foresight,' or of constructive criticism, in a pre-eminent degree. Real power will run any machine. Mr Hueffer said fifteen years ago that a certain unknown Bonar Law would lead the conservative party. Five years ago he said with equal impartiality that D. H. Lawrence would write notable prose, that Mr de la Mare could write verses, and that *Chance* would make Conrad popular.

Of course if you think things ten or fifteen or twenty years before anyone else thinks them you will be considered absurd and ridiculous. Mr Allen Upward, thinking with great lucidity along very different lines, is still considered absurd. Some professor feels that if certain ideas gain ground he will have to re-write his lectures, some parson feels that if certain other ideas are accepted he will have to throw up his position. They search for the forecaster's weak points.

Mr Hueffer is still underestimated for another reason also: namely, that we have not yet learned that prose is as precious and as much to be sought after as verse, even its shreds and patches. So that, if one of the finest chapters in English is hidden in a claptrap novel, we cannot weigh the vision which made it against the weariness or the confusion which dragged down the rest of the work. Yet we would do this readily with a poem. If a novel have a form as distinct as that of a sonnet, and if its workmanship be as fine as that of some Pléiade rondel, we complain of the slightness of the motive. Yet we would not deny praise to the rondel. So it remains for a prose craftsman like Arnold Bennett to speak well of Mr Hueffer's prose, and for a verse-craftsman like myself to speak well of his verses. And the general public will have little or none of him because he does not put on pontifical robes, because he does not take up the megaphone of some known and accepted pose, and because he makes enemies among the stupid by his rather engaging frankness.

We may as well begin reviewing the *Collected Poems* with the knowledge that Mr Hueffer is a keen critic and a skilled writer of prose, and we may add that he is not wholly unsuccessful as a composer, and that he has given us, in 'On Heaven,' the best poem yet written in the 'twentieth-century fashion.'

I drag in these apparently extraneous matters in order to focus attention on certain phases of significance, which might otherwise escape the hurried reader in a volume where the actual achievement is uneven. Coleridge has spoken of 'the miracle that might be wrought simply by one man's feeling a thing more clearly or more poignantly than anyone had felt it before.' The last century showed us a fair example when Swinburne awoke to the fact that poetry was an art, not merely a vehicle for the propagation of doctrine. England and Germany are still showing the effects of his perception. I cannot belittle my belief that Mr Hueffer's realization that poetry should be written at least as well as prose will have as wide a result. He himself will tell you that it is 'all Christina Rossetti,' and that 'it was not Wordsworth,' for Wordsworth was so busied about the ordinary word that he never found time to think about *le mot juste*.

As for Christina, Mr Hueffer is a better critic than I am, and I would be the last to deny that a certain limpidity and precision are the ultimate qualities of style; yet I cannot accept his opinion. Christina had these qualities, it is true—in places, but they are to be found also in Browning and

even in Swinburne at rare moments. Christina very often sets my teeth on
edge—and so for that matter does Mr Hueffer. But it is the function of
criticism to find what a given work is, rather than what it is not. It is also
the faculty of a capital or of high civilization to value a man for some
rare ability, to make use of him and not hinder him or itself by asking of
him faculties which he does not possess.

Mr Hueffer may have found certain properties of style first, for himself,
in Christina, but others have found them elsewhere, notably in Arnaut
Daniel and in Guido, and in Dante, where Christina herself would have
found them. Still there is no denying that there is less of the *ore rotundo*
in Christina's work than in that of her contemporaries, and that there is also
in Hueffer's writing a clear descent from such passages as:

> 'I listened to their honest chat:
>   Said one: 'To-morrow we shall be
> Plod plod along the featureless sands
>   And coasting miles and miles of sea.'
> Said one: 'Before the turn of tide
>   We will achieve the eyrie-seat.'
> Said one: 'To-morrow shall be like
>   To-day, but much more sweet."[41]

We find the qualities of what some people are calling 'the modern cadence' in this strophe, also in 'A Dirge,' in 'Up Hill,' in—

> 'Somewhere or other there must surely be
> The face not seen, the voice not heard.'

and in—

> 'Sometimes I said: 'It is an empty name
> I long for; to a name why should I give
> The peace of all the days I have to live?'—
>   Yet gave it all the same.'

Mr Hueffer brings to his work a prose training such as Christina never
had, and it is absolutely the devil to try to quote snippets from a man
whose poems are gracious impressions, leisurely, low-toned. One would
quote 'The Starling,' but one would have to give the whole three pages of it.
And one would like to quote patches out of the curious medley, 'To All
the Dead'—save that the picturesque patches aren't the whole or the feel
of it; or Süssmund's capricious 'Address,' a sort of 'Inferno' to the 'Heaven'
which we are printing for the first time in another part of this issue. But
that also is too long, so I content myself with the opening of an earlier
poem, 'Finchley Road.'

> 'As we come up at Baker Street
> Where tubes and trains and 'buses meet
> There's a touch of fog and a touch of sleet;
> And we go on up Hampstead way

Toward the closing in of day . . . .

You should be a queen or a duchess rather,
Reigning, instead of a warlike father,
In peaceful times o'er a tiny town,
Where all the roads wind up and down
From your little palace—a small, old place
Where every soul should know your face
And bless your coming.'

I quote again, from a still earlier poem where the quiet of his manner is less marked:

'Being in Rome I wonder will you go
   Up to the hill. But I forget the name . . .
Aventine? Pincio? No: I do not know
   I was there yesterday and watched. You came.'

(*I give the opening only to 'place' the second portion of the poem.*)

'Though you're in Rome you will not go, my You,
Up to that Hill . . . but I forget the name.
Aventine? Pincio? No, I never knew . . .
I was there yesterday. You never came.

I have that Rome; and you, you have a Me,
You have a Rome, and I, I have my You;
My Rome is not your Rome: my You, not you.
      . . . . . For, if man knew woman
I should have plumbed your heart; if woman, man,
Your Me should be true I . . . If in your day—
You who have mingled with my soul in dreams,
You who have given my life an aim and purpose,
A heart, an imaged form—if in your dreams
You have imagined unfamiliar cities
And me among them, I shall never stand
Beneath your pillars or your poplar groves, . . .
Images, simulacra, towns of dreams
That never march upon each other's borders,
And bring no comfort to each other's hearts!'

I present this passage, not because it is an example of Mr Hueffer's no longer reminiscent style, but because, like much that appeared four years ago in 'Songs from London,' or earlier still in 'From Inland,' it hangs in my memory. And so little modern work does hang in one's memory, and these books created so little excitement when they appeared. One took them as a matter of course, and they're not a matter of course, and still less is the later work a matter of course. Oh well, you all remember the preface to the collected poems with its passage about the Shepherd's Bush exhibition,

for it appeared first as a pair of essays in *Poetry,* so there is no need for me
to speak further of Mr Hueffer's aims or of his prose, or of his power to
render an impression.

There is in his work another phase that depends somewhat upon his
knowledge of instrumental music. Dante has defined a poem[42] as a composition of words set to music, and the intelligent critic will demand that either
the composition of words or the music shall possess a certain interest, or
that there be some aptitude in their jointure together. It is true that since
Dante's day—and indeed his day and Casella's[43] saw a re-beginning of it—
'music' and 'poetry' have drifted apart, and we have had a third thing
which is called 'word music.' I mean we have poems which are read or
even, in a fashion, intoned, and are 'musical' in some sort of complete or
inclusive sense that makes it impossible or inadvisable to 'set them to
music.' I mean obviously such poems as the First Chorus of 'Atalanta'[44]
or many of Mr Yeats' lyrics. The words have a music of their own, and a
second 'musician's' music is an impertinence or an intrusion.

There still remains the song to sing: to be 'set to music,' and of this sort
of poem Mr Hueffer has given us notable examples in his rendering of Von
der Vogelweide's 'Tandaradei' and, in lighter measure, in his own 'The
Three-Ten':

> 'When in the prime and May-day time dead lovers went a-walking,
> How bright the grass in lads' eyes was, how easy poet's talking!
> Here were green hills and daffodils, and copses to contain them:
> Daisies for floors did front their doors agog for maids to chain them.
> So when the ray of rising day did pierce the eastern heaven
> Maids did arise to make the skies seem brighter far by seven.
> Now here's a street where 'bus routes meet, and 'twixt the wheels
>   and paving
> Standeth a lout who doth hold out flowers not worth the having.
> *But see, but see! The clock strikes three above the Kilburn Station,*
> *Those maids, thank God, are 'neath the sod and all their generation.*
>
> What she shall wear who'll soon appear, it is not hood nor wimple,
> But by the powers there are no flowers so stately or so simple.
> And paper shops and full 'bus tops confront the sun so brightly,
> That, come three-ten, no lovers then had hearts that beat so lightly
> As ours or loved more truly,
> Or found green shades or flowered glades to fit their loves more duly.
> *And see, and see! 'Tis ten past three above the Kilburn Station,*
> *Those maids, thank God! are 'neath the sod and all their generation.'*

Oh well, there are very few song writers in England, and it's a simple old-
fashioned song with a note of futurism in its very lyric refrain; and I dare
say you will pay as little attention to it as I did five years ago. And if you
sing it aloud, once over, to yourself, I dare say you'll be just as incapable
of getting it out of your head, which is perhaps one test of a lyric.

It is not, however, for Mr Hueffer's gift of song-writing that I have reviewed him at such length; this gift is rare but not novel. I find him significant and revolutionary because of his insistence upon clarity and precision, upon the prose tradition; in brief, upon efficient writing—even in verse.

Harriet Monroe mostly let herself be persuaded by Pound's convictions and enthusiasms, but there were crises in his relationship with her. He often found her old-fashioned and provincial, and unwilling or unable to appreciate really valuable verse. His irritation led to threats to resign as foreign correspondent, and he tried in vain to get Ford to take over his place. In a brief note—which may turn out to be the earliest letter from Pound to Ford which is extant in its original form—he appeals to Ford to take over the job. (He used *Poetry* magazine stationery.)

P 2. ALS. 1 1. Chicago.

[London] [ante 12] Nov. 1913

Dear Ford:
   Will you please take over the foreign correspondence of "Poetry" & communicate with them to the effect that I have turned it over to you.

yr E. P.

Ford was not to be persuaded, and told Miss Monroe so in a letter dated 12 November 1913.[45] It reveals his amused and sympathetic attitude toward Pound:

Dear Madam,
   I have received the enclosed letter from Mr Ezra Pound who has gone away into the country without leaving me his address. I don't know whether he has the literary advisership of your organ to dispose of, but I am perfectly certain that I could not do his job half so well as he has done. Could you not make it up with him or reinstate him — or whatever is the correct phrase to apply to the solution of the situation whatever that may be? I really think he applied himself to your service with such abounding vigour and such very good results that it is a great pity that you should part company. Besides, if I tried to help you that energetic poet would sit on my head and hammer me till I did exactly what he wanted and the result would be exactly the same except that I should be like the green baize office door that every one kicks in going in or out. I should not seriously mind the inconvenience if it would do any good, but I think it would really be much better for you to go on with Ezra and put up with his artistic irritations; because he was really sending you jolly good stuff. That is the main thing to be considered, isn't it?

Yours faithfully Ford Madox Hueffer

Many people came to be the butt of Pound's impatience or anger; any irritation with Ford was tempered by loyalty and affection. He early showed a tendency to poke fun at Ford's pretensions—real or assumed— to distinguished heritages, be they familial or literary. He loved to spoof Ford's links to the Pre-Raphaelite heroes and heroines, as well as his German ancestry of—perhaps—baronial distinction. Ford's German extraction revealed itself also in his given name: Ford Hermann. Ford was not unwilling to recognize the possibilities of romance and dignity connected with the foreign name, if only for use as a humorous pseudonym in his collaboration with Conrad on the story "The Nature of a Crime." Polish and German elements were combined to make of the joint authors one "Baron Ignatz von Aschendorf."

Pound made fun of the traits of vanity and pompousness in this Fordian persona. A slight piece in *The Egoist* for 16 February 1914, "An Essay in Constructive Criticism," is, as Pound's bibliographer suggests, most certainly by Pound. Bearing the subtitle "With Apologies to Mr. F- -d M-d-x H- -ff-r in the 'Stoutlook,' " it may have been sparked off by one of the installments in Ford's series of "Literary Portraits" in the *Outlook*. (In "Mr Hueffer and the Prose Tradition in Verse" he praises Ford's faculty of "constructive criticism.") Pound signs his essay "Herrmann Karl Georg Jesus Maria" and adds to it a footnote in the name of "William Michael R-s-tti," that is Ford's uncle by marriage.

As time went on Pound was turning to other centers of force than Ford and his diminishing numbers. These prewar years were trying ones for Ford. His dubious German divorce and "marriage" scandalized and alienated several former acquaintances, a publisher's indiscreet misuse of the name of "Hueffer" for Violet Hunt brought about a libel suit; ill health plagued him, and he suffered from having lost contact with his children.

Pound, who served as Yeats's secretary in the Sussex countryside during the winter of 1913–14, was invited to spend Christmas with Ford and Violet in a nearby cottage. He reported to his mother: "Am down here for a week with the Hueffers in a dingy old cottage that belonged to Milton. F. M. H. and I being the two people who couldn't be in the least impressed by the fact, makes it a bit more ironical. [. . .] Impossible to get any writing done here. Atmosphere too literary. 3 'Kreators' all in one ancient cottage *is* a bit thick. [. . .] Play chess and discuss style with F. M. H."[46]

Pound enjoyed the company of Yeats, who was "much finer *intime* than seen spasmodically in the midst of the whirl."[47] The membership of Pound's new "little gang" reflected his interests in the arts: Wyndham Lewis, painter and writer, and Henri Gaudier-Brzeska, sculptor, now belonged to his closest associates; some of the old Imagist friends were still there: F. S. Flint, Richard Aldington, and his wife, H. D. A new force,

Amy Lowell, soon to be distrusted as leading the Imagists astray, was making her presence felt. A new poet, T. S. Eliot, arrived on the scene and was found to be "worth watching—mind 'not primitive.' "[48]

Pound was undergoing the transformation from Imagist to Vorticist; or was it only a change of name, accompanying a change of affiliation? With the launching of the Vorticist magazine, *Blast,* Wyndham Lewis providing the impetus and Pound the name, Pound was for a time firmly within the Lewis orbit. A new prose writer, James Joyce, invisible as yet, was from then on to profit by Pound's services as admiring and efficient champion. In an essay on Joyce, published in 1916, Pound strikingly omitted Ford from the ranks of significant novelists.[49] (Ford published *The Good Soldier* in March 1915; the beginning of the novel appeared in *Blast* for 20 June 1914.) In a letter to Joyce, written six months after the publication of *The Good Soldier,* Pound lavishes praise—to the point of "inane hyperbole," he fears—on *A Portrait of the Artist as a Young Man:* "In english I think you join on to Hardy and Henry James (I don't mean a resemblance, I mean that there's has been nothing of permanent value in prose in between." Was he thinking of Ford when adding the following: "I know one man who occasionally buries a charming short chapter in a long ineffective novel . . . but that's another story"?[50]

Pound may have had Ford, as the foremost champion of Impressionism, in mind when he wrote his review of Joyce's *Dubliners.* (This was before Ford published the whole of *The Good Soldier.*) While expressing his admiration for the Impressionist school of writers, he deplored certain tendencies to softness and lack of intensity in some of its members. Again one wonders who is the target of Pound's criticism: "There is a very clear demarcation between unnecessary detail and irrelevant detail. An impressionist friend of mine talks to me a good deal about 'preparing effects,' and on that score he justifies much unnecessary detail, which is not 'irrelevant,' but which ends by being wearisome and by putting one out of conceit with his narrative."[51]

Contacts
1915-1920

LONDON, SUSSEX

Ford was no longer at the center of things as he used to be; he no doubt felt left out by *les jeunes* and looked at this development, by turns, with self-irony and self-pity. He felt like a very old great-grand-uncle of the young rebels. In moments of self-irony he could say à propos of Wyndham Lewis and the group around *Blast:* "[. . .] I who am, relatively speaking, about to die, prophesy that these young men will smash up several elderly persons—and amuse a great many others."[1] True, he was still invited to the big literary events, such as Amy Lowell's *Imagiste* dinner in June 1914; he was asked to contribute to the anthology *Des Imagistes,* edited by Pound, and, later, to Harriet Monroe and Alice Corbin Henderson's anthology, *The New Poetry.* He was not included in Pound's *Catholic Anthology 1914–1915,* but then this volume, Pound declared, was put together in order to get a few poems by T. S. Eliot into print.

During the years 1913–1915 Ford often found occasion to put in a good word for Pound in articles and reviews in the *Outlook* and the *New Free-woman.* In September 1913 the outlook, he said, was full of hope, what with D. H. Lawrence and Ezra Pound coming up. He reminisced how he, as editor of the *English Review,* had come upon "suggestions of power in Mr. Pound's derivations from the Romance writers." He had to admit, though, that "Mr. Pound as often as not is so unacquainted with English id[i]oms as to be nearly unintelligible."[2] He praised specific poems by Pound: "Liu Ch'e" and "Letter of an Exile" [i.e., "Exile's Letter"]; he did not like his "Vortex." Not long after the publication of *Cathay,* Ford reviewed it in the *Outlook* for 19 June 1915. This is his earliest treatment in print of a book by Pound. It was authoritative enough for Eliot to quote from it in his *Ezra Pound: His Metric and Poetry.* The first part of the review "From China to Peru" is devoted to another book, dealing with the South American beverage maté. After a paragraph linking the two "exotic" books, Ford turns to Pound's poems; in the introductory paragraph of the review he asserts: "[. . .] if these are original verses, then Mr. Pound is the greatest poet of this day."

[. . .]

The poems in *Cathay* are things of a supreme beauty. What poetry should be, that they are. And, if a new breath of imagery and of handling can do anything for our poetry, that new breath these poems bring.

In a sense they only back up a theory and practice of poetry that is already old—the theory that poetry consists in so rendering concrete objects that the emotions produced by the objects shall arise in the reader—and not in writing about the emotions themselves. What could be better poetry than the first verse of "The Beautiful Toilet"?

[Quotes from "The Beautiful Toilet."]

Or what could better render the feelings of protracted war than "The Song of the Bowman of Shu"?

[Quotes from "Song of the Bowmen of Shu."]

Or where have you had better rendered, or more permanently beautiful a rendering of, the feelings of one of those lonely watchers, in the outposts of progress, whether it be Ovid in Hyrcania, a Roman sentinel upon the Great Wall of this country, or merely ourselves in the lonely recesses of our minds, than the "Lament of the Frontier Guard"?

[Quotes "Lament of the Frontier Guard."]

Yet the first two of these poems are over two thousand years old and the last more than a thousand.

And Mr. Pound's little volume is like a door in a wall, opening suddenly upon fields of an extreme beauty, and upon a landscape made real by the intensity of human emotions. We are accustomed to think of the Chinese as arbitrary or uniform in sentiment, but these poems reveal [them] as being just ourselves. I do not know that that matters much; but what does matter to us immediately is the lesson in the handling of words and in the framing of emotions. Man is to mankind a wolf—homo homini lupus—largely because the means of communication between man and man are very limited. I daresay that if words direct enough could have been found, the fiend who sanctioned the use of poisonous gases in the present war could have been so touched to the heart that he would never have signed that order, calamitous, since it marks a definite retrogression in civilisation such as had not yet happened in the Christian era. Beauty is a very valuable thing; perhaps it is the most valuable thing in life; but the power to express emotion so that it shall communicate itself intact and exactly is almost more valuable.

Of both of these qualities Mr. Pound's book is very full. Therefore I think
we may say that this is much the best work he has yet done, for, however
closely he may have followed his originals—and of that most of us have
no means whatever of judging—there is certainly a good deal of Mr. Pound
in this little volume.

Although Ford for some time remained in the periphery of Pound's
attention, mostly owing to the war, they still joined forces in trying to help
other writers, such as Joyce and Eliot. "F. M. H.," Pound wrote to Harriet
Monroe, who had been reluctant to accept Eliot's "Prufrock," "was just
as quick as I to see that Eliot mattered."[3] Ford was among the poets Pound
wished to see in *Poetry*. He was pleased to get Ford's contribution to *The
Little Review,* a series of essays appearing in six issues in 1918, later collected into the book *Women and Men.* We also note that Ford figured
among permitted writers on the "list" that he approved for his young pro-
tégée, Iris Barry.

Writing in 1917 of a few "beautiful poems that still ring in my head,"
Pound again singled out for praise lines from Ford's translation of Walther
von der Vogelweide, his "Three-Ten," "the general effect of his 'On
Heaven'; his sense of the prose values or prose qualities in poetry; his
ability to write poems that half-chant and are spoiled by a musician's additions [. . .] ."[4]

Ford's activities as critic also stimulated Pound, to agreements and
disagreements. In his essay on Henry James for the August 1918 issue of
The Little Review Pound often refers to Ford's views of his great predeces-
sor, especially as they were expressed in Ford's monograph *Henry James.*
He may have reread it when it was reprinted in 1918. In a letter to John
Quinn he writes: "Hueffer on James spatters on for 45 pages of unnecessary writing before he gets started. I think there are good things in his
book."[5]

Pound may have had reservations about Ford as novelist and poet—
less so about Ford as critic—but there was never any wavering in his admiration for Ford as an oral commentator on literature. He knew full well
that many of his own dicta on verse derived from Ford, and he used them
so frequently that we tend to forget their source. In an analytical assessment of the *status rerum* in London in the mid-1910s, he pinpointed Ford's
lasting contribution: "Ford Hueffer, a sense of the *mot juste.* The belief
that poetry should be at least as well written as prose, and that 'good
prose is just your conversation.' "[6] Other remarks on Ford and quotations
from his works reappear in Pound's memoir of Gaudier-Brzeska and in
Pavannes and Divisions, which collected pieces published in various magazines before and during the war.

The only piece directly dealing with a work published by Ford in the war years is a very brief and largely unfavorable review of Ford's *On Heaven and Poems Written on Active Service*. It appeared under the general heading, "Books Current. Reviewed by Ezra Pound," in the *Future* for July 1918.

HUEFFER

> The Preface to Mr. Hueffer's volume of War poems is a misfortune, both for the author and his friends. Time was when he held a brief for good writing; he has now fallen into the Chestertonian bog. The title poem "On Heaven" was, however, composed in a happier period, and later events have not interfered with its placid and leisurely charm. It is impressionist, and Mr. Hueffer himself tells us that it is "too sloppy." Most impressionism is too sloppy. But this particular poem, despite its general looseness, has patches of great charm and very well-written passages; and it has some sort of individuality, and is not like "every other poem in the language." One turns back with pleasure to the excellent Essay which appeared as Preface to Mr. Hueffer's "Collected Poems" of 1914.

Several of the poems included in this volume were, as the title suggests, treatments of a war that the author had seen at first hand. Ford went into the army in August 1915, and after several months of training in England, left for service in France. In addition to other, patriotic, reasons for Ford's voluntary joining—he was overage for compulsory service—this act meant an honorable breaking out of the saddening situation of his private life.

Others among Pound's associates were taking part in the war: Henri Gaudier-Brzeska, who never came back, Richard Aldington and Wyndham Lewis, who did return. Eliot made several vain attempts to offer his services in the war effort. Pound's daughter, Mary de Rachewiltz, has shown (in "Fragments of an Atmosphere," Autumn-Winter-Spring 1979/80 issue of *Agenda*) that Pound, too, made moves to join, but that nothing came of these attempts. What strikes one, however, in Pound letters available from the war period is how comparatively little they deal with the war, whether it be as a political issue, as a defense of a certain civilization, or as a human tragedy. One comment occurs in a letter to Harriet Monroe, written in the first autumn of the war: "This war is possibly a conflict between two forces almost equally detestable. Atavism and the loathsome spirit of mediocrity cloaked in graft. One does not know; the thing is too involved. [. . .] One wonders if the war is only a stop gap. Only a symptom of the real disease."[7] He shared Ford's views of an aggressive Prussian civilization, especially of the damage it had done to the young: its principles of education, which were geared to the advancement of applied science and philology rather than pure science and humane learning, were fated to kill all sense of joy and mystery in the young. He evidently comments on Ford's analysis of Prussian culture, *When Blood Is Their Argument,* in a letter to his mother (on 23 May 1915): "The book is very good. I trust the faculty of my rotten University will read and digest it. The preface contains a number of statements similar to those which I have made repeatedly any time for the last ten years." In his preface Ford denounced several phenomena which were also objects for Pound's hatred: academicism and materialism, while he expressed his deep love of French culture.

On Gaudier-Brzeska's death in 1915, Pound felt deeply the loss to art: "Gaudier-Brzeska has been killed at Neuville St. Vaast, and we have lost the best of the young sculptors and the most promising. The arts will incur no worse loss from the war than this is. One is rather obsessed with it." Ford's involvement in the war also meant, to Pound, a hindrance to art: "Hueffer up in town on leave yesterday. It will be a long time before we get any more of his stuff, worse luck. He is looking twenty years younger and enjoying his work."[8] His mention (in July 1916) of Ford's subsequent shell shock and hospitalization in France is, if anything, lighthearted, granted that his correspondent, Wyndham Lewis, was no great sympathizer with Ford and, furthermore, had adopted a rather cynical style in his attitude to humanity at large.

Pound's writing in the last year of the war and immediately after reveal new thoughts and concerns; articles in *The New Age* in 1919 reflect his changed ideas on economic and political matters. It was in the office of *The New Age* that late in 1918 he met Major C. H. Douglas, founder of Social Credit.

Pound's disgust with the spirit underlying the war and his deep regret at the loss in human values, which we can glimpse in his letters, were most clearly expressed in *Hugh Selwyn Mauberley.* It is a farewell and a settling of accounts. For the portrait of the dedicated artist, who refuses to compromise his art for material goods and earthly glory, he drew on Ford, who was at this time living the life of the Small Producer cum Artist—or the other way around.

> Beneath the sagging roof
> The stylist has taken shelter,
> Unpaid, uncelebrated,
> At last from the world's welter
>
> Nature receives him;
> With a placid and uneducated mistress
> He exercises his talents
> And the soil meets his distress.

> The haven from sophistications and contentions
> Leaks through its thatch;
> He offers succulent cooking;
> The door has a creaking latch.[9]

1919 was a year of readjustment and a new beginning for Ford. He had revived his old dream of living peacefully in the country, producing his own food and pursuing his intellectual and artistic interests. His new companion, the Australian painter Stella Bowen, found a ramshackle cottage for them, called Red Ford, near Pulborough in Sussex. Ford moved there in April. Later Stella joined him. (This was the dilapidated cottage that Pound immortalized in *Mauberley*.) He changed his surname to "Ford" by deed poll on 4 June.

Pound had welcomed Ford's re-entry into the London world after the war. In a letter to William Carlos Williams he reported on the "situation": "Fat Madox Hueffer in last evening [. . .] ."[10] Did they discuss Pound's plans for a new literary quarterly? Ford had begun to write again, in spite of all protestations that he was through with writing as a profession. *No Enemy*, which summed up his reactions to the war, was written at Red Ford. (It did not find a publisher until 1929.) He began "two immense Novels."[11]

The preoccupations that Pound noted in his portrait of the Stylist are reflected in the slighter prose pieces that Ford published in various periodicals during these months spent in the country. He reminisced about the war and gave expert advice on kitchen gardening; he surveyed the contemporary literary scene and revisited the prewar years, praising the literary *group* as an important support for the writer; for writing "is such a solitary business," he said.[12] *Les Jeunes* was such a group, Ford pointed out, with Pound, Lawrence, Lewis, and Eliot as its most prominent members. Even the urge to write poetry was slowly coming back to him; he finished a long poem "of a Fairy Tale type";[13] this was "A House," which Pound tried to place in *The Dial*. It finally appeared in *Poetry*, whose award it earned, and in *The Chapbook*. He augmented his meager income by occasional reviews, among them one of Pound's *Quia Pauper Amavi* in the *Piccadilly Review* for 13 November. His comments on Pound come at the end of the article, after several rambling paragraphs on *Les Jeunes* and related matters. There is also a brief mention of a book by the Russian-born poet-journalist John Cournos.

[. . .]

Something Different.

    As for Mr. Pound——No, don't imagine that words fail me! They never do; but courage—sometimes! For Mr. Pound is the Bertran of the

modern world. Like Dante, he takes all knowledge for his province; but,
like the Lord of Altaforte, he carries a terribly knotted bludgeon. If I praise
him, he will bludgeon me for praising him wrongly; if I find fault with the
shape of his columns, he will break my legs with rocks rolled down the
summit of Mont Vedaigne. That is the right spirit for a young man mad
about good letters.

It is the only spirit. . . . For years now Mr. Pound has pursued rhythms,
ideographs, knowledges, revolts, learning, remote languages. He has pursued
them incomprehensibly, with incoherences, with dazzling flashes of insight,
in Provence, in Rome, in Philadelphia, in Islington, in the Underground of
Paris, in the Auberges of Toulouse, Poitou and Granada. He has made
essays in the forms of Guillem de Cabestanh, of Propertius, of Meleager, of
"Sordello," of Laurent Tailhade, of Rimbaud, of de Régnier, of de Gourmont, of Ri-ha-ku![14] I can think of no one who has more patiently pursued
a living erudition or more preserved a fierce vitality. His "Cathay" is an
exquisite and consummate rendering of an atmosphere that may or may
not be invented or authentic; and his proud boast at the end of his present
volume—which contains too many debatable "forms" to be touched on at
all cursively, for I seem vaguely to remember that Mr. Cournos has bashed
Mr. Pound somewhere, and no doubt Mr. Pound has hit back in some other
periodical, so that they will each want to do dreadful things to me for
bracketing them together. What a lot of wigs upon the green! Nevertheless,
since no one has so rendered the soul of Propertius as Mr. Pound has done
in "Quia Pauper Amavi," the proud boast of the last lines of this volume
is justified—

Here Ford quotes the end of section XII of *Homage to Sextus Propertius* (from "Like a trained and performing tortoise"). The "boast"
ranks Propertius—Pound's persona—among the great classical poets who
have sung of love.

The Red Ford cottage turned out to be too primitive for permanent
living, and Ford and Stella bought another place, Coopers Cottage in
Bedham, a small village near Fittleworth in Sussex. It was some time before they could take possession of the house; they moved there in September 1920.

The move from Red Ford to Coopers looms large in Ford's letters to
Pound in the summer of 1920. This is in fact the earliest period in their
correspondence that is extensively documented. Ford's withdrawal to the
country had made letters more important as a means of communication.
Ford and Stella had been receiving many visitors to their secluded haven,
Ford tempting his friends with "the most amazing French dishes,"[15] and
in July we find him entreating Pound to come down to discuss *vers libre*
and other literary issues. The letters show that there was a fruitful give
and take; Pound with his useful association with literary magazines served
as Ford's contact man.

In the late spring Pound and his wife had been vacationing in Italy. (Pound and Dorothy Shakespear were married in 1914.) He had managed to arrange a meeting with Joyce at Sirmione in June, and his services were next directed to helping the Joyce family get settled in Paris in early July. On the twenty-first of that month Pound returned to London, determined to make a last attempt at earning a living in England. He felt optimistic enough to have stationery printed with his address, 5, Holland Place Chambers, Kensington, W., to be used as the London address of *The Dial*.

For lack of extant letters—many must have been written—we are plunged without mediation into the discussion between Pound and Ford. We do not have Pound's replies to the first three of Ford's letters written in 1920. Ford opens on an exasperated note; he is irritated by Pound's handwriting, by the blunders and inadequacies of *The Dial,* for which Pound is the provider of European material, and by what might be a minor disagreement between Pound and F. S. Flint about a common statement on Imagism. *The Dial* was serializing Ford's "Thus to Revisit" articles—also appearing in the *English Review* in approximately the same form but with additional installments.

These first few letters reverberate with Ford's indignation at being treated like an obscure or dated writer. His "dancing on the Athenaeum," referred to in one of these letters, resulted in a letter to the editor of that august journal (16 July 1920); in it he criticizes a negative assessment of Flint's book of poems, *Otherworld: Cadences.* He defends Flint's use of *vers libre* as being based on the way ordinary people actually express emotions such as joy and sorrow. In "The Battle of the Poets" section of the book version, *Thus to Revisit, vers libre,* Imagism, and Mr. Pound figure prominently. With humorous bravado Ford claims to be "the doyen of living, Anglo-Saxon writers of *Vers Libre* [. . .] ."[16]

With his letter of 12 July Ford enclosed a message to *The Dial,* for Pound to send along to the editor.

F 1. TLS. 2 11.

Red Ford Cottage, Hurston, Pulborough S U S S E X.
12/7/20

Dear Ezra;

All right! I have however been so used for so long to taking parades for a friend — not to mention an enemy — that it seemed a natural request, understood as I understood it. But put it how you will I am much obliged. I have sent them a longish, simplish domestic poem [i.e., "A House"] — another [On] Heaven, about 750, mostly shortish lines. I will write them a couple more articles on the state of affairs in England —

Squire-Athenaeum-Sitwell people who seem to me to be all much of a muchness viewed from here and on poetry generally. It seems to have gone back four hundred years while I was away — poetry, I mean. I have been dancing on the Athenaeum all this week-end — they are worse than anything I ever saw: Academics perpetually sneering at the French; just like the old paper of the '80's.[17]

   As for you and Flint, God bless you both: I can't make out what it's all about. Anyhow, don't cut my throat just yet over it all. Your handwriting is more incomprehensible than your type-script and that says a great deal; Stella and I spend all our spare moments deciphering your last letter. I expect we shall get to the end of the job before I write again. In the meantime, much more power to your elbow.

                                                          Yours F

P.S.: Whilst you are in Paris would you very kindly go or write to the Imprimerie Gourmontienne — I can't discover the address — and ask them to send me their periodical for a year, giving the 15 frs that are necessary which I will return to you by return. Love to Dorothy.

F 1. Enclosure. TLS. 1 1.

                         c/o Captain Ford **RED FORD COTTAGE,**
                                HURSTON, PULBOROUGH
                                              12/7/20

The Editor, *The Dial*

Dear Sir;
   I seem to have understood the terms of my contract with Mr Pound wrongly; it appears to have been for six monthly articles instead of three. I write these things, however, slowly and with difficulty and, as I thought you wanted — or he — only three, I have not got another ready and may not have for some time. He asks me therefore to send you the enclosed instead. I hope you will like it. As far as it goes it is the sort of thing of mine that America has liked best, and I had intended it for another American magazine that wanted something ⟨Attention of E.P.⟩[18] — but rather than let down Mr Pound — for the mistake was rather mine than his, I send it along.
   I have not yet had the decency to acknowledge and thank you for your cheque and your kind letter; I am incorrigible when it comes to the minor courtesies of life; but let me thank you now. I am much obliged.
                         Yours very sincerely Ford Madox Hueffer.

F 2. TLS. 1 1.

RED FORD, HURSTON, PULBOROUGH
26 [July] /20

Dear Ezra;

Alas, I never come to town and am almost certain not to do so before November, though Stella was shopping there last week. I can't afford to come; and I don't like it when I get there and animals die if I don't look after them and crops go wrong. But I'd like to see you. Couldn't you run down for a night? You shall be guarded from the weather like a day old child and fed exactly as you are fed in Soho . . . I am just finishing a novel about La Vie Litteraire.[19] It is turning out rather finely macabre.

Love to Dorothy; bring her with you

Yrs   F.

F 3. ALS. 1 1.

=Man Falls on Nose=In great haste.
Red Ford 27/7/20.

Dear Ezra:

Your heart is golden: so are yr. words. But the latter are normally — even when they can be read — incomprehensible. Remember that you deal with hempen homespun wits. Does "for a minute" = "at present":? or that you wouldn't think for a minute of honouring[20] our establishment? If the former: we abandon this place — hoping to let it furnished — for a month on the 4th prox, or six weeks: then we return to pack up & move. In Nov. we shall be in town for a short time — so if you intend coming it must be next week end — I find by using this pen of Stella's I can write just like you! but refrain![21]

Thanks very much for the Mercures. All literature will be received very gratefully by

Yrs. F.

I am going to write some stuff about Vers Libre for the Dial, immediately.

F 4. TLS. 2 11.

RED FORD, HURSTON, PULBOROUGH
29/7/20

Dear Ezra;

Het es al een seer invermaagliike vorstelling ! Dichteren en eht solkliik verruckten man siin net te verstahn! Nockni Vlamsk . . . . [22]

In other words we go on Tuesday to
Scammell's Farm

> Bedham
> Fittleworth
> SUSSEX

where a few books would be most earnestly welcomed and where I shall
be up to the eyes in painting, papering, plastering and bricklaying until at
least the incidence of the autumnal equinox. And I am afraid we could not
by any possibility put you up there. but I do want to see you. Could you
by any means come down to the pub — a very gorgeous and replete
one, for a night. An enthusiastic publisher has just commissioned me to
turn the Dial-English Review articles into a book which I shall do as soon
as I have got rid of my novel — I hope before Tuesday. I think it important that we should agree upon a formula for vers libre, non-representa-
tionalism and other things before I go any further. We want some
manifestoes. I mean, I might tread on some of your or X or Y or Z's
corns without in the least doing it intentionally unless as you would say
you or someone puts me right. You forget that it is six years since I
poured oil on these eaux puantes and I don't so hell of a well rem[e]mber
who were Imagistes and what it was all about. I can't afford, either for
time or money, to come up to Town before November, when I shall have
to, whereas you are young, mobile, affluent, fortunate — and interested
in getting the right thing said, almost more than I.

Anyhow: that is that.

As for writers. . . What do I know of them? There was Andre Gide —
but perhaps you have conspued him years ago. . . I used to like the prose
of a man called Tomlinson, but I do not know what has become of him.
Herbert Read also, I like. I miss from your list Cunny G[raham]; and
Hudson; but I suppose there are obstacles of age and the like. Wilfred
Blunt also. I also much admire George Stephenson — but rather for
matter and temperament than for manner. There is also Iris Barry who
should certainly be supported. . . Certainly. And of course Mary Butts.[23]

So you see, I am not much good. . . Why should I be? . . I have done
too much propaganda for too many years; I have rather to attend to
my own Art, in these my — you would say — Indian Summer months. . .
Nux gar erchetai![24]

I suppose the Dial would not like to serialise my novel for twopence
or three pence? It is turning into an Immensity — a sort of Literary Via
Dolorosa. . . I viewed it with suspicion at first; but it comes on.
God bless you.

F.

P 3. TLS. 4 11.

[London] 30 July 1920

H[och]W[ohl]G[e]B[orener]. Frejheer fon Junk:

Will try to get down for a pow-wow.

Will also lend you INstigations, with my latest pronunciamentos and bulls, calves, enclinicals etc.[25]

/ / /

Re/ vers libre etc . . May I summarize.

Dante: "A poem is a composition of words set to music."

That bloody well differentiates prose and verse. Now vers libre simply discards a fallacy that french or English need be versified by a metronomic regularity in smacked and non-smacked, or "long and short" syllables.

The details can be left to Abbé Rousselot and experimental phonetics and the phonoscope.[26]

All one can claim is the right to use the musical component with a musicians freedom.

(Indicated in orig. manifesto by me in Poetry in the year I.[27])

The Apostacy of the Fecal and Excremental band of self-styled Imagists is in their neglect of the Second Commandment:

"Use absolutely no word that does not contribute to the presentation".

This of course has nothing to do with the musical component, it wd. apply irrespective of whether verse was "regular" or "free".

/ / /

Eliot has pointed out that "No vers is libre for the man who wants to do a good job".

/ /

I have pointed out, the obvious, that any art is a mixture of a constant and an inconstant elements [sic].

In verse one can take any damn constant one likes, one can allitterate, or assone, or rhyme, or quant, or smack, only one MUST leave the other elements irregular.

The rhimm, rhamm, rhuff, became INTOLERABLE when people abandoned the utterly libre Ang-Saxon metric, and tried to fit REGULAR assonance, with French regular-syllabic verse.

/ / /

You will, ultimately find my, phanopoeia, melopoeia, and logopoeia discrimination in "Instigations" ⟨p. 233–4⟩

/ / /

You can quote this letter if you so deign. Better it shd. go as a quoted letter than that I shd. bring down any more graven tablets from Helicon.

You can also enlarge upon my:

China: Eye

Greece: Ear, onomatopoeia, quantity,
Provence: Rhyme, (vide Arnaut)
French prose: literary sense, which same has not been a bloody bogey
for former poetic eras, though a few latin poets had it. Notably Ovid and
Propertius. (Horace had got no further than Lionel Johnson or the 18th.
century.)
Ovid had heard of Flaubert, and Propertius of Laforgue.

////

Art: merde. I am fed up. There have been Piccasso and Wyndham
[Lewis], and there have been upon them their parasites. There was also
Gaudier, but he is d[e]ad and, propagandas will not fill his purse nor
his belly.

Willett[28] is interested in the Dial, or rather in its new stationary, and
thinks [John] Lane might take it on for England.
    Glad of any stimulus you can apply in that quarter. ⟨rather important
to get it in here. if N.Y. is to keep the pace.⟩
    Hudson telegraphed me not to come down to lands end to see him last
spring, and I am diffident about springing Dial on him. Wd. look as if my
visit of pure homage was merely a touting trip. Hadn't connected with
Dial when I proposed it.
    Wd. be glad if you cd. drop him a word, use Dial paper as enclosed.
    Also Cunny G. . . . . shd. like him very much indeed but thought he had
vowed farewell to letters.
    Enclose another sheet of stationary to interest him in project.
    Dial has already accepted a mss. from Mary Butts. Blunt is "with
O'Leary in the grave",[29] at least I think he is too old and too unlettered
and vague in his orientation.
    H. Read I never have swallowed, not as a writer. Don't know G.
Stephenson, shd. be glad to see mss. of Tomlinson, but dont in the least
know where he is.

Will try yr. novel on Dial. But probably wd. be bad editing to run novel
and your causerie at same time, and I think it absolutely essential that you
shd. do your general article in each number; . i.e. practically the editorial or
what is bound to become the editorial chunk of the magazine.
    I have started a general impression of Paris.[30]

Will send you my new versicul-opus [i.e., *Hugh Selwyn Mauberley*] to
yr. new address; believe it contains an "advance"; by no means as rich as
"Propertius" but has form, hell yes, structure, and is in strictly modern
decor. J[ohn].R[odker]. thinks both he and I will be murdered by people
making personal application of necessary literary constructions verging
too near to photography.[31]

My defense being that "Mr Nixon" is the only person who need really
see red, and go hang himself in the potters field or throw bombs through
my window.

Have already struggled with my in-laws. I have had to tell 'em a poet
ought not to have ANY friends and relations, and with the option of
lumping or liking they have decided to endure. ⟨Je prends mong bieng ou
je bloody well le trouve.⟩

That's that.

E

Remember Lane, to spur him on to nobilities.[32]

F 5. TLS. 2 11.

> Monday: [2 August 1920][33]
> Tomorrow 3/8/20 to
> SCAMELLS FARM
> BEDHAM
> nr FITTLEWORTH
> S U S S E X

Dear Ezra;

Your letter overwhelms me in a dismantled dwelling, on the point of
moving, I can't answer it all therefore, and what I do answer does not feel
as if it would come coherent. I don't feel that I am the best person to try
any of the writers you mention. I will however have a shot. ⟨— if you like.⟩
Nor do I feel that Lane is much good — Pinker at any rate, between
ourselves, is violently trying to get me to go elsewhere and as he will
probably get up a quarrel over my body with L. I probably shall. But how
would Chapman & Hall suit you? They are just now beseeching me to do
things for them and, if you approve, I will try them. But let me know just
what you want — an English imprint only, or more capital, or reprinting
here. Chapman would probably be better than Lane as they have a much
larger organisation — connection with booksellers and so on, that being
really half the battle . . But I don't want at all to influence you against
Lane if you think him all right.

You will see H.G. [Wells] and Ethel Mayne dancing over my corpse in
the English Review.[34] It leaves me only a little annoyed — but still annoyed! I will communicate my feelings as to Vers Libre and your letter's
manifesto about it when I get into more tranquil surroundings. I think I
rather — at first sight — dislike the "music" idea in the connection;
but no doubt we mean different things by the word.

Do you see your Athenaeum's "Henri de Regnier writes well"! And the
incredible Shelley stuff . . . It is the Hidden Hand of Professor Wircklicher
Geheimrath Putz coming back via the Cocoa Press![35] Mark my words.

By the bye: Why say in the Little Review that I am gaga![36] Is it the
voice of South Lodge [i.e., Violet Hunt] whispering across your great
Atlantic to reverberate here? Or what is the game? In a very few years,
mon vieux, you too shall be toothless, myopic and resemble Maclise's
drawing of Talleyrand . . . . But I suppose you have never seen it. So
continue to dance in your beflowered meads au son des fiffres de crotale.

I quite see the point of ⟨non-⟩serialisement in the Dial; don't suggest it to
them. I just thought it would give them cheap copy — but it would take·
four years to be put through, anyhow!

Let us know when you will be able to tear yourself from the great
metropolis and we will find you a room. Stella has been drawing vivid
caricatures of you inspecting the pigs.

Yours   F.

P 4. ALS. 2 11.

[London, 11 August 1920]

Cher F.

Your August stuff – very lovely — wish to hell you could write the
whole magazine.[37]

N.B. prière d'une vierge —

Don't stir up W[yndham].L[ewis]. = Those two "etc" in July are more
bother than they were worth.[38]

Must hang together until this show is established. = you can take it
out of me — & of W.L. ·— if you must — later on.

yr E

Secret sea-side conference — = oh much more than Flint (who. by the
way is now en-wroth'd with Richard [Aldington] (who'se ars poetica I cd.
spare) for his, R's saying that F.S.F. isn't a genius —)

The that which some people demand !!!

11 Aug.

Have not seen Ethel & H.G. in Eng. Rev. yet. = but they can't possibly
matter.

Ford and Stella had taken up temporary lodgings at Scammell's Farm
while they were doing up the cottage they had bought. Pound visited them
in Bedham possibly shortly after 11 August, staying at the local inn.
In *It Was the Nightingale* (p. 138) Ford describes his friend's arrival:

And Mr. Pound appeared, aloft on the seat of my immense high dog-cart,
like a bewildered Stuart pretender visiting a repellent portion of his realms.
For Mr. Pound hated the country, though I will put it on record that he
can carve a suck[l]ing pig as few others can.

Pound could presumably take the joke of having an animal named after him; Ford called his male goat Penny, the reason being that "he facially resembled (but was not) POUND, Ezra."[39] In spite of his dislike of the country Pound took pleasure in Ford's descriptions and analyses of country life, at least enough for a few words of praise: in an article on W. H. Hudson, the great naturalist-writer, he refers to Ford as being at his best "when he is least clever, when he is most sober in his recording of country life."[40]

With his newly acquired French contacts, Pound was able to propose new projects, which are mentioned in the next few letters. The internal debate between the two friends is continued, concerning questions such as preoccupation with Subject versus interest in Rendering, or their respective roles in the Battle of the Poets, one as an Impressionist, the other as a Vorticist. Pound is, in Ford's eyes, incorrigibly American, a fact which, Ford claims, shows itself in his assessment of, for example, Henry James. In one of the letters Ford undertakes an evaluation of Pound's *Instigations*.

F 6. ALS. 1 1.

Scammells Farm, Bedham, Sussex, 30/8/20

Dear Ezra:

Ref: Proust. It wd. amuse me to <u>do chez</u> S[wann] — & I would do it if yr. publishers wd. give me <u>plenty</u> of time, so that I cd. do a bit now & then when not in the mood for other work.[41] If they wanted a complete Proust I wd. edit it: i.e: go through anyone else's translation to see that it was all right, & write an introduction: but I couldn't translate the whole: it wd. bore me to tears. If as I say, they gave me lots of time I shd. not be exigent as to price: but I shd. leave that to Pinker — to get the best he cd. for me. That is that.

I am getting along with the <u>Dial</u> article — with interruptions from Violet who has planted herself in the neighbourhood & runs about interrupting my workmen & generally making things lively. I fancy she had you followed by a detective when you came down & so got the address. But I may be wrong about that, However, we flourish as the Abbey Theatre itself never did.

Yrs. FMF.

F 7. TLS. 1 1.

BEDHAM nr FITTLEWORTH S U S S E X
1/9/20

Dear Ezra;

I daresay it won't be easy to find suitable translators without frightful, eventual scrimmages; still, it can be done and my back is broad and my

skin tough. Any how some decent translation of a French Author is a cock
we owe to Aesculapius. You will have to do one yourself ⟨in that self
sacrificing spirit!⟩ — and certainly Aldington and Flint.

The Yale Review has written to ask me to write for them. I suppose
the DIAL does not consider itself as monopolising my services. Or does it?
The Y.R. seems to be solid enough. Do you know anything about it? I am
doing some underground work for the D. in the way of securing writers for
whom you wished; I will let you know results when there are any.

As for the disciple of Holmes's Watson, I had no idea of even suggesting that his appearance was any more than a coincidence (What an
assonance!) It is annoying of course as it is not good for Stella to have
shocks. I suppose I shall have to go to the police for protection, which
will be a bore. . . It is thus that we cultivate the Muses on a little thin
oatmeal.

Yours F.

F 8. TLS. 2 11.

Bedham 5/9/20

Dear Ezra;

Your forwarding to me of the DIAL correspondence is a nuisance. . .
For obviously I do not 'submit' things to papers. I am commissioned. The
only course that remains open to me is to request you to cable to the DIAL
that I withdraw 'A HOUSE'. I should, in the natural course of things,
have nothing more to do with the Paper. However, I know you do not
want that — and indeed the Cause comes before personal mortifications —
so let that go.

I have written the enclosed with great haste so as to get it, if possible,
in time for the next number. If it is in your opinion, in time, would you
have a copy typed at express speed by some local typing person and send
it off. If you think it will not be in time, just send it back to me. It isn't
good — I need such an immense amount of leisure and reflection to do
anything nowadays, and, what with bothers and things, I do not get much
chance of either. It will do to stop a gap and the next one shall pick up
the strings and make a tidy pattern.

Essentials then: Cable the Dial: H[ueffer]. withdraws House. . . . Get a
copy of this stuff typed and returned to me post haste; forward the stuff
itself to the D. for the October No. and let the annoying matter drop. I
will write two more articles for them; afterwards things may be more
defined.

Anyhow, good luck to your efforts. I am sorry they are attended with
so many botherations. In frantic haste.

F

P 5. TLS. 5 11.

[London, 7 September 1920]

Abba, my father,

Forgive them, they know not . . . They are young men, of excellent intentions, who until eight months ago had no contact with writers.[42]

To cable wd. be to appear to show more interest in their actions than is well for them to receive the impression of.

The point is not whether they want 30 pages of poem; the point is does the Yale Review want it to such degree that your convenience is fostered by having it transferred.

I struggled for six months to get "Prufrock" into "Poetry". The present people are a far better outfit than "Peotry".[43] Educational campaign must begin in the office.

/// They sent back three of my cantos, then they cabled, then they wrote wd. I return same to them. Since then (yesterday, in fact,) comes letter that they haven't room for two poems of mine they have already paid for. "more especially as" they are printing a prose article of mine about Paris.

They are also "printing all they have room for" of Proust in October.[44]
///
They have however "advanced", really advanced with great rapidity during the last five month[s]. They have conspued the London Mercury; they have lost belief in the intelligence of the public. And they really eat from the palm instead of snapping at ones fingers.

They wrote very deferentially: You had said some other paper wanted "A House"; did I think etc. etc. it cd. be managed without lesé F.M.H. beings as how it was 30 pages. etc.

Do consider that their only fixed dimentions are those of page space; all else is fluid

They have clique-o-phobia and terror. AND ⟨the next job is⟩ to get them to understand that a magazine must be a concentration of the interest of a ten or twenty writers;

and one has got to make 'em see the not very obvious or superficial difference between this and running a clique organ.
///
Quae cum ita sint: I will, con permisso, write either that they are to send "A House" to the Yale [Review] as you can't be bothered waiting for them to get round to it.

Or I will continue the line I took with them in my first reply. Namely that they must stand to their guns; that, from ⟨point of⟩ their own interest they wd. lose more by my suggesting that you move on the mss., more of your interest in the magazine, "solidarity" than the space or three times it wd. be worth. (The position officially being that I have NOT mentioned their spatial difficulties to you.)

Their present "consideration", delib. before their parliament is whether they shall take on the motto
    "Laisser a ceux qui en valent la peine, franchement ecrire ce qu'il pense".
    (It looks like bad french, but Remy [de Gourmont] wrote it. and I dare say a gramatical eng. equiv. cd. be found.)

They must make|a "spiritual home" for say twenty of the best writers, after that the public be damned, it can trundle along when it gets ready (and will certainly be heard howling "Aihj. wite fer me, maaaaama" before many moons have deciduated.)

                              ///

    I don't think the prose is in time. The Oct. number comes out on the 25 th. ⟨of Sept.⟩ and today is the 7th. I am having three copies made, and will send the first copy to N.Y. that will hold the space in Nov. no.
    But think you will have time to make any emendations you want, and send on emended copy.
    I think it is a very noble Gallifet charge, at least that was first effect.[45] On second reading it seems cooler and more composed.
    Certainly excellent strokes in it. And the parable werry true.

First impression was that you were throwing yourself a bit too naked and reckless upon the spears.

                              ///

One or two minor points that I might raise, but probably better keep my mouth shut until you have completed the matter ??[46]
    A. I agree that the present lit. disease in U.S.A. is a confusion of
        self-expression with art. Wrote warning edtrs. of that fact, a few
        days ago.

        Possibly damnd ergotising plus personal complex, and not a contra-
        diction of anything in your essay: While "Homage to S. Propertius",
        Seafarer, Exile's Letter, and Mauberley are all "me" in one sense;
        my personality is certainly a great slag heap of stuff which has to be
        excluded from each of this [sic] crystalizations. And an expression
        of the "personality" wd. be a slag heap and not art.

        I wonder if you are right in saying "we" (yunkers) wanted to wipe
        out impressionism.
            Certainly one was full of academic bunk, and certainly you
        started the assault on it, so far as I was concerned.

I take impressionism as the first necessary assault on Fanny B[r]awn[e] and the Folios.

And certainly one backs impressionism, all I think I wanted to do was to make the cloud into an animal organism. To put a vortex or concentration point inside each bunch of impression and thereby give it a sort of intensity, and goatish ability to butt.

Structure, inner form, (thence departmentilization, which ultimately demands a metric, a rhythmic organization, each part necessarily of the whole, just as in prose (H.J[ames].) each word must have its functioning necessary part).

Forgive this endlessness.

Your way of putting the matter is probably wiser. Any damn thing I put down is so susceptible of being made into a new academicism.

Wish to gawd you cd. have a bit of peace and quiet.

yr E

Salut à S[tella].

F 9. ALS. 1·1.

Cooper's, Bedham 10/9/20

Dear Ezra:

I haven't a ghost of idea about translators' prices. How shd. I have? Anyhow it is a labour simply of love: it can't "pay" me & I don't care. Say £50 for translation & £20 for Preface, if you like. Or anything else. Or 9/– per 1000 & £20 — or anything else. I hate to put the burden on you but I simply don't know.

I like first glance of yr. Instigations very much. Particularly the James — wh. I think is the best piece of prose you have done. However I will write at length later. This is in haste.

Yrs. FMF.

If they haven't done that typing yet, just return ms. & I will type & amend as I go. I will attend to Varieties of Vortigious Belief in next no.[47] This one is only generalising & I note yr. personal reservations. I think the whole movement conspuait Impressionism.

P 6. TLS. 1 1.

[London, early September? 1920][48]

Dear Ford

[William A.] Bradley (vid. enc.) thinks he has now got terms from Nouvl. Rev. Fr. re/ Proust, which his firm will accept.

He "objects on principle" to leaving your fee to publisher's sense of
square deal. (After all he does write himself, and has to get his living
out of said firm.)

Also he wants me to telegraph your answer. It is a little difficult. One
doesnt want to alarm H[arcourt].B[race].H[owe]. and Co., and one must
think not only of self but of other translators, if any, and not cut the rate
below "liv[i]ng wage" and other trade union ethico-standards.

One might telegraph in form "Hueffer suggests . . . so and so", asking
goodish but not alarming figure and leaving loop hole for negotiations.

At present Bradley thinks your doing the "Cote de chez Swann" is as
much as he had better embark on; leaving question of complete edition
for the present vague.

He wants complete edition, but details can wait.

yr E

F 10. TLS. 2 ll.

BEDHAM nr FITTLEWORTH S U S S E X 19/9/20

Dear Ezra;

I have been too much cluttered up what with getting a novel [i.e., *Mr.
Croyd*] corrected for the typist and the continuing ⟨activities &⟩ incursions
of Violet [Hunt] and her agents — which are really bad for Stella[49] —
to write about Instigations which I will do in a full dress letter. Perhaps
now if no one comes down the chimney!

Firstly: It is a very good piece of work; full of good definitions and
makings clear. The JAMES I still think is the best of it; I don't know
whether it would gain or lose by being more carefully arranged; perhaps it
would lose in impressionistic value. . . There are one or two points: In
your appraisement of Henry's individual works you are too American (I
daresay I am too European) If you look them through again you will
notice that you cease to be interested in them as soon as the Trans-
atlanticism goes out of them and only take notice again with the American
Scene — after Antaeus had actually touched Western Earth again. You
are in fact bored with civilisation here — very properly; and so you get
bored with the rendering of that civilisation. It is not a good frame of
mind to get into — this preoccupation with Subject rather than with
rendering; it amounts really to your barring out of artistic treatment
everything and everyone with whom you have not had personal — and
agreeable — contacts. There is the same tendency in your desire for the
STRONG STORY and in your objection to renderings of the mania for
FURNITURE. You don't, as a cadenced verse writer, like prose at all and
want to be helped ⟨to read prose⟩ by being given stories written a coups de
hache; and, having no taste for bric a brac you hate to have to read about
this passion. . . But it is one of the main passions of humanity. . .

Stephen Crane used to say that he was not giving fancy prices for corner lots and battlefields — but he gave them all the time. . You might really, just as legitimately object to renderings of the passion of LOVE, with which indeed the FURNITURE passion is strongly bound up. . . Still, these are only notes; but I think you might think about them — because you might harden into the Puritanism of the Plymouth Rock variety — which would be a disaster. . . Anyhow it is a very valuable piece of work and I am very glad you have done it; some passages gave me real pleasure in the reading)) I mean pleasure in the language, which is a rare thing. . .

   Having got the nuvvle off my hands I will go through the DIAL article at once and send if off, probably on Tuesday. . . It occurred to me, ref. Bradley, that I really ought to have left the question of terms to Pinker. I wish I had; but I suppose it is now too late?

   I hope Dorothy flourishes.

Yours   F.

   Anyhow I'm a damn better typist than you! Quat [sic] do I owe you for those copies — and the Gourmont subscription?[50]

The rest of the letters exchanged in 1920 focus on the fate of "A House" and the "Thus to Revisit" series. In Pound's last letter for this year he reveals his dilemma: Where to go next? He had grown increasingly dissatisfied with his life in London. There was no longer any intellectual *life* in England, he felt, except what centered on his own "eight by ten pentagonal room." The question was, he told William Carlos Williams, "whether I have to give up every shred of comfort, every scrap of my personal life, and 'gravitate' to a New York which wants me as little now as it did ten and fifteen years ago. Whether, from the medical point of view it is masochism for me even to stay here, instead of shifting to Paris."[51] He found it difficult to earn a living by his writing; many of his articles and reviews—on music, drama, economics—appeared under pseudonyms. He decided to try Paris as his next base, at least for a year. Not long ago he had helped Joyce to settle there with his family; now the time had come for Pound himself to begin a new life in a new environment. It turned out to be the life of an exile.

F 11. TLS. 2 11.

COOPERS, BEDHAM nr FITTLEWORTH S U S S E X 10/10/20

Dear Ezra;

   For goodness' sake don't worry any more about the matter. I had my grouse about it out last month and that was nah poo finny.[52] I haven't a rancorous thought left — even as far as the DIAL is concerned; and never had any at all about your share in the business — for which, obviously I can have nothing but gratitude. I know how that sort of person lets one down — and for the matter of that I know something about the troubles of that sort of person, so I can make plenty allowances for them too.

The only point that remains is the question of the U.S.A. copyright. I fancy the HOUSE is the sort of poem that <u>might</u> have a popular enduring sale even in your country right or wrong. Munro [i.e., Harold Monro] is publishing it here with cuts by John Nash in November;[53] I am full up with the Yale for the next quarter. If you could get Poetry or the Little Review or something of the sort to take it — for nothing, if necessary — I should be rather glad. — But I daresay that is only my over-carefulness. Anyhow if there is anyone whom you might like to please by giving it to them, just give it to them. Perhaps Bradley has a periodical? It is merely the question of copyright which concerns me.

I shall be sending you the next instalment of THUS TO REVISIT tomorrow or next day. It is possible the DIAL may not want that either. If so, don't worry. It will appear here in the ENGLISH REVIEW and upset the people I want to upset all right, and the bookrights are contracted for with Chapman and Hall all right too. But again the matter of U.S.A. copyright comes in, for bookrights. Perhaps Bradley might consider those too. It would be all for the good of the Cause if he would. But in any case don't, pray, worry; I am absolutely calm about these things.

We are getting on with the rendering of this house less troglodytic; the Abbey Theatre note is fast disappearing; I have got some pedigree Large Black pigs; we shall be throwing timber next week and so on.

We shall be coming up to Town to the Coles' early next month and shall remain there for an indefinite period;[54] afterwards we shall be in residence here more or less permanently. (This information is for your private ear) I daresay we shall then meet.

Please thank Dorothy for writing; it was very nice of her but not really necessary ⟨except for friendship's sake⟩ . I am more like the White Queen than people think. Stella sends her love to you both; she is fairly flourishing.

Yours   F.

F 12. TLS. 1 1.

BEDHAM 11/10/20

Dear Ezra;

Here is that second article. You may differ from it in places: but I will right your wrongs — and those of Waller, Suckling, Lawes, Purcell and Arnaut Daniel when I come to section PHONETIC SYZYGY

It occurs to me that I wrote rather ungraciously, yesterday, when I uttered no thanks about your appreciation of A HOUSE — and Dorothy's.

The fact is that, writing after lunch and beer, I was a man of but one purpose — to assure you that I did not care about the DIAL contretemps; and did not even regard it as a contretemps . . . But of course I like your liking A HOUSE: I daresay, one day, I shall appear as a better [Coventry] Patmore[55] — Quien sabe? . . A patmore crossed with Grimm, Heine and — disons! — Gautier[.] For I begin to think we have let ce pauvre Theo be too much overshadowed by the others of the Soirees de Medan.[56] And now it looks as if the whole lot were about to disappear before the moonrise of Henri Beyle — of whom I wrote impassionedly somewhere in 1894! And then it will be the turn of the Goncourts — or me — or you! God bless you both!

F

P 7. TLS. 2 11.

[London] 21 Oct [1920]

Dear Ford:

The Dial is abs. chuck a block; they are printing your fourth article (don't make out whether fifth had arrived or not) at any rate they are printing what had arrived in N.Y. up to Oct. 8th.

After that I can't guarantee anything. I feel that anything further wont get in. . . . at least not for a long time, unless it <u>tickles</u> the editorial fancy.

Advise that you hold off next article until they ask for it; or until they ask me to send on for more stuff;

present indication is that they want "no more european copy until June" . . . unless it is twelve lines of Hardy. ⟨They observe that the shorter the poems the better "judging from the last that have appeared."⟩

Of the edtr. I will say only that he [has] more virtues than any other millionaire editor I know of.

They had accepted a lot of stuff before I sent in the french copy, which was evidently in excess of what they had anticipated, both quantitatively and, happily, qualitatively.

I wrote the other day to the New York Post about your work; they had written me, in vague terms about a hoped for improvement in their Lit. Sup. Canby is editing same.[57]

I also have hopes that they are improvable. They wd. be useful as counterblast to Times.

I wrote independently of Dialitions, and before rece[i]pt to [i.e., of] Thayer's letter last night.

inter tenebris.

E

F 13. TLS. 1 1.

COOPERS, BEDHAM nr FITTLEWORTH S U S S E X

24/10/20

Dear Ezra;

I have received the reverse[58] — by the same post as, apparently you received the letter to which you refer. This seems to be a matter of strategy — unless you think the letter is only a circular, it seems to call for some reply direct, from me. Shall I send them the third article and say I want special rates, for which they seem to ask. It is no particular trouble to send them carbon copies of the stuff, which goes into the English Review in any case and ultimately to Chapman and Hall and I should prefer them to finish this [as number] three because the first two are rather senseless without the winding up: but I don't want to do anything to queer your pitch in any, any way at all!

Thanks for writing to the POST; I don't know why you should take all this trouble; but I'm just as grateful as if I did!

We expect to come to Town on the 4th. inst, if strikes do not make it impossible. We have got a motor, so the railway does not matter; but I suppose there may be difficulties about food. So, if that does not intervene we shall meet about then!

Yrs F.

Verso of *F 13*. Scofield Thayer to F.
Dial letterhead. TLS. 1 1.

[New York City] Oct 8, 1920.

Mr. Ford Madox Hueffer,
% Captain Ford,
Red Ford Cottage,
Hurston, Pulborough,
Sussex, England.

Dear Mr. Hueffer:—

It may be of interest to you to know that we have raised our rate of payment for prose to two cents the word. In exceptional cases we shall pay more than this.

Yours truly, Scofield Thayer

P 8. TLS. 2 11.

[London] Monday [25 October or 1 November 1920]

Dear Ford

Have not been on writing terms with that idiot bitch in Chicago [i.e.,

Harriet Monroe] for some years, but have sunk the hatchett and written her a cooing note; hope it works.[59]

Didn't say Dial had refused, but that poem was about to appear here, Dial full, and I in deep regret to lose mss. which her printing of On Heaven gave her next right to.

It seems to me one will have to try to start a magazine here. Cant perpetually run Eng. lit. from N.Y. and the wilde peerayrieeeeee.

Anything the Dial does to increase Am. circ. above certain point will damage its sale here. (non-extant as yet.).

Moi je deviens idiot. Whether twere better in the jettison of noncombustibles to treck for Paris, and forget the natural idiom of this island, or in the face of all too damn tumultuous seas and boat-rates emigrate, and on the quayed and basket-covered banks of bleak Manhattan, chase the trade of letters !!! Balls that itch not, etc. or in the teeth of Rhonda suffer printers pension corporations weekly to bombard me?[60] Et bloody cetera.

Have you any idea how far [Austin] Harrison has gone in his relentment to me-ward?[61]

The Dial has turned off a rather amusing thing by [Philippe] Soupault and I have some more [Paul] Morand stuff that it has no room for.

Am also less ferocious than I used to be. I shd. have to talk to Harrison viva voce before one cd. come to anything. His business manager was very prompt and affable re/ exchange of ads. ⟨with Dial⟩ but don't know that that means anything.

Still if Austin is for an anglo-french entente I am in position to assist.

///

What you might, if it isnt too bloody a bore, say, is that enc. list shows what I did for Dial in six weeks visit to Paris; that I am mecontent with them re/ your poem, and that they are full up for six months, and that here's all this connection under my hand, to say nothing of my own energies.·

If he wants to talk he cd. send me word where & when to call on him

yr E.

Contacts
1921-1924

SUSSEX, PARIS

One of the few outlets that remained to Pound was *The New Age.* Its editor, A. R. Orage, commented in the issue for 13 January 1921 (p. 126) on Pound's decision to leave London. Mr. Pound had been "an exhilarating influence for culture in England"; he had "left his mark upon more than one of the arts [. . .] ." But, Orage stated, "like so many others who have striven for the advancement of intelligence and culture in England, [Mr. Pound] has made more enemies than friends, and far more powerful enemies than friends. Much of the Press has been deliberately closed by cabal to him; his books have for some time been ignored or written down; and he himself has been compelled to live on much less than would support a navvy."

When being interviewed by the *New York Herald* shortly after his arrival in Paris, Pound denounced England as suffering from the same "poison" as existed in German "kultur" and in the American university system, that is, a senseless and insensitive propagation of *facts,* at the expense of developing an understanding of the workings of facts. Particularly deplorable he found the English neglect of two books on credit control and economic power by one Mr. C. H. Douglas.[1]

Before settling down in the French capital, Pound and his wife went to the Riviera, staying part of the time at the Hotel Terminus in St. Raphael. By mid-April he was back in Paris, taking up temporary residence at rue des Saints-Pères, while his wife visited her family in England.

While staying at St. Raphael, Pound attended to the business of getting Flint to prepare a joint Flint-Pound-Ford statement or history of *Imagisme* as it once was. They had been laying plans for such a document, over dinner at a London restaurant and via letters. (Apparently these plans for a book came to nothing.) Flint expected more assistance on the project than Pound was willing to give. In a letter of 23 January Flint suggested that Pound "write the first rough draft of our joint screed, and send it on to me to fill up." Pound wrote the first part of a letter to Ford on the verso of Flint's "epistle."[2] He replied to Flint's letter the same day he wrote to Ford, probably enclosing a "schedule" similar to the outline he sent to Ford.

The question of the origins of *Imagisme* was a sore point in the relationship between Pound and Flint; they had quarreled—Flint with a great deal of asperity—about who had been the most important of the originators and about who had belonged to the group. It was Flint's essay, "History of Imagisme," in the 1 May 1915 issue of *The Egoist* that had caused the disagreement to flare up. Among other things, Pound had found fault with Flint's essay for its failure to mention Ford's role in the affair: his insistence on the significance of "simple current speech" ought to be considered as one of the sources and influences.

P 9. ALS. 2 11.

St Raphael. Jan 30. [1921]

Address. via. 5. H. Place Chambers W.8.

Dear Ford:
In <u>verso</u>. epistle from F.S.F.

=

As near as I can remember I gave him an outline, the day we all dined in Addison Rd.

—

Am now sending him an outline for a book — or very nearly a book

=

as I think you agreed he wd. do that sort of descriptive prose rather well.

—

Don't know how he will take the outline

—

but if you see him you might encourage the product

=

There is a lot of Hulme's <u>mss</u> that Orage will lend him

—

as further "nucleous".

=

Roughly = the cenacle.
        Hulme.
        Eng. Rev.

me — Imagisme
Various shades of symbolism —
your impressionism (more or less what Flint himself believes.)

—

& my ticks for <u>centre</u>, intensity, vortex — hardness

hokku — as an aside. etc.

I'll annotate the work, or do introd = or <u>not</u>, or whatever he likes —
except write it.

=

    cd. say certain things in notes that might be amusing — but not impor-
tant enough to use as text — at least not <u>cause</u> for a book.

                                               Love to youall, E.

Harriet [Monroe] says "House" is appearing shortly.

    Ford and Stella had spent the last few weeks of 1920 in London, and
as a matter of course they had seen Pound off and on. They returned to a
wintry and muddy Bedham. The farming adventure had turned out to be
an expensive experiment, and Ford also suffered setbacks in his attempts
to place his writings. He found consolation in the admiration of visitors
who came to pay homage to "Cincinnatus," the role his old collaborator
Conrad saw him in. Stella Bowen, in her reminiscences, characterizes Ford
as needing "more reassurance than anyone I have ever met. That was one
reason why it was so necessary for him to surround himself with disciples.
[. . .] In exchange for the help that he gave Ford received something very
valuable—something that was good for him and without which he could
scarcely live. He received the assurance that he was a great master of his
art."[3]

    Ford's "Thus to Revisit" articles were brought out in book form in the
spring of 1921, with several minor alterations.[4] These rambling reminiscences deal with writers and writing since the nineties and center on his
own involvement with the new literature. It was, he asserted, a book of
Propaganda for Creative Literature.

    Pound's presence in the book is quite strongly felt. Ford opens his
chapter, "Mr. Pound, Mr. Flint, Some Imagistes or Cubists, and the
Poetic Vernacular," by quoting, approvingly, Pound's "Don'ts," including
his jab at a line from a very early poem by Ford ("dim lands of peace"
from the poem "On a Marsh Road [Winter Nightfall]"). He then sets

about to explain to the less Instructed Reader how these rules for poetry came about as a protest against derivative poems written in the Great Tradition. His remarks suggest *vers libre* as the remedy for the dying art of poetry. He even advocates the use of slang, when slang can express shades of meaning which have become lost to sanctioned language. Browning and Hardy "showed the way for the Imagiste group."[5] To illustrate the "cleanness" of the Imagistes, he quotes, among others, Pound's "Liu Ch'e" and the opening stanzas of his own "In the Little Old Market-Place." He finds his own lines more "conversational" than the other specimens quoted; they have "the sound rather of a man talking amiably to just any company." Mr. Pound is a very great poet, Ford attests, with an immense, whimsical erudition. The prose of his critical writings is another matter, though: his aphorisms are "like sharp splinters of granite struck off by a careless but violent chisel." Pound's habit of *rendering* rather than *commenting* lends his critical writings "an atmosphere of restlessness." They are "craftsman's notes" rather than the balanced prose of "the Born Critic." But "whatever Mr. Pound is or is not," Ford concludes in a quick survey of Pound's career to date,

> of this the Reader may be certain: Wherever two or three Men of Letters— of Printed Matter—are found united in irritations some splinters from one or other of Mr. Pound's chippings will be found at the bottom of their poor, dear abscesses. The kindest-hearted man that ever cut a throat [. . .] this American son of all the Troubadours has kept up [. . .] a ceaseless substrife throughout distracted Europe. [. . .] The uninstructed Reader should imagine this Rufous Terror, with an immense physical vigour and the restless itch of a devil, pursuing the Irritating-Beautiful—in the disguise of a cattle-hand across the Atlantic, in an Islington doss-house, on Montmartre; as a tramp on the Montagne Noir, in Venice, in Madrid, in Barcelona—and, God knows how, through an infinity of scripts, parchments, Romance notations, volumes, ideographs, libraries, Quellen, documents inédits and the wrappings of fried fish. And of this I am sure: I could not say that I have never written an insincere word "for the sake of a little money or some woman." But I will give Mr. Pound that character.
>
> There can have been few men whose deaths have so often been announced.

Pound was pleased by the testimony; he told his mother (31 May) that "Old Hueffer" had been "very amiable" in his last book. He wrote to Ford complimenting him on the book.

Throughout *Thus to Revisit* Ford brings in likes and dislikes shared with Pound: an enthusiasm for Henri Gaudier-Brzeska and *vers libre* in English; an aversion to the Typical Academic Critic and dead language. He formulates a dictum on the art of poetry that Pound was to make his own: looking back on his apprenticeship as a poet Ford says, "I had to make for myself the discovery that verse must be at least as well written

as prose if it is to be poetry." As evidence of his early discovery he intro-
duces his poem "The Great View," which was written in what turned out
to be *vers libre* and which was based on observations of everyday life and
written in "exactly the same vocabulary as that which one used for one's
prose."

Some of the disagreements between Ford and Pound regarding the
theory and practice of poetry are only hinted at in Ford's banteringly affectionate treatment. He implicitly places Pound among *Les Jeunes* who
once attacked Ford's Impressionism. He touches lightly upon the relative
importance of subject and technique in writing; Ford extravagantly insists
that technique—the how to write—is the only thing he cares about. But
the overall picture shows the two of them fighting side by side on the
barricades.

While preparing his articles for book publication Ford was struck by
his many contacts with American writers in the course of years. In a letter
to Harriet Monroe he writes: "[. . .] I have a book coming out in the
Spring. It is going to get me ostracised here—but on looking it through
it is astonishing to me to observe how, from Stephen Crane to James and
from him to Ezra and T. S. Eliot, your country right or wrong figures in
one's reminiscences."[6]

Pound found Paris to be a good place. True, even here fools abounded,
but they were "less in one's way" than in London.[7] He was in close contact with Eliot and Joyce, blue-penciling the poems of the former, boosting
the latter. Eliot ought to be got out of England, he suggested, and William
Carlos Williams was advised to take a year off and come to Europe to
meet some interesting people. He renewed his contacts with *The Little
Review;* he became interested in new sculpture and new music, working
himself on an opera incorporating texts of François Villon. He eked out
his income by translating and signed an agreement with Boni & Liveright
to deliver such translations as the publisher requested. An important paragraph was added to the contract to the effect that the publisher agreed
"not to demand Mr Pound's signature on the translation of any work
that Mr Pound considers a disgrace to humanity or too imbecile to be
borne."[8] On the successful revision of *The Waste Land* manuscript he extended his "complimenti" to the author, at the same time suggesting what
he still saw as the major problem with his own epic: the problem of
structure.[9]

It is clear from Pound's correspondence that there was steady contact
between him and Ford during these early Paris years. There are no surviving letters from Ford to Pound for the year 1921; there are indeed
very few Ford letters from Pound's Paris period. They maintained their
mutual services: Pound as contact man, Ford as general adviser and critic
of work in progress. Pound took his poems to other masters as well: he

humbly consulted Hardy on "Homage to Sextus Propertius" and "Mauberley"; he had also asked his friend "Bull" Williams to comment on them.
By concerted efforts of Poundings and Hoofings they tried to get things
done; some people, like Flint, evidently did not give off any signs of life
and energy.

Some remarks of Ford's (now lost) on "the Grand Manner" called
forth a slightly peeved response from Pound; they were no doubt of the
same nature as Ford's 1911 "groan" and later critiques of his friend's
hankering for the medieval or Pre-Raphaelite touch. Pound felt slightly
guilty about this tendency in himself to "go into nacre and objets d'art."
Even so he was asserting his growing independence of Ford's preachings
about contemporary speech and the *mot juste:* "Some day I shall lose my
temper, blaspheme Flaubert, lie like a – – – – and say 'Art should em-
bellish the umbelicus.' "[10]

P 10. ALS. 3 11.

Hotel Terminus St Raphael. 6/4/1921

Dear Ford:

Is the "Grand Manner" what we have been trying to cure me of for so
long? — or is it something desiderandum. I have just had another longer
& more gracious letter from Maximus Thomas [i.e., Hardy] of Dorchester
who don't however mention the G.M. — — I don't think it had occured
to him.[11]

He says the S. Prop. ought to have been called "S.P. soliloquizes" or
zummat o' thet zort. = by which small phrase he pokes the weak spot in
most writing of the last 30 years. = what a dam'd lot of aesthetes we
are. =

One almost comes to believe that the artist ought to be too damnbloody
stupid to be able to perceive anything but his subject. = all of which
tallies with various things you have grown weary of reiterating. I shall be
happy to bask in your showered glory when I get to Paris = shall
probably carry "Thus to revisit" in place of pass port, saying to all &
sundry "Thus am I" (Ozymandias) = The local tennis club has presented
me with an silver ash tray ⟨with 12 enameled blue & green fish⟩ (note the
G.M. in "an silver") in token of my victory of my rheumatism. = For
the first time in years I have had a real rest & written nothing — not even
book rev. for Dial — pendant trois mois.

The sun sets like a blazing barrel head, orange & stage pink. — all the
unrealities of the musical comedy stage — being evidently the authentic
tradition of some damn mediterranean realist. = Paris next week & a
plunge into gawd knows wot. — certainly a change of life

I can't recall Percival Gibbon — the last ½ of the name suggesting munino, I fancy I did meet him in the days of the multi-secretaried Eng. Rev. but there is no ineffaceable or individual dent in my memory. nor have I heard of a Rheyr[12] = It is possibly John[Rodker]'s turn to look after such phenomena.

Hope to see the home made illustrations as well as "Revisit". when I get to Paris.

New book on "Constantin Guys" — full of interest. Cocteau, Morand, Proust, have new stuff out. – & also the skittish Piccabia — whose [Jésus Christ] Rastaquouere I haven't yet seen.[13]

Flint I dare say sparks only under repeated & steely impacts, Poundings or Hoofings — then no steady combustion = Primate instrument probably not thirsting in se for your gore but merely tacit. = "No one" seems to have heard from him. (at any rate our Times confrere hasn't.)

With salaams to Stella & Esther.

y E

Address for letters. H.P. Chambers until I get a roost in Paris

P 11. TLS. 2 11.

59 rue des Saints Peres [Paris]
11th May. [1921]

Deer Foord:

In viewwww of the fffffacts that: the Dial has finally sacked me; and that the Little Review has been most noble in getting suppressed for Joyce, even unto the nth. time; we are making the L.R. a quarterly, and I am bringing out a special summer number.

20 photos of Brancusi's stuff (more to it than to anything except Gaudier's, and more mature in some ways.)

The whole of Cocteau's "Cap de Bonne Esperance" (tr. by Jean Hugo, and rediged by me.)

Collaboration promised from Morand, Cros, and Picabia.

Features for the year, one essay each number by me on the Artist, i.e. four numbers with 20 reprods. Brancusi, Picabia (blocks probably borrowable for this)

Lewis and Picasso. ⟨(probably book on 4 mod. artists as result.)⟩

Cocteau has also written to Cendrars, who is in Rome. If he isn't too slack to answer that will about clean up the active element here.

3d number to contain a small anthology (sel. by me) of active french poetry since 1912 (i.e. where I about end in Instigations).

///

In view of which facts, do you feel free to collab. there is no pay for
anyone. But you belong in the ring and are certainly younger than the
junior pundits of Times, Chapbook, Eng. Rev. etc.

I wish you wd. also, if it aint too much trouble, pick up stray stuff in Eng.
I mean IF Flint or Rodker does anything interesting.

S.V.P. the L.R. is still "American" and the local talent shouldn't be
crowded out by European stuff; not right to send stuff which is no better
than what can be done in Greenwich Village. I won't have H.Reed[i.e.,
Read], he is too bloody dull.

Also your damn Island probably needs him; this safety valve in
Hesperia probably reduces pressure on England's dying engines ANYhow.

I see the Irish Times is offering £100 prize for nice clean novel of
Irish life, really "true" and neither kiltartan nor psychoanalytic. . . . .
whoopeee.

/ / / /

Do you want me to wangle you a review copy of "Ulysses", for say review
in Eng. Rev. or elsewhere ???

/ / /

Re/ L.R. present address is
Miss M.C. Anderson, 27 W. 8 th. St. New York
Love to Stella.

your Ezra.

Pound's turn came to offer a critique of Ford's recent work. From his
lodgings in Paris he sent complimentary remarks on *Thus to Revisit,* followed by an outspoken, critical "lecture" on his friend's faults as a writer:
his cluttering his writings with outdated, sentimental stuff. (As per August
1918—writing on Henry James in *The Little Review*—he had found only
"exceptional moments" of great awareness in Ford's novels.) Ford was
apparently hurt by these criticisms—protesting against this " 'ymn of
'ate"—and Pound hastened to assure him of his love and admiration.

P 12. TLS. 1 1.

59 rue des Sts. Peres Paris VI e.
22 May [1921]

Chere Vielle Feve[14]

You have done a very charrming book, and have also and at last got
over your bloody point . . . . NOT that prose an potry are the same, but
the remarks on provincialism, takin' information for granted, and for
mots justs etc. ⟨p. 74–5, 77–93⟩

At any rate several pages of the only criticism that has been in England.

I dont know that it will "do any good" in England, it is a comfort to a
few enlightened spir[i]ts, perhaps three or four Amurkns will get the point.
I shall any how try to administer it to them as they arrive sul questa riva
(Sher. Anderson, Kreymborg, Thayer etc. one by one like leaves in
autumn). Seder tra filosofica famiglia, Aliscans,
   with me for a bloomin Farinata among the less solid shades of the
Ang-Sax world.[15] Metaphor dont quite work, as one seems rather to have
emerged from the murk of England a riveder le stelle.
   Brancusi, Picabia, Cocteau all more free and flightful than the moulting
vultures of W.C.2.

I daily ask myself why the hell I stayed in Eng. so long; and then comfort myself with reflection that one cdnt. have left during the war, and that
I probably escaped as soon as possible, or very nearly so.
   Two country cousins (Wyndham (P. Wyndham Lewis) and John
(Rodker)) have descended upon me during the course of last week . . . . . It
is ridiculous after so short an immersion here, that one shd. suspect
ᴏoneself of being about to feel about english visitors here, as one did
about Americans in London.

I don't know what to do about Stella's request for an art paper. There's
L Amour de l Art, which is a sort of French Burlington; and la Vie des
Lettres, Anthologie Internat. that reproduces Lipschitz.

The new L.R. shd. be better than either IF it goes. Picabia has been
down with near-pneumonia, so the Kangaroo [i.e., "Kongo Roux"] is
delayed a week or so.[16]

There is the intelligent nucleus for a movement here, which there bloody
well isn't in England.
   Wd. Chapman H[all]. send review copy of Revisit, not to Dial, but
to Dr W.C. Blum care of Dial ??[17]
   God knows when I'll get a flat. Have very pleasant high balcony in
this hotel — but not much space.
   Love to you both.

                                              E.

P 13. TLS. 2 ll.

                           59 rue des Sts Peres Paris VI[e]
                                   26 May [1921]

DEER old Bean
   To continue lectures begun by Holman 'Unt, despite present outrageous
postal rates.[18]
   WOT you dont bloomin' see is that wot you do with ideas is just as

bad for the reader's morale as wot Bridges does with langwidge.

I.E. you hang onto a lot of old tarabiscotage Sancte Foi Catholique, Tory party, etc. O the hell of a lot of it; and that not only is it necessary to have the mot juste, and the order of words simple, without interjected digits obstructing, and grampion hills gramping etc., it is equally necessary that the writer shdnt have his <u>citron</u> filled with semblable clots of ancient furniture sentimental, traditional, purely decorative et bloody cetera. (even if one isn't treating the same in immediate paragraph it, the clutter, causes a slide-around just as deliterious as the slide-around (verbal) in the Times lit sup.)

In return for the blessings conferred upon me in 1911 by your lecture of, let us say Aug 7 th of that year, these presents.

And that my ancient Feve is why Mr Conrad who writes worse, and all the bloomin others who write worse, sell more.

And also possibly why old Hardy gets through despite his funny way of writing verse. Have just had a poem from him, full of every sort of inversion verbal, but so DAMN straight in thought. Just like the straight-ness you say is in Huddy[i.e., Hudson]'s prose (though it very often ain't IF one is lookin fer it)

And that My Dear Col. Blood[19] is where you bloomin well listen to me (if you really want the 'knack', and aren't merely throwin' amical roses), the little places where the reader <u>glisses</u> on yr. so charmin' verbal surface.

I admit it is better to meander than to put up a fake structeure in rectangles pretendus, (Kip[ng]. and H.G. [Wells])

No, mong cher, you are full of suppressed forsooths and gadzookses of ideation. For which reason some liar has just said yr. book is not a treatise on the art of writin'. etc.

AND it aint any use, not to you it aint, no more than my early clingin to "forloyn"s and swevyns.

It rises and dances in [The] Young Lovell, i.e. rises to the verbal surface, where it is better than when druv in. Perhaps yr. very struggle to get the lympid verbal surface has druv it in'nard.

In any case, continuin' the late 'Olman, I send my analyst's dossier, fer wot it is wurf. As my belief as to why you don't swat the beadsighted fly at thirty yards.

And so they begat each other.

Or so at least it is up to you as the sole jeune in England to start your bloomin little movement sur l'isle

> Il y avait un jeune type sur l'isle
> Who had not the universal appeal.

> There Bennet and Wells
> Is the bookies that sells
> in spite of our stylistic squeal.

You are all right as long as you are talkin abaht prose or style, when you
get off that you go all right until you strike a bit o somfink decorativo,
after which you rabble like a bloody brebis.

Benedictions & Greetings to Stella.

yE

P 14. TLS. 1 1. Enclosure.

59 rue des Saints Peres Paris VIe.
[June-July? 1921]

Dear Gruberroruntopus:
I wrote you a long but incomprehensible letter to say that you[r] talk
of a 'ymn of 'ate was nonsense. I was only writing you because of the
great love an' admiration and admiratio that I manage to bear you.
I enclose some remarks of Mr Liveright. He appears to pay his authors.
At least he has just sent me a cheque, and that is very nearly a blood test.

Will you let him know what you have to sell him. I cant answer his
letter u[n]less you tell me what there is unsold. I take it the Good Soldier
and most of the novels have already gone to them bloody states. What
about the heart of country, and men and women. etc etc. etc.[20]
s.v.p. Either write to him, or send me a letter I can forward.

Love to Stella.

Ezra

[Horace Liveright to Pound. Encl. with *P 14.*]

I've been thinking a good deal about Ford Maddox Hueffer these days.
Would you mind letting me know again at great length just what you
think of his would be best for this country, and before you write, make
sure that what you suggest has not already been published in this country.
I think a volume of his, if it's the right one, should go very well this
coming Spring.

After this little contretemps things returned to the normal exchange of
ideas on where and how to get published and paid. They were both hard
up; Quinn came to Pound's rescue after the latter had bravely declined
financial aid, while Ford's situation as Small Producer and Writer was
becoming even more precarious.
Pound tried to arrange a reunion in London during a hurried visit in

the fall of 1921; he seems to have brought it off, for shortly afterward
(22 October) he reported to his mother that "Hueffer [was] about as
usual." Yeats was "somnolent."

P 15. TLS. 2 11.

59 rue des Sts Peres [Paris] VIe.

[August? 1921]

Dear Ford

That son of a bitch Canby offered me 40 bones for an article[21] and
has just sent me eighteen; as you have been dealing with him for some
time, perhaps you can tell whether this is a special pleasantry on his part,
or a fixed habit.

He asked if he might cut the article, I replied that he cd. if he didn't
alter sense or reduce the price. He has of course removed most of the
sting, in fact nearly all of the sting.

However, passons. As I persuaded you to write for his weed, and took
further trouble for him when he first wrote me, I am inclined to regard his
character with disfavour.

2.

Will any bleeding son of a whore's behind publish a book by me on
Brancusi (the beautiful genius). He is doing what Gaudier might have
done in thirty years time. The saurian Lane claims to have sold about 215
copies of the Gaudier (since when he has done the £2/2 abortion on
Yakobstein) [i.e., Jacob Epstein].[22] The Brancusi ought to have about
100 illustrations, and about half as much letter press as the Gaudier. (Wd.
back down perhaps to 60 illustrations if cdnt. manage the 100.).

The Brancusi might restart the sale of the Gaudier, as I shd. naturally
refer to Gaudier and to the book on him, fairly often. (Argument for
Lane, but not for any other barabas.)

As usual, I dont expect to make anything by the job, amt of royalties
being negligible I dont see that it much matters what the percentage is
called in contract. Suppose one had better demand 60% in order to make
barabas think one expects to acquire.

I think the size and format of, type etc. of the Gaudier is o.k. for a book
on sculpture. (The Vandieren "Epstein" too expensive, snob de luxe
a'mmosphere, that cd. be avoided.)

Will the fact that I am about to appear in Mercure de France, Les Ecrits
Nouveaux, La Revue Mondial, be of any use? (Dont mention this save as
priviledged communique, to publisher's agent, it wd. only provoke more
hard feeling and anti-french outbursts in the gutter press.)

When I say "what G. might have done in 30 yrs. time" expression naturally inaccurate. B. is at least fifty, and there is the accumulation of wisdom; one is first annoyed at his saying that "sculpture n'est pas pour les jeunes hommes", and that Gaudier "avait enormement de talent" but hadn't time to get results. But the fact is on his side, and after knocking about his' studio for a while one sees what he means.

Zadkine has ability, but is still years ages behind Gaudier. As for Brancusi, it is a comfort to find a man who knows more about his own job than oneself does about it (his).

═══

Salutations to Stella & Blessings on the house, the pigs, the etc.

yr E.

P 16. ALS. 1 1.

[London] Tuesday [October 1921]

Dear Ford

Am here on rush visit of 3 or 4 days. Is Stella still in town?[23]

My belle-mere says her cook is hopeless — but she (belle-mere not cook) wd. be very pleased if you & Stella cd. lunch here on Friday at 1³⁰·

──────────────

[Jonathan] Capes not wildly optimistic about books on AHT.

yrs ever Ezra

Sorry to be so abrupt. only got in last night.

In December 1921 Boni & Liveright published Pound's *Poems 1918–21,* containing three "portraits" and four cantos (Cantos IV–VII). He needed frank criticism of his epic, which so far refused to yield a satisfactory design, and in January 1922 he sent the draft of what was then Canto VIII to Ford, asking for incisive comments. A highly significant exchange of views and arguments is documented in the correspondence between the two in the early months of the year. This exchange reveals that, contrary to what has been generally believed, Pound discussed this canto before its publication in *The Dial* for May 1922.[24]

Ford was at the time busy completing his first postwar novel to be published, *The Marsden Case.* After putting the finishing touches to his own manuscript, he went through Pound's draft very carefully and sent him detailed comments, possibly in more than one letter. His criticism concerned "zoological" and other improbabilities and Pound's unfortunate predilection for archaisms. He had nothing to offer on the subject of structure. The canto as it was published in *The Dial* may not have differed from the version sent to Ford, with one minor exception (see *P 18*). Pound was not satisfied with the canto, however, and later reworked it: he deleted the first fourteen lines—perhaps as a result of Ford's criticism of the repetition of cadences—added a couple of new lines and fitted the whole into his epic as Canto II.

P 17. TLS. 2 11.

> 70 bis, rue Notre Dame des Champs, Paris VI e.
> [13 January 1922]

Dear Ford.
    Note address.

Death breeding struggle for simplicity. I dont know whether you have had a shot at my bloody cantos. You wont have liked much of 'em. I wish however your infinite patience could persuade you to go through the enclosed with a red, blood-red, green, blue, or other pencil and scratch what is too awful.

    I've done fifteen or more versions, all worse or less or more. I wonder if the things I think will draw your "My Gawds" are the same things that I fear will do so.

    At any rate, as you know, there is no possible way of getting any criticism, and one goes blind, deaf after a time.

    Dido and the, 'elenaus, 'eleptolis, have to stay, they are the links with the preceding canto. Up to now it has been mainly hash, necessary beginning if I am to reconstruct the various ichthiosauri that I need later in the poem. Hope to confine it to American language from now on (with possibly a very verreeee few lapses into Chinese, choctaw, greek, provençal etc.)

    However, not for me to say what I want to do, but, if you are so amiable, for you to say what has got onto the paper. It damn well needs a fresh eye. And les jeunes, etc. are no use, ⟨to me for these matters. All see less than I do.⟩

Liveright has been here, advantage over other publishers is that he was in wall street first, not an office boy in a boite d'edition.

    Dont know that will be much use to you, but he seems ready to take more chances than the others.

    Greetings to Stella.

> yours ever Ezra

13th Jan

F 14. ALS. 2 11. Lilly Library

[Bedham, Sussex] 21/3/22

Dear Ezra:

I put yr. m.s. away in an exceptionally safe place while I was finishing
my novel – & have spent the fortnight or so since I finished in searching
for the m.s.. Here it is at last however, pencilled according to yr. com-
mands.

Pardon if the suggestions are mostly zoological. That is how it falls
out. Zoological mistakes don't matter a damn, serving to give Reviewers
a few more pence for a few more lines — but zoological questionabilities
⟨.A.⟩ do because they arrest the attention of the Reader of Good Will &
that arresting of the attention blurs the effect of the poem. One says:
"Do waves, wirling or billowy things run in the valleys between hillocks of
"beach — beach-grooves? I don't think they do: they are converted into surf
"or foam as soon as they strike the pebbles & become wash or undertow in
"receding & then run."

Per se that does not matter — but the weakening of the attention does.

It is the same with your compound words like "spray-whited" & "cord-
welter." — But as to these I am not so certain: my dislike for them may
be my merely personal distaste for Anglo-Saxon locutions which always
affect me with nausea & yr. purpose in using them may be the purely
aesthetic one of roughening up yr. surface. I mean that, if you shd. cut
them out you might well get too slick an effect.

A. applies of course to Snipe : vine-must : lynx & slung oxen &
pulling seas:
i.e: the vine is the stock, tendrils, leaves etc on wh. grow the grapes
    from wh. the must is made.
Pulling seas would not matter if you did not have oarsmen in the next line
Slung oxen ditto, if there were no shipyard in the line before suggesting
    oxen being taken aboard an At. transport liner in slings
The same with lynx & tail.

I wouldn't bother you with these verbal minutiae if you hadn't asked
for them; the latter part of the poem — of the first page & a half is a very
beautiful piece of impressionism, as good as anything you have ever done &
that is what really matters. I do hope you'll go on & get the whole thing
together in volume form as soon as possible. It'll get onto the world a
feeling of big achievement.

Of course, I think that, in essence, you're a mediaeval gargoyle, Idaho
or no! And it's not a bad thing to be.

Things here are much as usual except that it's snowing on one side of
the house & the sun shining on the other which is not an absolutely
everyday thing.

A fellow has written asking for the French rights of four of my books:[25]
I take it I owe that to you. He wants me to quote him a lump sum for
the four. Have you any idea what wd. be a proper amount? I'd be glad
if you'd let me know.

Glad too to have yr. news!

God keep you any how. Stella sends her respects: E[sther].J[ulia]. will
soon be old enough to do the same.

Yrs. FMF

P 18. TLS. 5 11.

70 bis, rue Notre Dame des Champs Paris VI e.
[post 21 March 1922][26]

Dear Hesiod:

Thanks orfully. It is only the minute crit. that is any good, or that prods
one. First to rebuttals. Ox is slung. At least my recollection is that I saw
in Excideuil a sling and wondered wottell it was until I actually saw an
ox in it. D[orothy]. also thinks I told her at THAT time of seeing the ox. I
don't believe this is an hallucination born of seeing the sling and building
hypothesis that it was for ox.[27]

Can't think everyone has seen army transports, or that they wd.
superpose modern derrick & classic ship.

Thank heaven the points that worried ME, have got by your eagle optic;
that's some relief.

Now Snipe?, arent they the damn longlegged barstards that scurry along
the sand in N.J.? I can hardly go in for reed-birds or more scientificly
differintiated orniths. I wuz told as a kid that the damn things were snipe.
BATHIAN BRIMFUGL BRAEDAN FAETHRA, is the general text.[28]

I tried a smoother presentation and lost the metamorphosis, got to be a
hurley burley, or no one believes in the change of the ship. Hence mess
of tails, feet, etc. will condier [? i.e., *conduire,* "suggest"] shifting the tail,
but it don't need to be taken as part of next animal. some of the other
mammifera are certainly tailed. That not the pint, I know.

Re/ The double words, and rep. of cadence. The suffering reader is
supposed to have waded through seven cantos already: MUST bang up
the big-bazoo a bit, I mean rhythm must strengthen here if he is to be
kept going.

KHRRRIST, To make a man read forty pages of poetry, and with
prospect of 300 to follow ????

As to Gargoyles, some one has got to make the plunge, decide whether the Epic, or wottell of cosmographic volcano is extinct or not. It will take me another thirty years at least. Shall probably do vol. of first ten or fifteen cantos.

The problem of Coeur Simple and the Gt. American desert is still before me.[29]

If you remember the VII th at all, you will remember that I did get as far as Soho and Bayswater. Am not really interested in anything that hasn't been there all the time.

That probably dif. between prose and poetry. Prose can be made of something that merely occurs once in a given setting, or if you Flaubert-eneralize, of something that a lot of people are doing "in a given way", Feinaigle, Amoros, etc.[30]

//

(Am up on that work, as have just passed an enormous article on Joyce and Bouvard to Mercure.[31] They say I am not "assez vulgarisateur" and want a few paragraphs added.

Very dif. from London, where they wd. merely tell you to go to hell if you weren't assez mosche.[32])

Surely one speaks of "receding wave".[33] It may be a technical looseness of phrase, but it is certainly "english". "Wash" is impos. Homophone with laundry. (which is used both of the institution and of the wash).

No use old bean. There is def. an association or aroma of words, apart from the justness.

English simply hasn't the mot juste in the french meaning. And french is abs. paralyzed and dying from a too strict logicality.

Cocteau of interest because he is the only one who dares beard the syntax bogey in its arid lare.

///

Re/ pulling. Surely, you must have been at sea in storm and know how the bloody wave pulls the whole boat. Boat makes a heave at wave, cuts in a bit, then gets dragged off course.

Gorm, I've spewd eleven times onto the broad gray buttocks of the swankin Atlantic.

It is anything but a "run", its a pull,
Are you thynxxing of a lynx or a hyena?

Thanks eturnully, for going over the thing.

Snipe, long legs, long beaks, certainly on Jersey shore, lepping about the pools left in the sand. Fond memory of cheeildhood.

Will have another go at the matter.

///

About [Victor] Llona. I dont know whether it is possible to get more than 3000 fr. gross from a french publisher for author and translator. I am, as you know, always timid in these matters. I think if you got 10,000 fr. down for four novels it wd. be about what might be expected. May Sinclair is the only author I know who can give you any more exact information.

Joyce got 1000 for the Portrait, and his translator got 1000, and was annoyed because Joyce hadn't held out for more.[34] On enquiry I found out that the MORE meant 3000 instead of 2000 ⟨for the two of them⟩.

That's private.

Dont see that "surf runs in beach groove" wd. do. surf is definitely the curving over and the foam,. Wave runs up beach, <u>and then runs back,</u> "receding wave" is surely english.

Can't read your note on splay. The bird spreads wing, and nips with beak. Preen, I suppose, is verb you want. To preen IS to nip at feathers with beak.

/ / /

Question of "joints", not of bird but of poem. Cant be really determined until the thing is done, and one goes back over it. I know there is waste in the "get away" at beginning of this, but main incident, has got to set in the whole. Lynx with preceding. Poor old Dido is the coupling.

May be able to eliminate some of these things later. It helps in a way to print the single cantos, and get 'em out of the shop. Also one sees better on printed page.

AND the damn thing acts as accusation much more strongly than if it were in desk in typescript. Also draws more objections.

Disadv. of starting in Idaho, one never hears of 20 th. or XIX th century, until one is too old. Joyce lucky in copping form of Odyssey. But it wd.nt have done for me ANNYhow.

I dare say it wd. be easier to cut the 7 preceding cantos & let Acoetes continue = only I dont see how I cd. get <u>him</u> to Bayswater.

Love to Stella & benediction of E[sther].J[ulia].

yr. E.

Pound had arrived at a point to take stock of his own work and his literary debts. In a letter to his old teacher Felix E. Schelling, he summed up his total debts to date: he owed thanks to Robert Bridges, for caution against homophones; to W. B. Yeats, for encouragement "to tell people to go to hell, and to maintain absolute intransigence [. . .]"; to Hardy, for a suggestion regarding the title of "Homage to Sextus Propertius." Ford receives the widest recognition: "Any amount of good criticism, chiefly in form of attacks on dead language, dialects of books, dialects of Lionel Johnson, etc., recd. from F. Madox Hueffer."[35]

He continued the stocktaking in an article published in *The Criterion* for January 1923, "On Criticism in General." He acknowledges the same debts, chief among which the one to Ford. This debt, he writes, "should include some sort of historic survey of Hueffer's critical writing, as found in the preface to his collected poems, and in stray criticisms of Henry James and other prose writers." It might be summarized, he suggests, "by saying that he believes one should write in a contemporary spoken or at least speakable language; in some sort of idiom that one can imagine one-self using in actual speech, i.e. in private life." Pound's growing self-confidence is seen in his assessment of Ford's Impressionist ideas on writing; he recognizes Ford's praiseworthy attempts to find "some possible and lucid basis of criticism, some gauge applicable to literature as a whole," but finds that his ideas have opened the doors to mediocrity and lack of commitment. Ford the Impressionist goes wrong, Pound states, "because he bases his criticism on the eye, and almost solely on the eye. Nearly everything he says applies to things *seen*. It is the exact rendering of the visible image, the cabbage field *seen*, France *seen* from the cliffs."[36] Pound completes this part of his discussion by pointing to the value of other qualities and ways of perception than those of the Impressionists, such as intensity and musical properties.

By January 1922 the Pounds had found permanent lodgings in Paris: 70 bis rue Notre-Dame-des-Champs. Their studio was on the ground floor, looking out on a courtyard and garden. It was furnished and decorated partly with specimens of Pound's own skill and enthusiasm, among them pieces of sculpture which, Ford said, were "of the school of Brancusi."[37]

That summer Pound met Ernest Hemingway who, in addition to initiating him into the art of boxing, introduced him to William Bird, another American with literary interests. Bird had recently established himself on the Île Saint-Louis as a printer of select books; this was the Three Mountains Press. He asked Pound to choose a series of prose booklets to be printed by his press in collaboration with Contact Editions, published by another American, Robert McAlmon. Pound set to work on what he intended to be a "strictly modern" series,[38] and he enlisted Ford as one of the contributors. Pound's final list contained his own *Indiscretions,* which was a reworking of articles he had published in *The New Age* in 1920; Ford's *Women & Men;* B. M. G.-Adams' [i.e., Bride Scratton's] *England;* Hemingway's *In Our Time;* W. C. Williams' *The Great American Novel;* and B. C. Windeler's *Elimus.*

P 19. TLS. 2 11.

70 bis rue N.D. des Champs [Paris] VI
1 Aout [1922]

Dear Ford:

There's a printer here who rather wants to do a series of ⟨prose—⟩

booklets, ⟨private⟩ limited edtn. under my gen. supervision.

Wot abaht it. They're to be about 50 pages each. To pay £10/ at start, and then another £10/ wdnt. interfere with later publication of same stuff in public vols.

I think "Men and Women" might fit. Although it wd. be interesting perhaps, and better to use something that hadn't appeared in a lump. I mean three or four ⟨essays⟩ collected from dif. periodicals; with a few new pages.

Strikes me such a series wd. give one a chance for intimite not afforded by the more blatant reviews.

Also one wd. not be limited by implications of other contribs. to series.

One might do a selection from yr. criticism. I dont quite see where I'm to get time to select it. BUT if it amused you you might collect 30 pages to indicate doctrine, or forty pages, and do a ten page preface.

OR in short, any damn thing you like.

Revolve idea. of this leetle series in your battered old coco

Strikes me one might be more effective thus, than in contributing to stray reviews, where the company is uncertain.

                                                                    yr E.

Love to Stella

Women & Men appeared in April 1923. It consisted of essays previously published in *The Little Review* in 1918. Some of the material went as far back as 1911, that is, a time when the suffragette movement was in the focus. Memorable sections of the book are sketches of "undistinguished people" Ford had met.[39] There are portraits of tough old country women who had earned his admiration for their endurance and realistic attitude to life and to their fellow beings, including husbands.

Pound evidently liked these pieces. He refers to them in his obituary of Ford. He had drafted some notes on Ford not long after the essays were published in book form, probably in early 1924, and he did so again in 1926. These notes were part of what apparently was meant to be an essay on the entire series, which Pound referred to as "The Inquest." The later draft, which is part of a somewhat more ambitious assessment of the series, is very brief on Ford's book.[40]

Extract from Ezra Pound, "[The Inquest]," TMs, 6 11. [1924?]. Yale.

In reply to questions. "The Inquest" is not a book by me, it is a series of books, selected by me. pub. rather more slowly than I had anticipated, with rather more sp[l]endour of format,

[. . .]

2. Women and Men, Portrait of Meary Sears, and anthithetic male figure,
"classic examples", or shall we say rep[r]esentat[ive], specimens of Impressionist mode at its best, as disting. from the discursive, (Indiscretions) and
later innovations.
  Appr[eciation]. of F. difficult for those not in eng, at least from 1908–20;
varied uneven product, fine chapters, as for example, in coming through
ether in L[adies]. W[hose]. B[right]. E[yes]. or of hotel scent in later [The]
Marsden Case (abominable piece of wk, as a whole)

Reasons. Prose, on back of envelope, form of A Call, awareness to what
constitutes good writing, this unique in Eng. of his time.
  Service to letters, ⟨merit⟩ etc, not to be dragged in discu[ss]ion of actual
writing. general estimate of his function in hist of Eng. lit.! but not to be
dragged into question of actual writing.

awareness, unique, successful novelist, follow law above, not too much per
page, nothing not to be seized by the average reader.
  neglect F.'s various sometimes incoherent preachments, take the ideas,
fact he has occasionally thought, I mean def. and precise concept or precise
shade or tone, not merely grandiose abstractions, mainly eronious.
  Local problems of S[ome].D[o].N[ot].; and the gd. soldier, memory of
scenes from earlier hist. novels, amusement of [Mr.] Fleight, and [The]
Simple Life ltd. both in surface technique, presumably brilliant, and but for
levity, wd. be recognized as hist. docs. are so recog. by those who know
how close their apparent fantasia was to the utter imbecilities of milieu they
portray. Unbelieved because the sober foreigner has no mean of knowing
how far they corresponded to an external reality.

[. . .]

Extract from Ezra Pound, "The Inquest, and other, in varying degrees
neglected, writings," TMsS (copy), 6 11. [1926]. Yale.

[. . .]

For a definition of the state of prose I found:

[. . .]

2. A fragment of F.M.Ford's eminently lucid and fluid writing, which I had
always enjoyed, and which could not be fitted to the standard commercial
size[.] The portraits of Mr T. who said "That exactly reminds me of my
days."; and of Meary Walker have always seemed to me very useful ammu-
nition in any argument concerning Mr Ford's right to his place; and if they
are not more used as such I can only suppose that his admirers are accustomed to finding him in six shilling novels "properly published" by Duck-

worth . . . so accustomed, in fact, that they refuse to search for him in tea houses of other venue.[41]

[. . .]

After two winters in Bedham, Ford and Stella were ready to escape the unpleasantness of mud and wind, so in the late fall of 1922 they dismantled the household at Coopers Cottage in order to spend the winter on the French Riviera where a friend had lent them his house. In a long, satirical poem, *Mister Bosphorus,* Ford took *his* farewell of England: both the intellectual and the physical climate of his home country were by now insupportable to him. Their first stop was Paris, where he was happy once more to mingle with brothers—and sisters—of the trade. "Ezra is here, going very strong [. . .] ," he reported.[42] He showed Pound his new poem; it was soon to be "shot at" him, Pound told his mother.[43] In mid-December Ford and Stella went on to Cap Ferrat, and there he began *Some Do Not... .* He was working well, and he felt that he was regaining his energy and the faculty of memory that he had lost as a result of the war.

In March Stella visited the Pounds, who had gone down to Rapallo in January. In Dorothy Pound's company Stella saw Perugia and Siena. Later in the spring she visited them in Paris, where she went to take painting lessons. In late April Ford and Stella moved to the Hôtel Terminus in Tarascon, but soon Tarascon was too hot, and they sought refuge in the Ardèche.

Ford was hard at work on his novel, and when they were all gathered again in Paris in September, he read out to Pound from the manuscript. Pound approved: it was the "best he has done since *Good Soldier,* or *A Call.*"[44]

Pound, meanwhile, had definitely lost his well-paid job with *The Dial.* (There had been no lasting break with the magazine in 1921, as he had feared then.) Now that Pound's "last [public] link" with America had been "severed,"[45] he had to establish other connections. Pound and Ford again did each other a good turn: Ford helping Pound to save face, Pound apparently helping Ford financially. Ford agreed to have an article he had written for *The Criterion* wait till the fall (evidently "From the Grey Stone") in order to make room for a contribution by his friend (the Malatesta Cantos). Pound offered to advance him for the article out of his own check. Ford's brief message of 28 June—perhaps never sent in this form—may be a thank-you note for such a favor.

P 20. TLS. 3 11.

70 bis, rue Notre Dame des Champs Paris VI e,
[May? 1923]

Dear Ford:

I begin this sideways in the middle. The Dial having said they thought
there wd, be no trouble about simultaneous ⟨Am. & Eng⟩ pub, of my new
cantos in July;

has subsequently fired me, and is, I think trying to shit on my honoured
head even re/ this earlier arrangement.

It is therefore rather important for mine honour and glory that the
Criterion should go through with their part of the matter and print in
July as per schedule. ⟨Dial break means my quasi complete exclusion
from U.S. magazines & is serious financially but not moraly⟩

///

Eliot's wife was at the point of death for three weeks during time when he
wd, otherwise have been making his calculations. for July contents. Consequently he has got to break his promise to someone IF he is to save me
from extinction, ⟨I mean he has promised more space than he has.⟩

////

I asked Stella when she was here, IF you were in any special haste about
appearance of yr, article. She said she didn't know, but didn't think it
mattered a GREAT DEAL.

My pome is 30 pages.

My suggestion is that I advance you the price of your article out of MY
cheque. so that your date of receiving payment may remain unaltered.

But the attempt of Thayer and co utterly to submerge me be frustrated.

////

Is this clear? NO, it is not clear.

Begin again.
AS Eliot is so fussed and flustered AND weary, I said I wd, undertake
the negotiations with YOU re/ postponement of the appearance of yr,
article.

AND ALSO that this postponement should not affect the date of yr,
gatereceipts.

ONLY as the Criterion treasurer is not particularly friendly to US this
arrangement can remain private.

Send a p,c, in answer IF you get this, as Stella did NOT leave us your
address.

Your article will appear in October; unless you raise HELL unlimited re/
its not appearing in July,

In any case the fault is on my head, not Eliots, and please write to me, not to him if you are en-wrothed.

The energumens of the Little Review are HERE [.]⁴⁶ I can't see how it is to be ressurrected as a paying proposition.

But may be tempted into larking. At any rate am collecting illustrations for 'em.

You're not likely to meet anyone in Provence who wants to capitalize a RED RED RED magazine.

Anything I get will go to myself and contributors, no printing expenses to deduct.

Quarterly publication.

yr Ezra

F 15. AL. 1 1. Cornell. (Letter never sent?)

Hôtel Porte, St. Agrève, Ardèche – 28 June [1923]

Dear Ezra –
   You're a brick.

Beside his work on the novel, the great literary event of 1923 for Ford was the founding of the *Transatlantic Review*. It was the combined efforts of the two instigators that led to the creating of this new magazine. "Letter from Pound saying Hueffer and he starting paper," Lewis told Eliot.⁴⁷ It was intended to be international in scope and outlook. Deprived of his American channels, Pound was eager to secure a dependable and tolerant outlet where he could publish at will. Ford visualized himself again as the successful editor of an influential literary magazine. Pound mobilized the wealthy John Quinn, who arrived in Paris in September. The gathering in Pound's studio—of Ford, Quinn, Joyce, and the host—is immortalized in a famous photo, presumably taken on 12 October.⁴⁸ Quinn put up about half of the money needed, Ford and Stella as much, and the magazine was launched. The first issue, dated January 1924, was out in December. The magazine was managed from an improvised office in the shop of Bird's Three Mountains Press at 29, Quai d'Anjou. Before it sank (its device was "Fluctuat") the review had published an impressive list of writers, among them such diverse figures as Conrad, Paul Valéry, Tristan Tzara, Joyce, Gertrude Stein, Hemingway, William Carlos Williams, Dos Passos, and Djuna Barnes. The *Review* will perhaps be remembered as the magazine which confronted the literary world with Joyce's "Work in Progress" (a title improvised by Ford and gratefully adopted by Joyce).

Ford was now once more in the center of things. He frequented the hangouts of the artistic and intellectual circles; his favorite restaurant was the Nègre de Toulouse. He entertained and arranged dances. Hemingway's portrait of Ford and Stella (the Braddocks) in *The Sun Also Rises* is not a very kindly one; the scene of the bal musette that he describes at the beginning of the novel supposedly owes its locale and some of its characters to the Ford milieu. In spite of his rather disdainful attitude to Ford, Hemingway saw fit to use some of Ford's anecdotes in his *Torrents of Spring*.

Harriet Monroe visited Paris and had tea with Ford; he praised French civilization as the only hope for mankind. She also met Pound for the first time. The general mode of verbal exchange may have been rather extravagant in the Pound-Ford circles. Quinn evidently misunderstood the way Pound addressed Ford, and commiserated with him: "Poor fellow. . . . You're an honest man. . . . I hate to see you in that position. . . ." Ford, according to his own recollections, assured him that it was not as "uncomfortable" as it looked.[49] But there were also those who felt that *Ford's* influence on *Pound* was unwholesome. In a letter to Quinn, Eliot regretted that Pound in his articles showed a tendency to imitate "Hueffer, who writes vilely and who never omits to mention that he is an Officer (British) and a Gentleman."[50]

Ford helped promising writers in countless ways. Some were grateful; for example, Nathan Asch, who testified to Ford's many services in trying to get him launched. He wrote forewords to the books of unknown authors; this was probably also an easy way to earn some money. His interest in one of his disciples led to complications; Stella Bowen has told the story of his infatuation with the young Jean Rhys, who shared their household for some time.

Pound was becoming more and more dissatisfied with his situation in the French milieu. The more he saw of Italy—and he had been traveling around quite a bit, with the Yeatses and the Hemingways and above all with his wife—the more he was drawn to the country. He spent most of 1924 in Italy, intermittently at Rapallo, which from 1925 on was to be his home for the next two decades. When he left Paris for good in October 1924, it was as if he "added another ten [years] of life."[51]

It has struck observers how comparatively little impact the Paris years had on Pound. It may be significant that Paris and France are largely omitted from the passage in Canto LXXX where he lists the symbolic gifts received from the various places and cultures the hero has passed through. Leaving America he took with him a sustaining (but insufficient) $80; from England a single cherished letter from Thomas Hardy, representing a literary tradition; from Italy ("if I go") a eucalyptus pip, embodying nature and growth (and a young daughter as well). Even before the Pisan perspective, he had taken a backward look at this period. In "Retrospect

Interlude," dated 6 December 1935 (included in *Polite Essays*), he concluded that the Paris years did not amount to much.

After his initial assistance Pound did not take a very active part in the running of the *Transatlantic Review*. Most of his own contributions were on music. From his temporary lodgings in Rapallo he may have suggested for editor Ford's consideration the work of a French writer. (Ford evidently did not take the hint, or he thought the candidate not worthy of appearing in the *Review*.)

P 21. Paige 659 (copy). Yale.

Hotel Mignon Rapallo 19 Feb [1924]

Dear F:

If you are keeping up with French publications, quoting or citing, it wd. be worth yr. while to look at

Stephane Lauzarine's stuff in Les OEuvres libres for Feb. 19[2]4, p. 271 etc.[52]

Readable. Several clichés still left in his mind — nationalism, etc. — but if you want to cite some current french lit, might as well be this as anything.

yrs. E.P.

Moving about as he did, Pound was not easy to get hold of during these months, as Ford found to his great irritation. In the spring of 1924 the finances of the *Transatlantic Review* were very bad, and views and votes of Pound, as a member of the Board of directors, were needed for important decisions. In an impatient letter written at the height of the crisis Ford addresses board member—and perhaps prospective shareholder—Pound, and in a note (or possibly postscript) written a few days later he voices his exasperation with the distant supporter. Pound gave the information requested.[53] From Assisi, where he was recuperating from appendix trouble, he sent in a letter to the editor, offering mixed praise and criticism of the latest issues. Ford magnanimously printed the message, signed "Old Glory," in the June number, adding some wry remarks of his own.

F 16. TLS. 1 1. With autograph notes by Pound. Lilly Library.

[Paris] 8/5/24

Dear Ezra,

Would you please signify to me as director of this company that you agree to the following motions and empower me to act as your proxy in voting for them?

1. That the capital of the company be raised to 150,000 francs by the
issue of 115,000 francs of further shares.
Or in the alternative
2. That the publication of the Transatlantic Review be discontinued
from the 1st prox
3 That the Administrateur Delegue be empowered to delegate his
powers to Mr Robert Rodes or any other person he may select.[54]

Do please answer this at once as this makes the third time I have written
to you on the subject and having these matters held up all this time is
mentally very harassing besides being absolutely ruinous. I am sorry to
trouble you but a general delegation of your powers to another director is,
as I have already explained to you, insufficient to cover these particular
matters.

Yours Ford Madox Ford

Would you, please, also let me know, for a return of directors that I
have to make, the place and year of your birth?

[Autograph notes by Pound, in lower and righthand margin of Ford's
letter, recto. In lower margin:]
I hereby empower F.M. Ford to act as my proxy in voting on these
propositions.

[In righthand margin:]
I assent to these propositions.

Ezra Pound

13/5/1924

[On verso after words "the place and year of your birth?" in Pound's
hand:]

Oct. 30. 1885

Hailey. Idaho.

F 17. TLS. 1 1. With autograph note by Pound. Lilly Library.

[Paris late May 1924]

Have just got your letter from Assisi so send this there[55]
Your criticism of the Review is an admirable bit of personal friendship
for selected friends – but you can not run anything on concentrated juice
of logs rolled . . nor catch any bird with a net set in its sight
I repeat: Trees, Well, I'm tired of them![56]

FMF

[Autograph note by Pound, after Ford's text:]

Re. 2nd. letter:
my earnings for 5 months have been = ZERO = am not in condition for immediate action

[In Pound's hand, beside Ford's signature:]

Buncomb

COMMUNICATIONS

We have received the following Communication. It reveals the proper Protectionist spirit of the tough old Yankee inheritance, the contributors unfavourably referred to being uniformly British. These comments we have taken the liberty of pruning. (A chance international litterateur has just this *very* minute walked into the office and said: "By Jove what amazingly good stuff that is of Dash's", this being the item, marked (1), so violently objected to by our American correspondent.)

To the Editor, *The Transatlantic Review*
Assisi, May 17th 1924

Cher F.
April number good. Especially Hem[ingway]. and Djuna [Barnes].
Want more of them and of McAlmon and Mary Butts.[57]
May Number not so good.
So and So: Nix. (*British Contributor.* Ed.)
Blank. Not sufficient. (*British Contributor*).
Dash (1) Oh Gawd. This village Idyll stuff. (*British Contributor*).
The chap on Palestrina, Cingria, quite intelligent.
H. Z. K. T. = *Times Lit. Sup* rubbish. He "enjoyed articles" = plus his personal biography, touching British delight in landscape—failed to grasp point—ghost of Clutterbrock. (*It adds to the enjoyment of this that H. Z. K. T. and Cingria are one and the same gentleman. Ed.*)
The So and So is regular ole magazine stuff. (*British Contributor*).
Pore old Bill Exe trundling erlong: quite good on Doubleyou, but rot on Why.
Best action you have is in McAlmon, Hemingway, Mary B., Djuna, *Cingria,* K. Jewett.
Will come back and (?) manage you at close range before you bring out any more numbers.

Yours

Old Glory

The above—by the bye, is a real letter.

An undated letter from Pound, here conjecturally dated October-December 1924, reflects his general disgust with the English and American literary world at the time. The target of the present attack seems to be critics connected with the British periodical the *Spectator,* where his *Quia Pauper Amavi* had been unfavorably reviewed. The book that he is referring to as a review object may be *A Draft of XVI. Cantos,* which was published by the Three Mountains Press in late January 1925. The Egoist Press distributed copies of the book in England, along with *A Draft of the Cantos 17–27,* in 1928.

P 22. ALS. 1 1.

Hotel Mignon Rapallo. [?October–December 1924]

Dear Ford:

<u>No</u> – I dont feel that as critic he is a great & good man.[58]

Possibly a syringe through which a few drops of our wisdom can be inserted in the siphylitic public.

====

Wd. surely be fatal to let the Strachey female <u>see</u> actual text of Hom. Sex. Prop.

If they'll write to the Egoi[s]t, they'll get a review copy = I oughtn't to intervene. I cant ask them to review me = at least I dont see how I can.

My position is <u>that</u> they are damned and abominable; you say they want to reform; I indicate a possible step in the right direction, but cant exactly exhort 'em to take it.

D[orothy]. will write to S[tella]. re/ dates, on receipt of S's letter.

yr E

Ford managed to steer the *Transatlantic Review* out of the perilous waters after the crisis in the spring of 1924, but because of Quinn's illness and death in July, it was necessary to find a new backer. While Ford was in New York in a Quixotic effort to settle the poor finances of the *Review,* Hemingway functioned as editor. He even found another wealthy American willing to back the magazine. The *Review* was kept going for a few months more, but by the close of the year the *Transatlantic Review* adventure was at an end. The failure left Ford heavily in debt for several years to come. Practically all commentators agree that he was a poor businessman. Pound apparently had no illusions about Ford's business talents; he wrote to his father shortly after Ford had left for New York and warned him against investing in the shaky *Review:* "Ef yew see Ford; feed him; but dont fer Gawd's sake put any money into the Transatlantic Review."

Many of the younger American expatriate writers, among them Hemingway, felt that Ford did not keep up a sufficiently modern style of editing; nor did all of them appreciate his personal style of self-advertising Literary Master and Central Force of Operations. Certainly after Hemingway began to have a hand in the business, the repertoire became more advanced, for example, with the serializing of Gertrude Stein's work. But the publication of Joyce's "Work in Progress" was Ford's decision.

Although Ford had hopes, evidently quite unfounded, of being able to restart the *Review,* his editorial for the December 1924 issue was actually his farewell address. The founders of the *Review,* Ford wrote, had had two main objects in view: "to promote greater cordiality in international relationships so that the arts might work in a better atmosphere" and "to provide a place for publication for such sincere commencing authors as the world might hold."[59] Who is to blame them for failing to realize the first aim? and who can deny that—if we limit "the world" to the Anglo-Saxon one—the second one was more than adequately fulfilled?

Contacts
1925-1934

PARIS, TOULON, RAPALLO

Ford was now past fifty, heavily in debt and with little prospect of establishing himself in an economically safe position. Conrad, once a friend and collaborator, had died—Ford's memoir of him had been well received. Pound, another—and more constant—friend and co-worker, had left the country. Old ghosts had begun to stir: Ford's legal wife Elsie and Violet Hunt had revived their feud over the right to the name of Hueffer. Violet Hunt's book of memoirs, *The Flurried Years,* caused some uneasiness. Still, now began the period when Ford was to write his most important work, the tetralogy *Parade's End.* Into this psychological panorama of the collapse of the Edwardian world and the emergence of a new, more brutal and more banal one, he put all he knew about the painful and passionate relationships between men and women, about the conflicting values of the old and the new. If he wished to see himself as the battered but sane and gentle Christopher Tietjens, this was certainly *one* view of Ford Madox (Hueffer) Ford, and not necessarily a false one.

Ford and Pound most certainly communicated by letter in 1925 and 1926; there are, however, no extant letters from these years. In June 1925 Pound sent to Ford an inscribed "author's proof" copy of *A Draft of XVI. Cantos,* which had appeared in January.[1] His work on the *Cantos* continued, "that chryselephantine opus," as he called it,[2] but otherwise both this year and the next were less productive than usual for Pound the literary artist. While preparing a volume intended to be *The Collected Poems,* he took a critical look at his early poetry, discarding the " 'soft' stuff" and the "metrical exercises."[3] The result of the screening process was *Personae: The Collected Poems,* published in December 1926. He was growing more and more critical of his home country, although he had not given up every thought of setting foot there again. He may have felt a bit tired of being the proverbial crusader for literature and was drawn toward other dynamic centers. His old interest in music had been strengthened by his relationship with the American violinist Olga Rudge. She was part of the ensemble that performed, for the first time, selections from his Villon opera, *Le Testament,* in Paris in July 1926. The year before she had born him a daughter, Mary, and they were to remain very close till his death.

The Pounds had now settled for good in Rapallo—a protracted stay in Paris in 1926 was due to the birth of Omar Shakespear Pound. By September 1925 at the latest, they had found their permanent home in Via Marsala 12, an address that was to figure in the letterhead of Pound's stationery for close to two decades.

Ford and Stella reportedly visited the Pounds at Rapallo in early 1926. They had been spending the winter at Toulon in the company of painter friends; around Easter they returned to Paris. This was a time of much partying, with Ford and Stella entertaining the crowds in their rue Notre-Dame-des-Champs studio.

Ford now put his hope in America for publishing his books and for the appreciation he felt was denied him elsewhere. In October 1926 he went to the United States to promote his work by a lecture tour and to negotiate with publishers. During his prolonged stay he visited Chicago, where Harriet Monroe gave him a warm welcome. He dumbfounded the *Poetry* staff by dictating, off the cuff, a two-thousand-word article that he owed the editor. He was celebrated at a P.E.N. club dinner in New York. A certain amount of repair was done to his bruised self-confidence.

It was most likely during this stay in the United States that Ford wrote an article entitled "Some Expatriates." (It does not seem to have been published.[4]) Among the expatriates Pound figures as a promoter of *avant-garde* music. He is a patriot and a fighting one, "a very Ajax," Ford writes, when it comes to championing American music. Ford gives us a vivid glimpse of Pound loudly supporting George Antheil, the American "bad boy of music" (to use his self-designation). At a Paris concert, in the midst of catcalls and other forms of demonstrations against Antheil's music, "Mr Pound arises in his place and shouts: 'Dogs! Canaille! Unspeakable filth of the gutter!' [. . .] ."

Ford goes on to tell of his own experience as a booster of Antheil. Being asked to produce a character reference for the composer he found that somebody "occupying some sort of minor official position" in the American colony in Paris countered his favorable testimony by a negative one. Argument: Mr. Antheil was a friend of Mr. Pound! Ford writes: "[. . .] I do not know Mr Antheil very well. But I meet him in drawing rooms where he would not be admitted if there were anything against him. That is enough for me and for any sensible human being. But Mr Pound I know very well indeed—as well as it is possible for one man to know another. And I will vouch for it that no more sober, honest, industrious and wholly virtuous American is to be found on this or the other side of the Atlantic. To know him is to know that – and to know him is an honour. That that minor American official does not know that is due to his not knowing Mr Pound: that he does not know Mr Pound is due to the fact that Mr Pound does not suffer fools gladly. That is perhaps a fault."

Treating American artists in the Philistine manner of the "minor official" makes the United States appear ridiculous. As a possible remedy Ford proposes that "America should read the poems of Mr Pound and see that the works of Mr Antheil are performed often and with applause. That is bound to come some day. It would be well if it came soon," he concludes, "for that would really be the New World redressing the balance of the old."

While he was in New York, Ford wrote a review of *Personae*. He titled it quite familiarly "Ezra"; it appeared in the issue for 9 January 1927 of the *New York Herald Tribune Books* and became the fourth essay of his *New York Essays*. In several messages Pound had alerted his parents to the review, which was to contribute to his "glory and immortality." He was pleased with it—the author had sent him a copy—and he felt that Ford deserved "the Grande Cordon of the Order of St. Michael and Ananias."[5]

E Z R A

PERSONAE: THE COLLECTED POEMS OF EZRA POUND
By Ford Madox Ford

It is now over fifteen years since Miss May Sinclair brought "Flaming Youth" to the decorative offices of "The English Review." "Flaming Youth" brought with it a poem called "The Goodly Fere." . . .

> A master o' men was the Goodly Fere,
>   A mate of the wind and the sea,
> If they think they ha' slain our Goodly Fere
>   They are fools eternally.

> I ha' seen him eat o' the honeycomb
> Sin' they nailed him to the tree.

And the ballad of "The Goodly Fere" set the Thames on fire.

It set the Thames on fire and then incomprehensible rows began. They were to me incomprehensible and they so remain. "The Goodly Fere" had not been published a week when the late Edward Thomas, a scrupulous and delicate poet, wrote for me a review of it, in which he declared that it was one of the greatest poems that has ever been written; but the review had hardly got through the press before Thomas wired to me asking me to withdraw the review. Ezra had been treading on his toes. And let that stand for the whole career of Ezra. To-day, once more, "The Goodly Fere," with his companions, falls on my no longer editorial desk, and here I am, hoping that it may cause the incineration, if not of the Hudson, at least of the East River. Then Ezra will stamp on my toes good and strong, and so shall history repeat itself.

I have been accustomed to say in my haste that of all the unlicked cubs whose work I have thrust upon a not too willing world, Ezra was the only one who did not subsequently kick me in the face. And so he was a good fellow. I do not mean to say that during sixteen years of close intimacy he has not caused me pain that has amounted to anguish. To begin with, his accent is so appallingly Pennsylvanian—let those who fear expatriates be reassured!—that with all the experience I have had of cis-Atlantic intonation I invariably fail to understand one-half of his talk. He, living in Europe, is so aggressively trans-Atlantic that, mild Briton as I am, I have found him trying at times. In this country I seldom hear America mentioned. But in Paris, God bless you. . . . Once, overwhelmed by, buried under the swarms of Middle Westerners mostly, that there beset the landscape, fill the coffee cup and deafen the ear with endless talk of the wonders that happen where Old Glory flies and of the meagernesses characteristic of places where she doesn't—overwhelmed and exhausted I seized a pencil and wrote on the restaurant tablecloth:

> Heaven overarches earth and sea,
> Earth-sadness and sea-hurricanes;
> Heaven overarches you and me;
> A little while and we shall be,
> Please God, where there is no more sea
> And no—say—Middle Westerners.

I forget the rhyme. . . . Mr. Ernest Hemingway, I dare say, was holding an immense fist under my nose and assuring me that English is written only to the west of Nebraska, or it may have been Chicago. . . . He was insisting that *we* English change the name of our tongue. . . .

At any rate, the Paris-American, the Rome-American, the London and the Berlin-American could give any fervent home-stayer seven lengths and a beating in the way of patriotism. It must be like that if you think of it. So do not imagine that I am preaching treason to you when I say that you will be something less than a reader of poetry if you do not read the poems of Ezra Pound.

But, indeed, that man has made me suffer. . . . I have had a try at most things, and there was a time when I aspired to be the *arbiter elegantiarum* of the British metropolis. So, of a morning I would set out on my constitutional, arrayed in the most shining of top hats, the highest of Gladstone collars, the most ample of black-satin stock ties, the longest tailed of morning coats, the whitest of spats, the most lavender of trousers. Swinging a malacca cane with a gold knob and followed by a gray Great Dane I used to set forth on a May morning to walk in the park among all of rank and all of fashion that London had to show.

Now, to the right of me lived a most beautiful lady.[6] She was so beautiful

that Mr. Bernard Shaw broke up the City Socialist Club by drinking cham-
pagne out of her shoe. But when she was not wearing shoes she wore sandals
on bare feet, draped herself in a tiger's hide and walked bareheaded and
slung with amber beads. Of a morning, being a faithful housekeeper, she
also carried a string bag, which usually contained red onions, visible through
the netting.

Well, almost as soon as I stood on my doorstep Fate would send that
Beautiful Lady bearing down on me. At the same moment from the left Ezra
would bear down. Ezra had a forked red beard, luxuriant chestnut hair, an
aggressive lank figure; one long blue single stone earring dangled on his jaw-
bone. He wore a purple hat, a green shirt, a black velvet coat, vermilion
socks, openwork, brilliant tanned sandals . . . and trousers of green bil-
liard cloth, in addition to an immense flowing tie that had been hand-painted
by a Japanese Futurist poet.

So, with the Beautiful Lady on my left and Ezra on my right, Ezra scowl-
ing at the world and making at it fencer's passes with his cane, we would
proceed up Holland Park Avenue. The Beautiful Lady in the most sonorous
of voices would utter platitudes from Fabian Tracts on my left, Ezra would
mutter Vorticist truths half inaudibly in a singularly incomprehensible Philadelphia dialect into my right ear. *And I had to carry the string bag. . . .*

If only he would have consented to carry it, it would have been all right.
I have never objected to being seen in the company of great poets and beautiful ladies, however eccentrically dressed. As it was, few of the damned can
have suffered more.

· I understand that Mr. Pound had to leave London because he sent a
challenge—to fight a duel with swords—to Mr. Lascelles Abercrombie, a
poet, because Mr. Abercrombie had published in the "Times Literary Supplement" an article in praise of Milton.

In England it is a crime to send challenges to British subjects. I am sure
Ezra has committed no other misdemeanor or laches in the course of his
career. He is the swashbuckler of the Arts. I rather wish he was not. But
most poets take to drink, narcotics, lechery, meanness—to some form of
derivative. Ezra takes it out in writing abuse of fools in hideous prose that
is seldom quite comprehensible. If there is an abuse to remedy Ezra dis-
charges a broadside of invective in unusual jargon at the head of the op-
pressor. There is no abuse in the world that he has not sought thus to blot
out.

Instead of drugs he stupefies himself with the narcotics of reform. In that
he is very American—but what a poet!

For me the most beautiful volume of poems in the world is Ezra's
"Cathay"—poems supposedly from the Chinese, but does it matter whether
they are from the Chinese any more than it matters whether Fitzgerald's
Omar or Baudelaire's Poe are from the East or the West, respectively?

[Quotes from "The River Merchant's Wife: A Letter" and "Poem by the
Bridge at Ten-Shin."]

Now, is not that delicate? Is not that beautiful? Are not the lovely words arranged as only a master of language could arrange them? . . . And if you want the Literature of Escape, to where better could you escape than to Cathay?

The quality of great poetry is that without comment as without effort it presents you with images that stir your emotions; so you are made a better man; you are softened, rendered more supple of mind, more open to the vicissitudes and necessities of your fellow men. When you have read "The River Merchant's Wife" you are added to. You are a better man or woman than you were before.

My ears are continually deafened by those who object to the work of Mr. Pound—by those who allege that he is erudite! Just heavens! he is no more erudite than any man of considerable knowledge of the world. In literature it is no matter whether your knowledges arise from an intimate knowledge of life in the Bronx or the Tombs in 1926, or from an intimate knowledge of life in China to-day, in France in the fourteenth century, or in Carthage of the time of Hannibal. I have never heard of any one objecting to Miss Mary Johnston because she displayed an erudite knowledge of the seventeenth century, or to myself because I have written novels about the fourteenth, or to Mr. Erskine because he is a classical scholar.[7] It would appear then to be merely captious to object to Mr. Pound placing his poems among the troubadours, the Chinese, or in the days of Sigismondo Malatesta. Time—any given moment of time—goes so swiftly and so irrevocably that there is no day that can proudly claim immortality for itself. The Broadway trolley of to-day is no more permanent a type than was the old horse stage that I can remember running down Fifth Avenue, and the Bowery slang of Stephen Crane is as *fade* as the prose correspondence style of the 1820's. So that it matters very little where or at what date a poet places his poems. What is requisite is that he should be erudite in his knowledge of the human heart.

You *can't* limit literature to New York or even to the Middle West and the year 1927; *Europam expellas forca tamen usque recurret.* And so will Asia and Africa, and no doubt one day Australia; and so will the age of Pericles, and of Augustus, and of Edward I. And our day will extend its tentacles into the next decade and the next half century, and young Australian poets in the year 2050 will be complaining of the fatal influence of the poems of Ezra Pound on antipodal verse. But the heart of man will remain eternally the same as, back through endless centuries, it has manifested itself.

I have always myself when writing verse tried to make it like the utterances of an English gentleman of to-day, speaking quietly and intimately into some one's ear. That is my personal ambition, but it has never been my ambition to limit poetry to the utterances of English gentlemen, and I cannot see why the New Yorker or the Middle Westerner should seek to imprison the Muse exclusively in his *parages.*

That is an ambition to me incomprehensible.

And what amazes me in reading right through at a sitting or two the collected poems of Mr. Pound is that more and more he assumes the aspect of a poet who is the historian of the world and who is far more truly the historian of the world than any compiler of any outline of history.

In the "Cantos," that immense work, of which only a portion has been published in the stately and beautiful volume that Mr. William Bird printed in Paris, Mr. Pound is avowedly writing a history of the Mediterranean basin. The "Cantos" are not included in the "Collected Poems," because presumably their series is not completed, but even the "Collected Poems" cover and illuminate a great space of time and of ground. To read "The Goodly Fere" is to make the intimate acquaintance of a companion of Our Lord. To read the "Impressions of Voltaire" is to have a flashlight thrown upon the personality of the author of "Candide," and to read the "Alba" that follows is to know a great deal of the frame of mind of the troubadours:

[Quotes "Alba" from "Langue d'Oc."]

As for modernity, from "Les Millwin" to "Mr. Nixon," the "Collected Poems" bristle with it, and what is the "Homage to Propertius" but a prolonged satire upon our own day, as if Propertius should come to New York or London or any other Anglo-Saxon capital?

For me, indeed, glancing rapidly through the pages of these "Collected Poems" is like taking a look through a newspaper. The aggressive titles of the poems give you tidings of wars, atrocities, murders, adulteries—of heaven knows what, taking place heaven knows where. Indeed, should the long-awaited visitor from Mars arrive at last and desire the news for the last two thousand years he could not, if he desired a rapid impression, couched in vivid and often violent phrases, he could not do better than buy and read Mr. Pound's beautiful volume. Let us take "Mr. Nixon" as a final example of Mr. Pound's satirical methods. It should go home to the hearts of all young poets. Certainly it would go home to mine were I young and a poet.

> In the cream-gilded cabin of his steam yacht
> Mr. Nixon advised me kindly to advance with fewer
> Dangers of delay. "Consider
>   Carefully the reviewer.

> "I was as poor as you are;
> When I began I got, of course,
> Advance on royalties, fifty at first," said Mr. Nixon.
> "Follow me, and take a column
> Even if you have to work free.

> "Butter reviewers. From fifty to three hundred
> I rose in eighteen months;
> The hardest nut I had to crack
> Was Mr. Dundas.

"I never mentioned a man but with the view
Of selling my own works.
The tip's a good one; as for literature,
It gives no man a sinecure.

"And no one knows at sight a masterpiece.
And give up verse, my boy,
There's nothing in it."

Likewise a friend of Blougram's once advised me:
Don't kick against the pricks,
Accept opinion. The "Nineties" tried your game
And died; there's nothing in it.

So with his collected poems Mr. Pound sets out, another Bertran de Born, splendidly swaggering down the ages. Another Bertran de Born, indeed, poking out his flame-colored forked beard into the faces, menacing with his cane the persons of the Kings of England, of France, of Navarre and of all the big business and of all the meannesses of the universe. They will probably hang him as the Kings of France and Navarre and England so nearly did for Bertran at Alta Forte. But I don't know that one can ask for much better than to have lived a life of sturt and strife and to die by treachery.

One more picture comes back to me. Mr. Pound is an admirable, if eccentric, performer of the game of tennis. To play against him is like playing against an inebriated kangaroo that has been rendered unduly vigorous by injection of some gland or other. Once he won the tennis championship of the south of France, and the world was presented with the spectacle of Mr. Pound in a one-horse cab beside the *Maire* of Perpignan or some such place. An immense silver shield was in front of their knees, the cab was preceded by the braying *fanfare* of the city and followed by defeated tennis players, bullfighters, banners and all the concomitants of triumph in the South. It was when upon the station platform, amid the plaudits of the multitude, the *Maire* many times embraced Mr. Pound that I was avenged, for the string bag and even for the blue earring!

When Ford returned from America, he and Stella went down to Toulon, where they stayed at the Grand Hotel Victoria. At this point the documented correspondence between Ford and Pound picks up again. We see the two friends making—and rejecting—plans for each other's welfare and promotion. For the rest of his life Ford continued to insist on an American engagement for Pound. Pound was not averse to the idea per se, but any such engagement would have to pay well to be worth the effort and the unpleasantness. He resisted Ford's entreaties with growing irritation.

In a letter to his father (3 April 1927), Pound tells of the suggestion for a lecture tour in the United States; Ford is due in Rapallo to talk these plans over. He had proposed this meeting in a letter which was also a response to an offer from Pound of a new forum for their publications; he had recently started a magazine, defiantly named *The Exile.*

F 18. TLS. 1 1.

[Toulon] 28th March 1927

Dear Ezra,

I ought to have written to you before – but I have not, and that is that. I have such a tic against writing letters that I cannot do it – and yours are always so incomprehensible that it is as good as getting no answers.

I have not yet seen EXILE. I did not want to send you those poems for they are not good enough to appear amongst the offerings of your roaring lions & besides, you will have a much better chance with it if you keep it severely American.

I spoke to Lee Keedick[8] with empressement of your lecturing in U.S.A. I certainly think you ought to do so, now, or at any rate the autumn being the moment, for your star there is on the wax. I have hopes then that we might go there together – or at any rate togetherish as to boats – in September. I am finishing a book [i.e., *New York Is Not America*] now, and if you are to be still in Rapallo Stella and I might run over for a day or so in mid-April. Answer this, if you would like it, in comprehensible phrases. We could then discuss American plans and if you still wanted me to write something for EXILE we could discuss that and I would do it.

In any case may the God of Villon, Hearst and Big Business in general prosper you and yours

Yrs FMF

Judging from a letter from Pound to William Bird,[9] the visit took place during the last week of April; Ford apparently arrived on the 22nd. After the brief visit Pound could write reassuringly to his father, who evidently saw eye to eye with him on such plans: the main purpose of a lecture tour was to get paid well. He had not wished to dismiss his friend's proposal too bluntly, although the thing looked like a "rum show" to him, for Ford had after all been "nobly selling" his stock in the United States.[10] Ford persisted, and wrote again shortly before leaving Toulon for Paris, and he soon came back with fuller details and a ready plan for the American tour. Pound's reply put an end to Ford's plans, at least for the time being.

F 19. TLS. 1 1.

Hotel Victoria Toulon, Var   9th May 1927

Dear Ezra,

I think it would be better to leave Wells of Harpers till I see him.[11]

In the meantime Irita van Doren of the Herald Tribune [Books section]
has been here. She says that if you come to New York to visit me in the
Fall she would just love to have two articles of you of 1500 words each @
$150 a time whilst you are in Gotham and no doubt many more if you
at all suited her readers.

If you hold very much by Harpers' could not you let me have a look at
any fragment of your ms [i.e., "How to Read, or Why"]? I can, I think,
make Wells take anything I want him to, but I can make a much stronger,
an almost coercive, case if I know at all what I am talking about.

We leave for Paris the day after tomorrow.

Yours always   FMF.

F 20. TLS. 1 1.

[Paris] 15/6/27

Dear Ezra,

I now propose to report progress as to your American tour. I have not
been idle about this!

I purpose myself to arrive in New York towards the 25th September
and that you should follow arriving as near as possible on the 15th
October, staying with me till the 6th Nov. when you will proceed to
Chicago to lecture on that date at the Arts Club and next day at the
Woman's Athletic. Of course if you do not want to lecture you can stand
about and look eminent and I will do the lecturing. They will pay $250
at the Arts Club and I suppose about the same at the W.A. This should
pay your fare from Chicago to Philadelphia and back to N.Y.. and
Irita[Van Doren]'s articles will pay your fares back to Italy – I mean the
articles you will write for her for the N.Y. Herald-Tribune. I am also
presuming that you will want to stay with your parents in Philadelphia.
New York is not so easy to arrange definitely as Chicago but you can be
assured of a royal welcome. I have spoken to more than a dozen lights of
that city – from Elinor Wylie to Bob Chanler[12] and Canby and they are all
ready to put up entertainments for you. All you therefore really have to do
is to get to New York. I am hard up myself at the moment having had to
pay for my mother's illness and funeral and also having received no
money from Boni's who appear to be going to fail. Otherwise I would
propose to lend you your fare in the full confidence that you will make
enough in N.Y. to pay me back – or not if you did not want to. I daresay
I can do it in any case – but I cannot be absolutely sure. So I hope you
may be in a position to do it.

Anyhow, let me know that you approve of this scheme and I will go on
arranging things[.] I have fixed up the lectures in Chicago with the view to
your seeing if you can stand it. If you can you could then fix up others for
the following season; if you can't you can leave it alone.

But I really can assure you that every human being I have spoken to about it most enthusiastically desires your presence on the other side of the Atlantic.

So write me your views as comprehensibly as you can. In the meantime you have my prayers.

Yours always   FMF

P 23. ALS. 2 11.

Venice 23 June [1927]

Dear Ford:

All this endeavour is most noble of you. But I don't know how to make my intentions more plain than I already have done. I am not going to the U.S.A.

The min[im]um I will consider for the god damn bother of crossing the stinking ocean is $5000. ⟨⟨above expenses⟩⟩ absolootly guaranteed.

I should be annoyed to get such an offer as I should then have to think about going. I don't think one wd. be decently well PAID for the trip under $10,000. which seems unlikely to be offered.

As for interrupting my "work", or if you prefer the term "the even tenor of my life" for bare expenses dubiously guaranteed, fees not down in writing, the breakable invitations of editors who reserve right to reject stuff they consider "unsuitable" etc. TO HELL WITH IT.

If you want someone to hold yer 'and and keep you from feeling too lonely among the distant barbarians, I will give Favai[13] a letter of introduction to you.

He is going for the first time. Innocent, & I shd. think uncorruptable.

In any case he will provide you a respite from the local fauna.

Your expression "following season" is horrible. I might go once for some overwhelming reason, but not to make it a habit.

I don't wish to seem ungrateful for your interest.

I am sorry your mother is dead.

yrs ever – E.

Salut a Stella. Benedictions

Ford went to America as planned in the fall. He spent the winter there, lecturing and writing. He had trouble finding out whether Pound was booked for lecturing or not; in a letter to Harriet Monroe he assumed the role of a victim of Pound's breach of promise. "Here I am back in

New York," he wrote, "and, as is not unusual with me in a dilemma —
naturally on account of Ezra. That poet undertook to come over with me
and at the last moment did not."[14] He visited Pound's parents and found
them "delightful."[15] The appreciation he enjoyed in America, together
with a romantic attachment to an American woman, led him to plan a
divided existence, spending part of each year in the United States and
part in France. He could not, however, envisage becoming an American
citizen; at about this time he drafted an (incomplete) essay entitled
"Citizen or Subject: Why I shall never become an American citizen."[16]

On his return to France in 1928, Ford and Stella broke up, amicably.
Old and new friends brightened up his life as a bachelor in Paris. Pound
came, to attend a dinner given in his honor by Samuel Putnam. Ford was
prevented from delivering the speech of homage because of an unforeseen
incident: one of those present, who was under the influence of drugs,
threatened the guest of honor with a knife.

Pound had acted on Ford's advice and submitted a series of articles to
ʻrita Van Doren; after some confusion they finally appeared as "How to
ɹ˯ead, or Why" in the *New York Herald Tribune Books* in January 1929.

F 21. TLS. 1 1.

HOTEL BEAU RIVAGE, CARQUEIRANNE, VAR FRANCE
Sept 10th 1928

Dear Ezra,
All I can do is to write to Mrs van Doren and suggest that she should
pay you for the articles – which I suppose she will. I don't see how she
could publish them because they are really incomprehensible: I offered to
annotate them so that the ordinary reader might understand something
of what they treated. But it was beyond me. There is too much politics on
this planet!

Yours   FMF

From 1930 on Ford's personal life became more stable and happier.
He had met a young Polish-American painter, Janice Biala, who was to
share his life and work with great devotion. She had actually come to one
of his Thursday parties in the hope of meeting Ezra Pound. In one of
Ford's *Buckshee* poems, "Fleuve Profond," which renders impressionisti-
cally a Paris night of lively literary talk and music, we catch a glimpse of
Pound (*"It must be seven . . . Are you all going? / Yes, Ezra's going . . . Not one more hot-dog? / The* Halles *for breakfast!* [. . .] *")*.[17]
Both Ford and Janice loved France and tried against all financial odds to
establish a French existence for themselves, seeing Paris and Toulon as
their ideal seasonal homes.

Pound meantime was firmly established in Italy, dividing his time between Rapallo and Venice with occasional visits to Paris. He was drifting further and further away from his home country in the sense that he felt less than fully informed about the literary situation over there; he was disgusted with bureaucracy and censorship; he was beginning to be immersed in subjects that he could not discuss with Ford. He had begun to read the German anthropologist Leo Frobenius. He seldom left Italy for long stretches of time; in June 1930 he and his wife visited Paris, where they had dinner with Ford. Ford was excited at the prospect of seeing his old friend again. "Pound is coming," he reportedly kept exclaiming.[18]

There are no letters extant from the years 1929 and 1930, but as of 1931 we can again follow the vicissitudes of the two collaborators, in letters exchanged and in writings about each other.

F 22. TLS. 1.1.

VILLA PAUL, CHEMIN DE LA CALADE,
CAP BRUN, TOULON, VAR
6th June 1931

Dear Ezra,

This is to authorise and empower you without let, hindrance, fee, honorarium, deodand, infangtheff, utfangtheff freely to translate or cause to be betrayed any work of mine save only my commentary on the Book of Genesis into any tongue or language save only the dialects of the Isle of Man and of the City of Philadelphia, Pa in its pre-1909 variety or sameness.[19]

We may shortly be passing through Genoa and would like you to lunch with us at any there hostelry designated by you.

I had yesterday the agreeable news that my latest novel [*When the Wicked Man*] is a best seller in New York. As however the largest sale of any book in that city has not yet exceeded four hundred copies this year and since no publisher has more than $11 in his bank I do not – though they need it – propose to have the seats of my pants reinforced.

May God and your country pass you by in their judgments is the prayer of

FMF

F 23. TLS. 1 1.

VILLA PAUL, CHEMIN DE LA CALADE,
CAP BRUN, TOULON, VAR
18 August 1931

Dear Ezra,

Could you lend me a little money? Liveright has been owing me a lot for many months and there seems little chance of his paying till the end of October and we are now approaching literal starvation having been without enough to eat for many weeks. If you could lend me $100 that would keep us going till Liveright does pay – if he ever does. But any little sum would be an immense mental relief.

It worries me as much to write this as it will you to read it.

Yours   FMF

P 24. TLS. 1 1.

[Rapallo] 20 Aug. 1931

Dear Ford

Herez the hors d'oeuvres. I will try to make up the rest of the hundred bucks within a fortnight.

I am bloody damn sorry the strain has arruv at such point.

My own earnings are merely derisoire. Will plain eyetalyan chq/ serve for the balance? It will prob. have to anyhow.

Your note on Huddy [i.e., W. H. Hudson] has aroused several xpressions of approval and appreciation.

ever E

P 25. TLS. 2 11.

[Rapallo] 21 Aug. [1931]

Dear Ford

Sent you a Paris chq/ yesterday. Here is the remainder in some sort of a draft.

I heard you were writing memoirs, presumably under contract; and take it you do not want merely to do odd articles here or there. In any case I dunno any edtrs. that can pay anything weighty, and have in fact just sent off a swat damning most of the sonsofbitches by name.[20]

Your buggerin VanDorens [i.e., Carl and Irita] (according inside information) kept gettin requests fer back numbers of their damn [*New York Herald Tribune*] "Books" suppliment ⟨containing my articles⟩; but they have never had the decency to say so or to want anything more nor have the bloody american sharks taken the stuff for reprint, though at last, yesterday I recd. a letter from a (presumably young) guy who proposes to start a pamphlet series and do wot he is told. This concerns the in'nerlexshul life of murka, and dont mean more than about 5 quid per pamph to the authors. (theoretically about 5 quid per thousand copies . . . and we know how many millyums our stuff will sell.)

He"z got more young on his list than he is likely to print. I wonder,
howeffer, whether you have anything CONDENSED in the way of crit.
that wd. Go with the preface to yr/ collected poems. I spose he ([Kenneth]
Rexroth; the guy) wants mostly new stuff.
    etc/ętc/
    itza cockeyed woild

E

F 24. TLS. 1 1.

CAP BRUN   Sunday. [23 August 1931]

Dear Ezra,
    Thank you very much indeed. I got both your cheques together
yesterday and really slept well last night for the first time for a long time.
I do hope it does not mean that you will have to go short.
    It is not that I am short of work for I have all I can do and more. It is
simply that nobody in America pays. My present novel [*When the Wicked
Man*] is announced as a "best seller" all over the place but all I have had
for it hitherto has been $250 which I extracted by means of violent threats
from Liveright a long time ago. He owes me now for my reminiscences
[*Return to Yesterday*] and I cannot get the money out of him. Several
papers also owe me money but take no notice of my requests for payment.
Of course things are very bad in New York and they pay practically no-
one who is abroad and unable to sue them. I am putting a lawyer onto
them immediately and in a couple of months may squeeze something out
of Liveright at least. My English publishers pay regularly enough but of
course not much and what they do pay I have assigned to Stella.
    So that for a long time we have been living practically out of garden
but now the drought has brought even that nearly to an end. However,
thanks to you, we shall be able to get along for a long time and, before
the end I hope to have squeezed something out of Liveright and to repay
you. I wish you – who are the more mobile – could get along to see us.
This is one of the most beautiful spots I know and there are a good many
things I should like to talk to you about. I don't suppose you will, but if
you would you would be very welcome.
    Every so many thanks again.

Yours FMF

In *Return to Yesterday* (pp. 373 ff.) Ford described young Pound as the
author appeared when he first knew him in the days of the *English Review*.

> Then came Ezra, led in by Miss [May] Sinclair. His Odyssey would take
> twelve books in itself. In a very short time he had taken charge of me, the
> review and finally of London. That will appear later. When I first knew him

his Philadelphian accent was still comprehensible if disconcerting; his beard and flowing locks were auburn and luxuriant; he was astonishingly meagre and agile. He threw himself alarmingly into frail chairs, devoured enormous quantities of your pastry, fixed his pince-nez firmly on his nose, drew out a manuscript from his pocket, threw his head back, closed his eyes to the point of invisibility and looking down his nose would chuckle like Mephistopheles and read you a translation from Arnaut Daniel. The only part of that verse that you would understand would be the refrain:

"Ah me, the darn, the darn it comes toe sune!"

We published his *Ballad of the Goodly Fere* which must have been his first appearance in a periodical except for contributions to the *Butte, Montana, Herald*.[21] Ezra, though born in Butte in a caravan during the great blizzard of—but perhaps I ought not to reveal the year. At any rate, Ezra left Butte at the age of say two. The only one of his poems written and published there that I can remember had for refrain

"Cheer up, Dad!"

As a reaction against a sentiment so American, he shortly afterwards became instructor in Romance languages at the University of Pennsylvania. His history up to the date of his appearance in my office which was also my drawing-room comes back to me as follows: Born in the blizzard, his first meal consisted of kerosene. That was why he ate such enormous quantities of my tarts, the flavour of kerosene being very enduring. It accounted also for the glory of his hair. Where he studied the Romance languages I could not gather. But his proficiency in them was considerable when you allowed for the slightly negroid accent that he adopted when he spoke Provençal or recited the works of Bertran de Born.

His grandfather [. . .] had promised to send Ezra to Europe. Ezra was just making his reservations when his grandfather failed more finally and more completely than usual.

Ezra therefore came over on a cattle boat. Many poets have done that. But I doubt if any other ever made a living by shewing American tourists about Spain without previous knowledge of the country or language. It was, too, just after the Spanish-American War when the cattle boat dropped him in that country.

It was with that aura of romance about him that he appeared to me in my office-drawing-room. I guessed that he must be rather hard up, bought his poem at once and paid him more than it was usual to pay for a ballad. It was not a large sum but Ezra managed to live on it for a long time—six months, I think—in unknown London. Perhaps my pastry helped.

Pound took an interest in Ford's book of memoirs. In late 1931—the English edition was published at the beginning of November—he drafted an essay in Italian, taking the memoirs as an excuse for introducing Ford to his readers. Titled "Appunti: 'Return to Yesterday.' Memorie di Ford Madox (Hueffer) Ford," it was most certainly intended for the Genoese paper *L'Indice,* for which he wrote a series of "Appunti." The essay on Ford was never published. In a New Year's letter he offered further, frank and detailed, comments on the book.

NOTES

Return to Yesterday
Memoirs of Ford Madox (Hueffer) Ford[22]

This is yet another highly readable book by Ford which testifies once again
to that great sensitivity of his, although it is interspersed every ten or fifteen
pages by a passage of almost pure imbecility. For twenty years I have been
trying to find a critical formula to boost my old friend and his unquestionable
merit.

I have come to hold the view that the faults of an author "do not count,"
that is, in a certain sense and to a certain extent they do not count when
there exists a sustained will to achieve something good, an intention directed
toward a praiseworthy objective.

What counts, and counts above all to the critic, are the positive values,
once this good will has been assessed and evaluated. The rest falls under a
quantitative judgement; be the negative percentage as it may, and the reasons
for it of no consequence, IF! and this IF is an IF in capital letters, – IF only
the author wants to improve.

I am not being paradoxical when I say that more authors fail, or at least
I have seen more fail, through lack of good intentions than through lack of
intellect. This daring claim does not at all reduce the value of the intellect.

There are a few who do not understand, who *cannot* see or feel, and who
with a certain determination systematize their nonunderstanding; but this is
another matter. Those who are not willing are in the majority. There are
others who excuse themselves, instead of making an effort. How many
writers have not lost ten years of their lives as artists by being unable to
forget that they had grandfathers and cousins?[23]

God willing, Ford can have another thirty years in which to rid himself
of *idées reçues,* and suchlike rusty tools. How many books with 430 pages
contain 340 readable ones? It is not requisite that an author's merits should
be advertized on the dust jacket. Note that Ford is unaware of possessing a
true and valuable merit of his own. He collaborated with Conrad for many
years. At his death Conrad left £50,000 in the bank. Ford is not yet in
comfortable circumstances, but there is not the slightest trace or suspicion
of jealousy on account of Conrad's success and wealth. It's not just because
he was used to seeing Conrad in misery and anxiety, but because neither of
them was concerned about such things or had such petty feelings. And during
the more than twenty years that I have known Ford intimately I have never
seen the least prevarication, the least wavering in his loyalty toward Conrad,
a man who was probably somewhat less intelligent than himself.

It is difficult to ascertain the merits of a critic whose critical *sense* is so
much more respectable than his critical *writings.* I, for example, *know* how
important Ford's perceptions were in London from 1909 till 1919, but this
does not mean that I can recommend any particular books by Ford without
leaving myself open to interminable discussion. In short, Ford is perhaps a
critic for those who are endowed with understanding. That is, enough understanding to separate the good nuts from the bad ones, and not to swallow
the shell with the kernel.

X X X

In a pretentious and haughty generation Ford has displayed almost all his weaknesses openly on the page, and the jackals have not failed to fall upon every little bone, using them as an excuse for avoiding or disregarding the critical value of the Fordian sensibility and the soundness and insight of his critical essays. This is so, partly because he is a victim of his own merits, and his enthusiasms are damaging to himself, in his furious attacks on Freudianism (which he judges by its faults), when he storms against what it wrongly regards as "science," but which is simply a prevalent defect of mediocre scientists; etc., etc.

I don't know if this book will interest the new readers as much as those who have long sought an explanation of the conflict between the intelligent Ford and the naive or almost simple-minded Ford.

In these memoirs there appear at least two reasons for this conflict: The macabre nanny who told horror stories, and the generation of journalistic vipers at the time of [Norman] McColl; out of these poisons emerged the young man of letters Ford Madox.[24]

Will my kind or refined reader allow me to quote Dante, or at least refer him or her to Inferno XXVIII, 11. 26, 27?[25] There was once in England a wretched specimen by the name of Gifford,[26] who left a breed of epigones. Being merely blind sucklings, it was (and still is) their habit when criticizing a book to find a particular minor flaw, a typographical mistake or something of minute importance, and by attacking this to get rid of their bad mood, inferiority complex, irritation at any author who presented an idea which was not yet generally accepted, or who did not easily enter the narrow openings to their rabbit-cage brains.

The youngsters in the universities often have such a habit in early adolescence, such a preoccupation with detail, before they acquire a sense of proportion, or before they are capable of judging the weight or the overall structure of a book.

As a reaction against these scoundrels young Ford rigidly adopted a kind of antiprecision attitude for the next 40 years. He does not wish to, and perhaps he cannot, express the precise thing, if this thing does not have a corresponding meaning. He persistently falsifies trivial details. This is a danger in itself, but Ford has his own kind of courage. It is a sure way of making pedants angry. It certainly irritates *me,* and has done so for twenty years, but now that I see the explanation it irritates me less.

What does it matter to me, for example, if I was born in Idaho or Montana? The danger lies in this, that it is difficult to know when a detail is, or will be, trivial, and when it can become important.

Persisting in this deliberate falsification for 40 years, Ford finally "makes his point," that is, makes his intention clear, succeeding in confounding pedantry a little and stimulating a feeling for relative worth. This is not to say that this has been or will be the best method, but I owe him a personal debt of gratitude.

Ford was born in a bad year, in 1876 or thereabouts, between one generation and another. He wanted to become a soldier; his grandfather ordered him to become an artist of some kind—painter, writer or whatever—and to behave like an "English Gentleman," which hardly means a gentleman in the ordinary sense, but which had and still has a complex meaning: it is a medley of base stupidity, quixotism, failure to understand reality; in short, a complex of diverse noble and trivial elements, which, in the final reckoning, has no relevance, either absolutely or relatively, to "being an artist."

He does not care at all if the narrator is a fisherman or an emperor, just so long as he has interesting things to say. If he tells the secrets of a tender heart to those who perceive the true meaning of love, so much the better . . . . even when this entails looking for them in the twenty-seventh sphere of heaven;[27] the important thing, however, is that he tells with the clarity and the full awareness of a fisherman who talks about a dentex or an octopus.

Conrad, too, who, like every other *petit bourgeois* of Polish or any other nationality, was the son of 33 emperors, 141 kings, 6758 barons, etc., Conrad the novelist invented a fictitious seaman to tell a story, just so as to get away from his own social position. Henry James referred ironically to the falsity of this narrator by calling him "that monstrous master mariner."

When art fails to reach or does not seek the impersonal, when it fails to become the roving eye or the voice [of an impartial observer], one can use a persona, as Cervantes does, but the social position of Quixote or Sancho serves rather to render the ridiculous.

Assessing Ford's position in the "paideuma," in the mainstream of "English culture," if you like, one observes that, as the son of a German father and of a mother who was at least part Welsh, he made himself for thirty years the champion of certain (excellent) French ideas, and that he had received these ideas from two Americans (H. James and Stephen Crane) and a Pole (Jos. Conrad); that he maintained these ideas in opposition to English academism and the Pre-Raphaelitism of Rossetti and Wm. Morris.

The Pre-Raphaelitism of his grandfather (F.M. Brown), as well as the kind which can be found in the paintings of Rossetti, can in certain details (as distinct from the total effect), concern a search for truth. I seem to remember that Rossetti often crossed a river in the daytime in order to examine carefully the shapes of the leaves that he wished to represent in a painting depicting that same shore in the darkness at night. Truth, in other words, has different aspects.

In those distant times, other Englishmen borrowed from the picturesque style of medieval tapestries, or from that of French symbolism.

I notice that Ford got his French Flaubertian tradition from a group of foreigners (among them some Americans) and that he passed it on to another group of Americans, and that the English mentality became more and more diluted. Standing apart from this tradition is Thos. Hardy, worthy Englishman "in the old manner"; George Moore (Irish) who studied French literature, perhaps through smutty stories, and who will have a bidet for a tombstone; Arnold Bennett, chromium-plated and efficient *cash register* who acquired the French technique; D.H. Lawrence, discovered and launched by Ford. Lawrence has left works manifesting an undeniable talent, rich and all mixed together like *un civet de lièvre*.

Joyce (as I've said elsewhere) drank directly from the Flaubertian spring with a strong dose of Ibsen.

E.P.

P 26. TLS. 4 11.

This goes care o' Sal [i.e., Samuel Putnam][28] / cause I hear you're in Paris but dunno yr/ address.

[Rapallo] 27 Dec. anno X [1931]

Dear Fordie

Wall, yew ave got a funny kind ov'a mind. BUT the opusculus throws a bit'er light ⟨(meaning bit of)⟩ onto some of its underbrush.

I feel vurry much as an imaginably lucid member of yr/ granpap's generation (say Robt. B[rowning].) might have felt toward yr/ daft aberations (or however many bbs and rrs it haz).

Vurry readable/ vurry readable // less wildly inaccurate detail. (gettin over yr/ anti-Mccoll comp[le]X.)

Cunningham and gawd worth the price of wollum.[29]

Though the portraichoor nacherly more priceful than annecdote.

I shd. be glad to review it for some murkn/ periodicl/ if any were open. No english bloody goddam lie-sheet wd. stand my language on some of the pts/ I shd. have to disKUSS.

Thank god I was born ten years later than you were. Escaped a lot of god damnd nonsense. Not sure the beastly word gentleman hasn't caused more trouble in yr/ bright l'il life than all the rest of the lang. (lang. = langwidg)

Spose I am the first person to know what a g. is and have strength of mind to refuse the specifications and definitely want a term implying more general [*crossout:* decency] constructivity. (I upset the Dial a good deal by that so revolutionary proposal.

///

Anyhow, you seem to have got out of some of snarls in yr/ worsted.

havent yet finished the book/ but take a few moments off to wish you 'appy noo year etc.

AT any rate I have, I think, at last got at the dissociation of what Conrad meant in yr/ adolescent years to YOU, and what his results as printed may or may not be expected to mean to anyone else.

Conrad/ bringer of the light of a european point of view into the black
bog of britain. H.J[ames]. xpresses much of the same thing in . . . . which one
is it // story where there iz a novelist talking about Brit. view of the novel.

Next Day

I was about to remove the paragraph about the "gent" or at any rate
rewrite it// thinking it wd. prob. make you pewk over the floor/
    First idea of softening it was: Fordie, you AVE got a rummy job lot
of "idees recues".

and I come back to it that you HAVE bitched about 80 % of yr/ work
through hanging onto a set of idees recues.

    parenthesis / not as to <u>fact</u> but to language)

    ERROR an' shockin' error; my dear Fordie
    There never was and never will be a "horse-trolley"
    vide P; 315^{30}

The trolley is the "string" videlicet; loose wire that connects the battery
(transmutter) or at any rate electric device ON the car, with the charged
wire overhead/ supported by the trolley-pole.

"off his (or your) trolley", hind side beforeness, meaning
    "trolley disconnected."

horse-car / cable-car (when the electric connection made below ground) ,
Lexington Ave. "cable" Not sure that wasn't a rotating device "pre-
trolley".
    No one but YOU ever paid more'n a nickel (vide term "dime" P. 315).

The half of you that is english, conduces to englishness; namely tangential.

The god damn Briton do not go at a thing straight/ Shx. [i.e., Shake-
speare] play wright // mebbe began it.

However/// that damn wheeze about "impression" impressionist ⟨defence-
mechanism?⟩ (part of it conducive to virtue) but still; you are better
when, being scientific (re/ durability of birds), you object to a defect of
science, namely the failure to examine the evidence.

OF cour[s]e if you think a half-wit like Bertie ⟨Russel⟩ is a scientific . . .etc. . . . .!!

Two thing[s] have affected you/ That bloody minded nurse/ and the
utter shits like Mccoll ⟨of that epotch⟩ and the penny-wit fussing over
accuracy in unimportant detail, printer's errors etc.

Both James and Hud[son]. intent on the object//

Conrad, a writer of very considerably lower category; still burdened
with idees recues.

Etc/

May the grace mercy and peace

etc//

with ever enduring esteem & affexshun

E

Soon it was Ford's turn to do his bit in reviewing Pound's *How to
Read,* which had appeared in book form late in 1931. He did so in *The
New Review* for April 1932. Although the author was grateful for the
"kind an[d] extensive woids," Ford's mild criticisms later called forth a
rebuttal. In his preface to the *Active Anthology* he defends the method of
How to Read with the following argument:

> Madox Ford made a serious charge, but not against what is on the pages of
> the booklet. He indicated that a section of what would be a more nearly
> complete treatise on the whole art of composition was not included. You
> can't get everything into 45 pages. Nor did the author of *How to Read* claim
> universal knowledge and competence. Neither in the title nor anywhere in
> the text did the booklet claim to be a treatise on the major structure of
> novels and epics, nor even a guide to creative composition. (Reprinted in
> *Selected Prose,* p. 368).

POUND AND *HOW TO READ*
By Ford Madox Ford

When that I was a little, little boy and looked presumably like an angel
Raphael, I penetrated into an Eleusinian mystery and came off scatheless.
After my father's State TIMES dinners, we children were allowed to come
in for dessert and then packed off to bed. I crept under the drawing-room
sofa and there remained until the ladies came in. I was immediately discovered and, my mother arriving at the conclusion that I did not want to
go to bed, I was allowed to stand by her knee. Then spoke Lady Cusins,
wife of Her Majesty's Master of Music, a broadlapped, amiably-spectacled,
comfortably jovial priestess of mysteries. Her eyes went round the feminine
circle. She said:
"We are all married women, aren't we?"
Alas for you! That is all that I remember.
But, whenever I sit down to write anything sincere and thought about, I
find myself still glancing around me and saying:
"We are all—oh, say Popes—aren't we?" Because it is hypocrisy and
worse to write anything sincere and thought about for the general.

Ezra, then, gives us his notes of a craftsman, and I hope we are all . . . oh,
men who have thought with sincerity about one craft or another.

I don't have to say that I am in agreement with every word that he writes.
He and I have been proclaiming the different sides of the same sort of thing
in one wilderness or another for the last quarter of a century or so. He has
frequently banged me over the head when at the moment he had no one
else to bang, or because I would not bang, in the universal Bannaher that is
his world, someone or somebody who had not been nice according to his
ideas to some other some one or somebody who was for the moment occupying his boundless enthusiasms. For Ezra was born, practically, in Philadelphia. He was born thus, to put the world right by banging tyrants, pedants, orthodoxies, New Worlds or any windmill that is sufficiently imprudent
to protrude its sails over the horizon of any heath over which Ezra may be
pricking. I—in the image for the moment of Ezra's Sancho—never was anything but a pacifist. I ride my ass beside his Pegasus and wish we could get
on. I began organizing Movements before he did, but he has organized and
banged on the head seventy two to my two. He is, in short, far more—or
much less—of a politician than I, who years ago decided that it is best to
plough a lonely furrow.

So that, if there are defects in most of Ezra's critical writings, they arise
from excursions from his text to horizons where he imagines he has seen
windmills. Or bourgeois to be *épaté'd*. These excursions are a nuisance. They
take your mind off the text. If a text of critical work is worth reading—and
Ezra's are mostly worth reading—it requires all your attention. The bourgeois
is not worth *épaté-ing*. We are, I take it, beyond the stage where that will
o'the wisp is considered pursuable.

In HOW TO READ, Mr. Pound's Philadelphian sox are frugally displayed. I have noticed them only once. There are a page or two of attacks
on American professors. I should prefer to see them replaced by a page or
two on *Architectonics*—which, as it is, gets only three words. There are a
page or two about the (London) TIMES LITERARY SUPPLEMENT.
These could well have been given to instances of "charged" words. I do not
see why Mr. Pound should continuously give free publicity to the (London,
Eng.) TIMES. If he did not do it, I at least should not know that it still
existed. And I do not see why Mr. Pound should without ceasing roll logs
off American university professors. If he didn't, one would not know that
those woodlice existed either.

His book by itself is of extreme value. If he extended it, it would be one
of the most valuable books in the world. To extend it, he would have to
think about Progressions d'Effet. That he dislikes doing. So, we have a
lacuna as to the article *Architectonics*.

It is time that some attention was paid to literature—otherwise it will not
be until the Universal Soviet has been established for a century that Ezra's
Canto's will be read. For it must not be forgotten that Ezra is first and foremost his CANTO'S. At that immense and glorious work he toils, noiseless
and intent, a Robert of Gloucester,[31] situate in the Italian Riviera and endowed with supreme genius, supreme patience, unceasing gusto for the Arts.

If then it is time that we paid some attention to Literature, it is *pari passu* time that a complete, handy textbook to that pursuit was produced. Of this Ezra has given us one half. If a student of genius studied and exactly conformed to the precepts of the book, we should have half another Ezra. It is time we had another whole . . . textbook!

I repeat: We are, I take it, all Popes here. Let us open a secret consistory. It is not good that the general should hear too much truth. We must begin by conceding that it is for human beings that we write. The general should not hear that. He should be taught to think that our eyes are upon Posterity alone, our crops meagrely filled with thin oatmeal. (*Parva tenui avena,* Ezra would say. It is good that he should re-sound, and loudly, the note of classical-mediaeval and even Kon-Fu-Tzean erudition.) But human beings are the stuff on which we project ourselves. *Architectonics, Melopeia, Phanopoeia* and the rest of the screw-wrenches and claw-hammers of Mr. Pound's engineering bench are merely his formidable tools for monkeying with the screw-nuts of human consciousness; (I hear Pope Pound ejaculating Psshaw! SS; SS; Hille! HR. R. RUNK! BREK. EK.EK! Being from the city where the greatest Republic proclaimed itself, he is all for aristocracy. It is great pity that he was not born there before the Declaration was signed. Then he would re-act against the other aeon). The fact remains that you must write either for Humanity as a whole or, like Ezra, for a sublimated Ezra-Superman.

Our distinguished colleague has always hated prose. His reaction has always been, unconscious or conscious, something like a race hatred. We Popes have always been by turns aristocrats and peasants. Pope Ezra is the aristocrat. Verse, poetry is the Senior Service, as, in the Army, we used to say of the Navy. Elevated now above the world, he regards the prosateur—the pedestrian—with the feigned deference that Lord Chesterfield would have paid to Benjamin Franklin as first minister from the United States. He *constat's* in HOW TO READ the world ascendancy of prose since the days of Stendhal. But he does it in much the tone of that weary Titan, the Marquis of Salisbury,[32] when he said—oh, but years ago—"We are all Socialists now". And he neglects to *constater* the whole of the process by which he has become the predominating poet of our age. Possibly he wants to keep something up his sleeve. We all delight to have secret *arcana.* The final touch of my *rouelle de veau Mistral* is a secret that shall die with me. But ruthlessly I will tear the veil from *his* secret.

Browning and Ezra are the two great major poets of our and the immediately preceding Age. That Ezra reveals. I use the word "major" to designate verse-poets who can hold your attention with their verses during extended periods of time. There have been a great many—*atque ego in Arcadia vixi!*—who can hold it, say, as "gliders". Up against the strong wind of an emotion or an excitement, we can make our flights. It is only Browning and Ezra since Bugbear Shakespeare who have been able to make a non-stop flight from, say, Philadelphia to, say, Cathay, revictualling, as it were, in the air above Casa Guidi.

Their secret is the same as that of the Swan, of Dante, of the author of

the ROMAUNT OF THE ROSE, of Homer . . . of all the super-Popes, if
there are any more, of verse-writing. It is the simple one of making themselves interesting.

The moment Mme de Scudéry wrote ARTAXERXES, long official poetry
in verse was dead for the reader. In the same way, horse-drawn traffic died
when it was discovered that, by small explosions within a cylinder, vehicles
could be made to travel very fast. There remain, it is true, rare spirits who
prefer passing behind an old mare between the hedgerows to being precipi-
tated by blasts across deserts. I am one of them. So some people very likely
still read long verse-poems. I am not certain whether I can or can't.

I will now become for a moment the miserable reader before your awful
pope-hoods. I confess I never could read verse-poetry. I never, in my youth,
read long poems by Keats, Shelley, Milton or anything that I saw no call
to read. I never read Tasso or Petrarch or the RAPE OF THE LOCK. On
the other hand I possess a certain patience and, if I feel that I am going to
get anything out of it I can read *in* a prose or verse book for an infinite
space of time. At school I was birched into reading Vergil, who always excited in me the same hostility that was aroused by Goethe's FAUST. Homer
also was spoiled for me a good deal by the schoolmaster. The schoolmaster
did not contrive, however, to spoil for me Euripides. I have a good part of
the BACCHAE and some of the ALKESTIS still by heart. But so, indeed,
I have Books Two and Nine of the AENEID, so that those mnemonics form
no criterion. But for myself, I have read most of the books recommended
for the formation of my mind in HOW TO READ—excepting of course
"CONFUCIUS in full . . . " Your preceptor must have a cupboard for his
ferules. In addition, I have read Doughty's DAWN IN BRITAIN, an epic
in twelve books. And SORDELLO—indeed I was reading in SORDELLO
only last night. And CANTO'S.

But all these things are as good—are better—preparation for the prose
than for the verse-poet. (I take it that your Saintliness agrees that as much
poetry has been written in prose as in verse, or more.) And indeed, both
head and appendix of Ezra's curriculum are made up of prose.

I may as well copy out that Encyclical. Here it is:

[Quotes from *How to Read* Pound's "syllabus" of writers from Confucius to
Rimbaud, i.e., the passage "CONFUCIUS—In full [. . .] find them dependable." (*LE,* p. 38)]

There is nothing to cavil at in all this. It is a selection like another. Or
since it is what has given us Ezra for Pope, it is a selection beyond compare.

Various speculations rise in one's mind at the examination of the list—
but they are merely speculations, not objections. The allocation of only
thirty poems to the troubadours, minnesingers and Bion seems meagre unless
it is to be regarded as a mere footnote of historical tendencies. As if to
awaken the student to the fact that something was going on in the interval
between Dante and Ovid.

But the real incidence of this Papal Allocution is that here Ezra throws

up the sponge of the aristocrat. The troubadours of all the verse-poets that
ever were in the Western world were the most excruciatingly skilled in the
articles of metrical skill and rhyme. (The Meistersingers were in a different
category. Their work more approached that of the Anglo-Saxon nature-poet.)
But all the other names in Ezra's catalogue are those of prose writers. I
possibly except Ovid. He again is one of the writers who was possibly spoiled
for me by the schoolmaster and of him equally I have a good deal still by
heart.

> Filia consuetis ut erat comitata puellis
> Errabat nudo per sua prata pede
> Valle sub umbrosa loçus est aspergine multa
> Uvidus ex alto desilientis aquae.[33]

I daresay it is skilled poetry, with the nature note, internal rhymes, onomatopoeia and all . . .

But Homer, Dante and all writers of hexameters, terza rime, rhymed
Alexandrines, blank verse are in effect *prosateurs* who seek either to exhibit,
par surcroît, a little ingenuity in rhyme or to hasten the sense by employing
the rhythm of the mill-wheel or the railway train. But, by the time of
Stendhal, as Ezra adumbrates, the writer had—no doubt insensibly—sensed
that these devices slackened the speed. They detracted in fact from the interest.

In the end—low be it uttered—a reader has to be held by subject. Sustained interest in a subject is so hard to arouse that a writer who knows his
job comes in the end to see that anything that carries his reader's attention
outside the frame of that interest is detrimental. Even displays of his own
cleverness are detrimental. It is a fool fowler who lays his nets in sight of
the bird.

Upon the reader—not Mr. Pound's Reader-student—all we poor Popes
depend for our Peter's Pence of attention, of life. Very gradually down the
ages we have invented a collection—an immense collection—of devices by
which attention may be captured and the reader be held in a trance. We
resemble the other Pope—of Rome, the Pontifex Maximus. Like him we
have to build an immense bridge. Rome, the institution, keeps itself alive by
an infinite number of devices, borrowed mostly from the arts or from gold-
beaters. Our Church keeps itself going by devices as numerous. Yet, just as
in the end Rome, Byzantium, Mecca and the rest kept themselves going by
keeping alive the interests of the puerile, so we have to keep ourselves going.

Down the ages, writing has greatly progressed—in mechanics. Name of
Him of Croisset seems to stick rather startingly out of Mr. Pound's list of
names. Flaubert is so out of fashion in practising literary circles. Yet the
name is astonishingly apposite, since in his precepts almost as much as in
his work, practically all that is known of the texture of writing is embodied.
Indeed, it may be said to have sprung fully armed from his forehead.

Writing as it today is practised is—consciously or unconsciously—a sort
of *pointillisme*. You put point beside point, each point crepitating against

all that surrounds it. That is what Ezra means by "charged" words. They are such as find electricity by fiction with their neighbours. That was the Flaubertian device—the Flaubertian *trouvaille*. Before anyone discoverable in the corridors of the literature that preceded him, he perceived that words following slumberously—obviously—the one the other let the reader's attention wander. If someone writes of the flowing seas or the roaring waves, none's attention will be awakened. But if someone else writes "the waves were barbarous and abrupt" or even "aneerhythmon gelasma"[34] there is some possibility that they may be appreciated by some awakened soul.

Properly considered, single words in themselves have no magic beyond possibly that of a certain euphony. I had once all the difficulty in the world in persuading a Japanese poet writing poems in English from setting down that love was the glue that cemented the world. He said: "Why not? Glue sticks things together and the word has an agreeable sound". He was probably right. But that apart, no solitary word can be much "charged". On the other hand when you put two or three together they come to life—or die.

So much I take it is generally accepted. It is when you come to the larger aspect of the conjunction of phrase with phrase, sentence with sentence, paragraph with paragraph that the matter becomes more obscure. That is finally the tyranny of the subject—of the idea. In that too Flaubert codified—clarified—matters for us. The whole of BOUVARD ET PECUCHET, as of MADAME BOVARY and EDUCATION SENTIMENTALE, is one long protest against ideas following one on the other slumberously. He evolved the doctrine of surprise. The whole province of art is to interest, and interest is made to exist by a continual crepitation of surprise, minute or overwhelming.

If you mention Flaubert today to a French writer or a very young American who has learned of the French, they will utter execrations only less in degree than those evoked by the name of the late Jacques Anatole Thibault. But it is against the personality rather than against the technique of Flaubert that they will fulminate. That is how, fashions progressing, new markets are created. The Lost Generation cries out to be provided with faith, ambition and other warm toddies. That is natural: only the other night a Young Thing exclaimed shudderingly to me:

"Don't talk to me of Ezra Pound. He horrifies me. He never writes from the depths of great emotions".

Ezra, on the other hand, is a great Pope-poet because he works much as Flaubert did. He "charges" his words, watches his sentences, sees that his paragraphs make friction the one against the other. *Ceteris mutatis,* his CANTO'S might be a BOUVARD ET PECUCHET of the North Mediterranean littoral.

HOW TO READ is in short the final—and first—passport to glory of the *prosateur.* That is not what it sets out to be, for in places it announces itself to be the *vade mecum* of the reader of verse-poetry. But the irresistible forces of destiny and development have so made it. The mere fact that all the writers there recommended must, by the Anglo-Saxons for whom it is written, be read in translation makes it a recommendation to prose. No translator ever rendered the verbal felicities and tricks of, say, Guilhem de Cabestanh. Not to mention Confucius.

Ezra's CATHAY is I think the most beautiful single volume that the world has yet known. But how much it owes to China or to what extent it reproduces the verbal felicities or mere cadences of Ri Ha Ku in THE JEWEL STAIRS, who is to say? So that, if we read it for its literary garb, we read . . . . Ezra. We may have something of Ri Ha Ku in its content.

HOW TO READ is thus an induction into frames of mind rather than a literary text book. Its value is very great, even if it merely shews how Ezra arrived at being a Pope-poet. I hope no Anglo-Saxon University will ever include it in its Courses. Anglo-Saxon Universities spoil all that they touch. But I hope it will be immensely read by Young Things, Nordic, Meridional or Oriental, provided they be of good will and have virgin minds.

And so, my brothers of the Conclave, I salute you. We *are* all Popes here, aren't we?

P 27. TLS. 1 1.

[Rapallo] 12 Giugno [1932]

Deer Ford
I.
Thanks fer them kind an extensive woids.
2.
Thanks fer the kind invite. There aint no hot hells [i.e., hotels] in Genova:: can't you and th lady eat here with us?

ever Ezra

These minor differences of opinion had no dampening effect on their mutual boosting activities. Pound put in a good word for Ford in his obituary of Harold Monro, published in the July 1932 issue of *The Criterion.* Màdox Ford, he wrote, "knew the answer but no one believed him"; "Mr. Hueffer," he went on, "was getting himself despised and rejected by preaching the simple gallic doctrine of living language and *le mot juste.* His then despisers and neglectors are already more or less inexplicable to our (1932) contemporaries" (pp. 586, 587). Ford was represented by three poems in the anthology of verse that Pound brought out in May 1932, entitled *Profile.* He commented thus on Ford's significance: "[Ford's] critical influence was always enlightened and his insistence on clear and contemporary speech was of prime importance for the health of English and American writing (chiefly the latter, as the Britons were mainly incurable)" (p. 21). And in *ABC of Reading,* among the few other novels he recommends for students to learn about the form of the novel, there is one by Ford. After studying Fielding, Jane Austen, James, and a few others, so Pound recommends, "you would do well to look at Madox Ford's *A Call*" (p. 90).

Ford, who had eagerly been proposing a reunion, offered to visit Rapallo. The visit did take place in late July–early August and left both verbal and visual records. The Rapallo paper, *Il Mare*, in its 20 August issue, featured an "interview," set down by Olga Rudge and translated by her: "Madox Ford a Rapallo." It was later retranslated by her and reprinted as "Madox Ford at Rapallo: A Conversation between Ford Madox Ford and Ezra Pound." It is quoted here from *Pavannes and Divagations*. The visit was also immortalized in two snapshots of Ford and Pound, placed near a statue of Columbus.[35]

F 25. ALS (aman.). 1 1.

[Cap Brun, Toulon] [July? 1932]

Dear Ezra,

Are you still in Rapallo? If so it is very likely that Janice and I may drift in on you in about a fortnight's time. If you won't be there then would you let me know when you will be there? Our plans are fluid but could be altered within limits. Anyhow I much want to see you so let us have an answer as soon as you conveniently can.

Salutations yours, FMF

Dictated to [Richard] Murphy who never learned how to write and has hacked both my machine and his own.[36]

MADOX FORD AT RAPALLO

A CONVERSATION BETWEEN FORD MADOX FORD AND EZRA POUND
(Translated by Olga Rudge)

Ford Madox Ford, "grandfather of contemporary English literature", founder of the *English Review,* the *Transatlantic Review,* friend of Henry James and Hudson, a collaborator of Conrad's, etc., passed through Rapallo the beginning of August, 1932. We were present when his friend Pound attacked him, verbally:

Pound: What authors should a young Italian writer read if he wants to learn how to write novels?
Ford: (Spitting vigorously) Better to think about finding himself a subject.
Pound: (Suavely, ignoring Ford's irritation) Well, suppose he has already had the intelligence to read Stendhal and Flaubert?
Ford: A different curriculum is needed for each talent. One can learn from Flaubert and from Miss Braddon.[37] In a certain way one can learn as much from a rotten writer as from a great one.

Pound: Which of your books would you like to see translated into Italian and in what order?

Ford: I don't trust translations; they would leave nothing of my best qualities. Some writers are translatable.

Pound: What are the most important qualities in a prose writer?

Ford: What does "prose writer" mean? The Napoleonic Code or the Canticle of Canticles?

Pound: Let us say a novelist.

Ford: (In agony) Oh Hell! Say philosophical grounding, a knowledge of words' roots, of the meaning of words.

Pound: What should a young prose writer do first?

Ford: (More and more annoyed at the inquisition) Brush his teeth.

Pound: (Ironically calm, with serene magniloquence) In the vast critical output of the illustrious critic now being interviewed (changing tone) . . . You have praised writer after writer with no apparent distinction (stressing the word "apparent" nearly with rage). Is there any?

Ford: There are authentic writers and imitation writers; there is no difference among the authentic ones. There is no difference between Picasso and El Greco.

Pound: Don't get away from me into painting. Stick to literary examples.

Ford: Hudson, and Flaubert in "Trois Contes". Not all of Flaubert, let us say the "Trois Contes."

Pound: You have often spoken to me of "fine talents." Are some finer than others?

(Ford tries to evade a comparison)

Pound: Are there new writers on a level with Henry James and Hudson?

Ford: (After qualifying Henry James' talent at some length) Yes. Hemingway, Elizabeth Roberts, Caroline Gordon, George Davis. Read "The Opening of a Door" and "Penhally".[38]

Pound: But as artists? If James is a consummate artist, is Hudson something else? He may be called a pure prose writer, not a novelist.

Ford: The difference between weaving and drawing.

Pound: Now for the term "promising." What makes you think a new writer "promises"?

Ford: The first sentence I read. When two words are put together they produce an overtone. The overtone is the writer's soul. When Stephen Crane wrote, "The waves were barbarous and abrupt", he presented simultaneously the sea and the small boat. Waves are not abrupt for a ship. "Barbarous and abrupt"—onomatopoeic, like "Poluphloisboion" in Homer (when the Cyclops throws the rock).

Pound: (Concluding) How many have kept their promises since the *English Review* was founded twenty-five years ago?

Ford: Stephen Reynolds is dead. Ezra has become hangman's assistant to interviewers . . . I don't know what Wyndham Lewis is doing. Norman Douglas. D. H. Lawrence is dead, but kept on 'till the end. Rebecca West. Among the successors: Virginia Woolf; Joyce in "The Portrait of the Artist as a Young Man"; the [Richard] Hughes who wrote "High Wind in Jamaica", a dramatist's novel, not a novel writer's.

EDITOR's NOTE: (Above) From the original interview in Italian, appearing in "Il Mare" of Rapallo at the time of one of Ford's visits. Pestered the next day as to what a young writer ought to read, Ford groaned: "Let him get a DICTIONARY and learn the meaning of words."

The discussions between Ford and Pound seem to have stimulated further joint actions on behalf of Literature. There was an exchange of letters in which Pound's current enemy, the French writer and critic Valéry Larbaud, is mentioned. Ford's suggestion of a possible forum for Pound's reflections on literary form is rejected—in humility and irritation. Although Pound doesn't mention the *Cantos* in his reply, their failure to yield or promise an overall design no doubt caused a sense of inadequacy in him.

P 28. TCS. Initial typed.

[Rapallo, p.m. 29 August 1932]

Dear F/ you will have noted that I did NOT drag you into row re/ Lardbug[i.e., Larbaud][.] at the same time, one or two pages of typescript on the weakness of present french critical standards and the ignorumps of eng. lit/ wd. be vereeee useful.

Put it in as impersonal form as you like and conduce to as much general amity as you like//

ever E.

F 26. ALS (aman.). 1 1.

[Cap Brun, Toulon] Sept; 1, 1932.

Dear Ezra,

I have no idea who Lardbug is though I can hazard a guess and no echos of combat have reached these shores so I don't see what I could do about it. I don't either know much about French criticism of today. It seems to be trying to vieillir avec dignité — and as for English ignorance that seems to be hardly anything to write home about. Besides if Lardbug is who I take him to be I would as soon think of tilting against an open sewer.

Would you answer me two things? (a) Is your pamphlet on political economy available for serial publication? (b) Would you accept a commission from a periodical to write something in the vein of your How to Read once a month for a remuneration of fifty dollars a time? The length to be just exactly what you like as well as the subject matter — thus affording you a permanent pulpit. If this were agreeable to you I think I

could arrange it but I am not quite certain. Let me have an answer as
soon as you conveniently can.

Yrs FMF

P 29. TLS. 2 11.

[Rapallo] 5 Sett [1932]

Reverend F/
    The term Lardbug is a contraction of Boule de Suif and Larbaud.
/ / /
The " ⟨ABC of⟩ Economics" is indubitably available for serial pubctn. =
now in duplicate in hands of agent/
    Miss V. Rice
18 East 41 st. St.
Noo Yok
from whom haspirants can git it.
/ / / / / /
"Something in the vein of" How to Read ???

In the sense that "How to read" is the condensation of conclusions arrived at after 25 years search it wd. not be possible to repeat or even
greatly to extend it.

    (Apart from a treatise on major form, which not yet having produced,
I mean not yet having terminated any work containing shining example of
Form of the whole, I do not feel competent to tell the world about it.)

(Mauberley has got some structure . . . but I ain't ready to theorize about
major form YET.)

On the other hand if: "In the vein of", means a monthly article telling
the young how to grow up, in short, a monthly article on comparative
literature etc. and kindred subjects, I think I cd. probably produce same
⟨$50 a shot wd. serve.⟩

"Il Mare" affords me (I.E. is supposed to be about to afford me) a
fortnightly outlet, but if the murkn public wishes to retain me as a writer
of their uncouth lingo it wd. be advisable for them to offer me something
better.

I was saluted as a master of italian prose two weeks ago . . . . not meaning
uniform and poifik expression, but capacity for packing a punch.

Trusting this answers yr/ enquiry with courtecy and concision, to say
nothing of promptitude
    I remain

E. P.

    greetings to the Shulamite.

The topic of a series of articles by Pound is further developed in the next few letters. The forum proposed, the *Hound and Horn,* is one to which Pound had contributed in 1930 and 1931. It was not until 1934 that the periodical carried another article by him. Ford, who was doing his best to try to find a British publisher for *A Draft of XXX Cantos,* may have used proofs of the American edition in these efforts. Pound's reply to the first letter—in which Ford touches on this subject—is missing; Ford continued his clarification in his next. Pound's answer reveals his growing irritation and frustration with the publishing world.

F 27. TLS. 1 1.

[Cap Brun, Toulon, ante 6 November 1932]

dear ezra

i have cut off the top of my left thumb in a gardenin operation and writing is difficult to me

i am forwarding you the proofs by this post[.] they were "out" on loan or i would have forwarded them as soon as i got your post card

i have not been idle about those articles but transatlantic correspondence takes a long time: put shortly the situation is now this:

the conductors of the periodical that i approached say this: they are very anxious that the connection with you should last for ever but they are perfectly certain that if the connection is monthly you will be wanting their blood at the end of the first month and that thus any arrangement they might make with you would to their regret come summerily – i use the "e" to indicate your jauntiness – to an end which they would much regret[.] they are innocent people with an absolute admiration for your work which they want to present

they propose therefore that you should write something, extending how to read – which excites their special admiration – or enlarging on some point in that work to about the same length as that of that tractate: this they would publish in two successive numbers of their non commercial periodical paying you drs two hundred for same[.] if you do not then send hirelings of the mafia or facisti to murder them they would commission further articles and so the giddy dance might continue

the periodical in short resembles the lamented dial[.] one of the proprietors – the one with whom i negotiate[39] – is a very rich man and one of your sincerest admirers[.] i pointed out to them the drs fifty a month did not satisfy you and this is what they devised[.] they hope – not too sanguinely – that you will not use the opportunity for getting back on your washerwoman or drs [Henry Seidel] canby, parker (the late) or [S. Parkes] cadman[40] or on any other obscure character because it is difficult to be really interested in the soiled linen or cupboarded skeletons of the un-

known or almost but that you will cast light on the obscure and unknown
problems of your art

    with regard to cantos i have not yet been able to secure a british
publication for that work but i remain if not faint at least pursuing[.]
the other projects in its regard progress[41]

Yrs FMF

F 28. TLS. 1 1.

[Cap Brun, Toulon] 6 nov 1932

Dear Ezra,

    The final periodical is the Hound and Horn to which, true to your
character of liberal shepherd you give a grosser name.[42] I gather that they
would rather not communicate with you direct because – true to your
other character of a shooter of sparrows with a duck-punt-gun – you will
address insults to them. The proposition from the monthly[43] was withdrawn for reasons that must be better known to you than to me. I have
tried every periodical with whom I have any contacts and some with whom
I have none in the hope of getting you a regular contract and it all whittles
down to that of the above journal. They now say: "Let the essay be upon
the metric of Bion.[44] Length that of HOW TO READ" – about 10,000
words, I take it "Price $200".

    Dr Parker was the late pastor of the City Temple, Dr Cadman you say,
is dead. The mild witticism of my conjunction of those names was merely
that you seem to find fun in miscalling, blasting, blackmailing and putting
yourself about people not worth a charge of buckshot or duckshot. That
is merely a matter of your sense of values. If you get more vital suste-
nance out of attacking these nonentities than out of being published by
them or someone like them it is not for me to interfere.

    Anyhow the above is the only firm offer I have been able to get out of
several months of effort. The H & H is I gather perfectly – and as far as I
can judge, sincerely – ready to publish your reflections on Literature for
ever. They would, I think, be still better pleased to publish your poetry.

Yours   FMF

P 30. TLS. 2 11.

[Rapallo] 9 Nov [1932]

Reverend father in gawd, carissime mihi mentor:

    I am at loss to know why any bloody menstrual shd. have MADE
an offer, and not having had any dealings with, or mentioned, any mensual
during the past period in memory recorded I am still more at loss to
know why the sonzovbitches shd. have withdrawn it.

((Exception to the above being Arriet's paper [*Poetry*] which cdnt. offer 100 bucks and one other highly specialized pubctn/ with which I am on most excellent terms and which does pay whenever it can think of anything I can do for it, i.e. lying within its narrow field.))

As fer Bitch an Whiffle, I have done at least 300 dollars work for the young snots for which I have not been paid and have no reason to suppose that future relations with them wd. be less disgusting than those I was for a period of two years god damned idiot enough to put up with.

A clique review that represents everything you have as critic struggled for thirty years to eliminate.

I deeply appreciate yr/ six months struggle, but perhaps you by now believe that my statement to you re/ disponibility was not exaggerated.

I was precipitous enough to write out most of the ten thousand words (mostly yesterday morning), but at any rate I shall now be spared the bother of correcting the mss/ fer the printer.

respects to the Shulamite

E.P.

One of Ford's most energetic and successful drives on behalf of Pound was his campaign to enlist the support of prominent authors for *A Draft of XXX Cantos*. Begun in August 1932 it resulted in the pamphlet, *The Cantos of Ezra Pound: Some Testimonies* by Ernest Hemingway, Ford Madox Ford, T. S. Eliot, Hugh Walpole, Archibald MacLeish, James Joyce, and others,[45] which Farrar & Rinehart sent out in connection with the publication of the first American edition in March 1933. In addition to his "Editor's Note," signed with the initials "D. C." for his old pseudonym Daniel Chaucer, Ford contributed a "testimony" of his own. Pound thanked him for the "wreathes."

EZRA POUND'S CANTOS

Editor's Note

It is not uncommon to hear some one quote:

> 'Who killed John Keats?',
> 'I', said the QUARTERLY
> So savage and Tartarly,
> 'I killed John Keats.'

And when we think that Keats and Chatterton and Douanier Rousseau and Cézanne and Schubert and Bizet and Edgar Allan Poe and a host of other geniuses or masters went without recognition during their lifetimes we not infrequently say: "Ah, why did we not live in those scandalous times so that we might have set that wrong right!" Or perhaps have bought their first editions . . . .

It is to shield our own time from such shame that we have got together from 'type' authors these testimonials to Mr. Pound and his CANTOS. Each of these writers may be regarded as representing or as having behind him a group of others and a public large or growing towards largeness. So it would appear that a considerable number of the inhabitants of the world of today is at least prepared to be aware of the existence, and of some of the great merits, of Mr. Pound. The range in schools and territory here covered is wide . . . .

Mr. Walpole calls himself Victorian and claims to represent English Cathedral closes; Mr. Wilson stands for New York in its more thoughtful and advanced moods. Mr. Williams, the adept of verse, proclaims a strong carefree prose. Mr. Tate is the leader of a poetic school that inclines to gay and virile erudition. Miss Roberts is a beautiful prosewriter and charming lyrist of the South of North America; M. Morand, an accomplished representative of the reason and order that distinguished the North of France. Mr. Joyce, the most unrivalled virtuoso, leads the vanguard of the green, westernmost shores of Europe. Mr. Ford who must be Mr. Pound's oldest accomplice once led an international vanguard that by now is entitled to bestow an Academic blessing on the celebrator of Sigismund Malatesta; Mr. Eliot is the revolutionary become Doctor; H.D., the unrivalled singer of Greece, along with Mr. Ford and Mr. Williams once marched in the ranks of Mr. Pound's Imagiste phalanx; Mr. Bishop is one of the young lions of today's verse and prose in America; Mr. Bunting represents Mr. Pound's latest activities in the art of movement-founding. These diversified expressions of gratitudes, enforced admirations, enthusiastic analyses, affectionate reminiscence and prophesy thus do honour at once to Literature, to their contributors and to Mr. Pound. Few indeed are the literary figures who could have evoked the like.

For the secondary occupations of Mr. Pound are by no means ignored in these tributes. They could not be. The Part that Mr. Pound has taken in the literary activities of today can only be paralleled by the functions of the royalist ACTION FRANÇAISE in France. It is as anachronistic and as valuable. The ACTION FRANÇAISE has nearly as few readers as Mr. Pound but on account of its trenchant love of public virtue it is so feared by every French political grafter that graft is hardly attempted by any French politician whose necessities have not driven him beyond the fear of contempt. So, with knout, bowie knife and gall-infused pen, for a quarter of a century and in obscure periodicals, Mr. Pound has stood as Censor of Grub Street, clue-holder to Parnassus and Perseus for all chained Muses. The periodicals that have supported him have usually lacked readers but few to whom Mr. Pound's exhortations have been addressed have escaped reading at least that part of his voluminous prose writings. He has fathered Vers Librism, Vorticism, Imagisme and two score other movements between those and Objectivism. He will found two score more. For, with seven leagued boots, unfailingly, he arrives with unexampled velocity at new vantage points seen from which all his latest crop of cygnets resolve themselves into goslings. All but one or two. So you have Mr. Joyce's generous tribute.

For the last quarter of a century Mr. Pound has been not merely a Pride's Purge but·an undeviatingly guiding light and an unparalleledly stimulating irritant. The large and indifferent public has now the opportunity to take these things into account. It must do so or it will find itself regarded by its great-grandchildren as having been all one with the worst of the bored, boring or criminal generations that have preceded it—all one, say, with the generation that viewed with indifference the burning of Joan of Arc. So it is time to get on the band-wagon!

D.C.

From FORD MADOX FORD

The warm winter sun falls on my back as I sit writing. There is an orange on a tree that never yet bore. That is consolation. The winter is here; the world has become rather empty. One once had friends. The cities swarmed with them. One could go toward any of the cardinal points or between them in any direction to find joyous discussion. That is all done. The world's arguments are now grim. One falls back on the consolation of finding an orange on a once barren tree. One's friends have died, changed, gone . . . .

These are commonplaces. They come however in the end to the attention of all individuals and of all races. Nations and individuals arrive at a winter when there shall be no more spring . . . only waiting. Then the arts alone do good.

It is to me a great consolation in such a season to let my mind wander along the pinkish corrugations of these shores. Their rocks hardly fret at all the blue water and when the thoughts have sufficiently but not too far pursued the shore they will come to the place where Ezra sits, plucking—in the name of the Prophet!—figs from the dusty thistles of our winter world. So all in our civilization is not lost.

All that is civilised in our time comes from these shores. By one bye-road or another. Their winds enjoin reason, moderation, frugality,—and in due measure, saturnalia. So, if our civilisation is to continue, or even to be remembered, we must have our outposts not only in boreal or torrid wildernesses but beneath these tempered and undying suns. And we must have our spies into the past that inexorably governs us and that constantly changes its aspect. The giant Atlas to refresh his strength must constantly re-touch the earth of these Mediterranean shores. So must we.

Mr. Pound learned all that he knows of life and letters from, in the first place, Flaubert. Tactics he learned at Altaforte at the feet of Bertran de Born who incensed the whole world with his libels. Of strategy Mr. Pound never heard, nor yet, though he sits at the feet of a statue of Columbus has he permitted his mind to be opened by travel. He reclines in a remote fragment of Coney Island that has dropped from the skies near Porto Fino. There he pursues what Flaubert pursued in his solitudes under the Norman cliffs of Croisset. He pursues unceasingly the just—the "charged" word—in just and even more charged cadences. That is his pursuit.

His activities are . . . . activities. With them he keeps his muscles keyed up. Very likely without them he could not support the strain of his pursuit of the intangible. His activities corruscate in the spirit of Bertran de Born who had a scarlet forked beard, the moustachios of a tom-cat and a singular command of invective that defeated itself. Literature has gained much from the activities of Mr. Pound. It has also for the time lost a great deal. You must strike the balance to suit yourself.

I am told that Mr. Joyce attributes to the poet the fact that the world listens to him at all and that without Mr. Pound. Mr. Eliot would have had to wait longer before instructing the youth of New England as to the humaner letters. And a great many others owe this or that to the activities of the author of the CANTOS.

That makes a big item on the credit side. Against this it is mostly because of his saltimbanqueries that the world hardly listens to Mr. Pound himself. That is a matter for Mr. Pound. You cannot grumble at a talker if he does not want to be politic enough to ensure an audience. But it is a great temporary loss to the world since many people will die without having read the CANTOS because Mr. Pound has found it imperative to assail with the *sirventes* of a second Bertran a number of nonentities. Indeed our civilisation may go to the ground with the CANTOS unread and will leave to races unknown the task of redressing that balance.

To the other account we may put the fact that the world gains by including such a character. Mr. Pound's cursory pronouncements in prose may seem to you mostly nonsense, but even his nonsenses give one to think. The sacred emperor may not in very fact be naked but it does nothing but good if a child be found to say from time to time that he has no clothes. To keep the thought of the world sane extravagances too are necessary. It is not in vain that the Schaunards[46] of the '40–'90's wore beards, sombreros and waving locks and the tradition of *épaté*-ing the bourgeois is not one that humanity can afford to let die. In that tradition Mr. Pound has the secret of the fountain of undying youth. When you hear him, wrapped round in his *taleth,* triply high-hatted and seated on his Presidential throne, pronounce exhortations and excommunicate to right and left you need not agree with him. But if you are wise you will go over your arms—your metres, your idioms, your cadences and your not too easy soul. That is what Movements are for and Mr. Pound has founded and abandoned a mort of movements. They may possibly teach you little but they may well make you watch out and see that your powder is dry. For me, when Mr. Pound tells me, as he does three times a year—that he is holding the leashes of a thousand young lions who will shortly bound roaring along these shores to devour me, I scarcely believe him. But I remember that in times past Ezra has enrolled mildly protesting me in half a dozen of his Movements—from Imagisme and Vorticism onwards. So, in deference to the memories of those distant times I look back over the last ten words that I have written to see how I may better select and arrange them.

And under all these ululations, as was the case with Flaubert, hidden also under his ululating Correspondence, the CANTOS progress. The first words you have to say about them is: Their extraordinary beauty. And the last word will be: Beauty. Their extraordinary, their matchless, beauty. They form an unparalleled history of a world seen from these shores which are the home of our civilisation. In that they are incomparable and indispensable. And only one thing is more necessary to society than History. That is that there should be somewhere a work of art or someone producing a work of art that whenever you visit it shall unfailingly arouse emotions in you. This the CANTOS do.

I take them down from the shelf and open them anywhere and come upon anything—the denunciation of usury in Canto XV, or the adventure of the young lady who came into court in a shawl that the judge mistook for a veil, or on the complaint of Artemis in the last Canto or on Canto IX which begins:

> One year floods rose,
> One year they fought in the snows,
> One year hail fell, breaking trees and walls

At once there are beauty and emotion and excitement. For Mr. Pound is not only a master of rhythms and words. He has the secret power over the heartstrings that is given only to such poets as, having been blind beggars, yet save lost empires from oblivion and redeem races from ignominy.

St. Katherine's Day, 1932

P 31. ACS.

[Rapallo] 27 Feb. [1933]

Thanks for the abundant wreathes. [A Draft of] XXX [Cantos] recd. this a.m. from Rinehart

Salve. E

can you send me copies.

by the way, what poems have you writ since 1930? or inedits in England?

Immediately after Ford received Pound's postcard at his current Paris address, 37 rue Denfert-Rochereau, he sent out an SOS. Pound, as usual, was not slow in coming to his rescue. Ford could not comply with Pound's request for new poems to include in the *Active Anthology;* his most recent work, the "Buckshee" poems, had appeared in 1931. Pound evidently never reviewed *The Rash Act,* as he had planned to do.

F 29. TLS. 1 1.

Please address reply to
37 rue Denfert Rochereau   P a r i s   V.

[Paris] 2.3.33

Dear Ezra,

Could you once more lend me $100 for a short time? ⟨– or less!⟩ As usual my American friends have suddenly stopped payment. I have just signed another agreement with Lippincott but it may be a month before they make their first payment and in the meantime I am penniless and so is Stella whom I have to grubstake. It would be a great service.

Have you any news from Farrer & Rinehart – or have they stopped too?

Yours FMF

P 32. TLS. 1 1.

[Rapallo] 5 March anno XI [1933]

Dear Ole Fordie/

GORR dem it !!! Will dew what I can BUT // expected to lexchure in Nov. and it has been postponed till end of this month/[47] AND . . . heaven knows when I'll git paid AND paid six months rent on March Ist.

I have news that XXX is to be pubd/ on the 14 th. six copies recd. IF they remit I can share.

BUT I got teh have the money to keep meself in Milan WHILE I am lexchoorin'. which I will prob. have to borrow at least part of.

I may git in a chq/ sometime///// Have you any idear WHEN Slipping-cott will pay?

anyhow here is 600 fr/ that will last over the week end.

aint life just wonnerful.

E

F 30. TLS. 1 1.

37 Rue Denfert Rochereau [Paris] 8.3.33

Dear Ezra,

Thank you very much: I feel humiliated at having worried you – especially with the dollar collapse which probably hampers your father. Things however are a little better here. I have wrung £50 out of Cape for Stella whose complete pennilessness bothered me more than anything and Lippincotts have paid – with a cheque that cannot be cashed. If you do not mind I will keep your cheque by me till Stella has actually got Cape's money and will then destroy it wiring you the one word "burnt". We can I think dribble along till then in reduced circumstances. I ought to have plenty of money for there is plenty of demand for my writing in your country – but it does not work out that way. .

I wish I could send you some verse, but except for the BUCKSHEE series which has already appeared I have not written any verse since 1930. If BUCKSHEE would suit you although it has appeared I will ask the London publishers – I can't remember who they were and have not the book here – for permission. It was in a series got together by some fool whose name does not come back to me – Abercrombie, I should think.[48] I might write some verse in a day or two. I have felt the sort of birth symptoms lately and if the capers of your $ bankers do not cause abortion, something might come. I wrote the below in answer to somebody who said I could not find a rhyme for CLOSERIE DES LILAS;

> An elderly maid at the Lilas
> Emitted a horrible squeal as
> She found that a male
> With cheeks pink and pale
> Wasn't really a man but a he-lass.

It would be rotten luck if your CANTOS are really to come out on the 14th before all this financial uproar is settled. My RASH ACT which is more like what I want to write than anything I have done for years came out on the 24th ult and has naturally been absolutely submerged. Should not have minded if I had not put more into it than, as it were I could afford – I mean in the way of mental fatigue. You will find more in it about your country than in all the belchings poor Bob ever belched.[49]

Janice sends her love. She added something about your critical activities, but I have forgotten what it was and she has gone out. It is just as well because she is rather modern

Yrs FMF

P 33. TLS. 1 1. Initial typed. Enclosure.

[Rapallo] 10 March [1933]

Dear Ford

Damn glad daylight has dawned/ Dont bother about telegraphing. Am relieved to know that I neednt try to invent something to cover the rest of the 100 bucks you mentioned in anterior epistle.

There is the st[erlin]g/ as well as the dollar/ AND then some.

We all OUGHT to have plenty of money. I have thought so for twenty years.

Hope to see the RASH ACT / will the blighters send me review copy.
Forward 'em the enc. ???[50]

I think dollar chqs/ will be cashable by the time you get this.

My ole man / not suffered yet.

yrs E

P 34. TLS. 1 1. Enclosed with *P 33*.

[Rapallo] 10 March 1933

Dear Ford
   Will yr/ publishers send review copy of Rash Act, to il Mare preferably
in my care.

yrs E. Pound

EP

F 31. TLS. 1 1.

[Paris][51] March 27, 1933

Dear Ezra,
   I am ashamed to say that I cashed that check of yours after all as it
took a very long time to get the Lippincot money. Here, however, is a
check for the amount. I do hope it hasnt bothered you too much to be
kept waiting.
   As soon as I have found some paper and string I will send you a copy
of the Rash Act.
   I have delayed writing this because I have been angling with another
publisher to get him to publish the Cantos in England. The matter is still
undecided but as soon as it is actually decided I will write to you about it.
The publisher is one to whom you have written letters of violent abuse and
the chief obstacle is that he is afraid you might resort to violence if one
of the letters got printed upside down. As soon as I have convinced him
that this would not be the case, I think it may come off.

Yrs FMF

We return to Toulon on Saturday.

   In addition to trying to secure an English publisher for *A Draft of XXX
Cantos,* Ford made attempts to find other openings for Pound. A suggestion
that he translate the *Odyssey* caused Pound to explode. Perhaps *before*
receiving Pound's reply and knowing about his plans to visit Paris, Ford
sent off an undated note, scribbled on a visiting card. It is here conjecturally dated April 1933.

F 32. ALS. 1 1.

[Cap Brun, Toulon] Easter Saturday. [15 April 1933]

Dear Ezra:
   There is a sort of publisher of preciosa who wd. like to commission
you to translate the Odyssey.[52] When he spoke to me about it it seemed

absurd. But won't you contemplate it? If only as a sort of spare time job bringing in a little, regularly? If so drop me a p.c. — comprehensible par preference — & soon.

Yrs. FMF

P 35. TLS. 3 11.

[Rapallo] 17 April [1933]

Deer Fordie /
   I thought Tommy Lawrence just HAD.[53] Wdnt. it show gr'ear confi'ance if you wuz to name the mysterious moke?

Also HOW MUCH DOES HE OFFER ????

It all confirms the general tendency // EVERY god damn invitation one has ever had is an invitation to INTERRUPT one's work.

   God buggar all bourgeois siphylization ennyhow !!

Who is the bastud? and why doesnt he take on one or more of the two dozen jobs that damn well need doing?

WHY the Hell dont he bring out an Arnaut, similar to the Guido?[54]

If he'za greekist / might be good thing to have a trans (proper edtn/) of Bion's Death of Adonis ?? That IS on a list of things I wdn't mind doing. ⟨also there are things out of print that NEED reprinting. = I cd. do prefaces to Salel. or Golding.⟩[55]

Odyssey ????? HOW MUCH A YEAR FOR HOW LONG, and wd. he do a serious edtn/

WHAT THE H E L L with such a bloody lot of things that NEED to be done and published . . . . . .
   where and WHAT . . . . . and why hasn't the blighter a name and address?
///
Incidentally I dunno who is going to do the Folio of Cantos XXVIII to XLV (or thereabouts); There are 28 to 39 now ready, the second folio vol. ends with 27.[56]
///

There OUGHT to be a decent edtn. of the trans of Cocteau's Mystere Laic.

The Guido was intended as the first of a series / Arnaut and Bion: and some Chinese stuff NEED doing, much more than yet another Odessy.

HAS the blighter any intellexshul or licherary interests ??

DAMN it I haven't ANY spare time. From Oct. 1st. 1931 down to
March 31 this year I have not had ANY time off, whatsobloody ever.
SPARE me a . . . . !! Spare TIME bloody burrinkus !!!
   Wot about 61 more Cantos waitin to be did ??

SPARE me yunyuns !!!

Why dont he "commission me" to write Cantos ???????? By the way as you
were Ngineerin the Ausgab/ of XXX what do think of small commytee
to answer idiocies of wellmeaning reviewers /
   I take it i shdnt. save in moments of exuberence . . . .

I dunno that they matter/ Have seen three notices. Agent reports good
press/ sales stopped by N.Y. bank mort/er/arium but Xpected to revive.

"ABC" out in Eng.[57]

Needless to send the preciocitist to hell / but cdnt. he serve some slightly
ameliorated use.

Meaning I dont utterly refuse, but praps he cd. be stimulated to develp hiz
magination, or praps he's just sot /////
   howeffer . . . .

am usually or allus willink tew woik.

                                                                E

F 33. ACS (visit. card).

                                        [Cap Brun, Toulon, ? April 1933]

Dear Ezra: What has Cummings done? I have not heard.[58]

Ref Apts.:
Eugene Pressly (166 Bd. Montparnasse) might let. Rent 500 au 4e but
very attractive with view on convent garden. Quiet.
The studio we had – 37 R. Denfert Rochereau might possibly [be] to let.
Ground floor with Soupente f 450 – but no comfort. Gas but no water
and outside W.C. Very quiet on court. Stella might also let for May.
   If none of these suit write Walter Lowenfels, 6 rue Val de Grace. He
does real estate agency when he can get away.
Why not look us up for a night or so on your way up? You'd be welcome.
                                                          Yrs. FMF.

oh: for 37 r. D. R. write Peter Blume who is there at present.

   Ford evidently misdated the next letter, in which he explained the
"mystery" of the printer who would commission a translation of the

Odyssey. A few days later he reported that he had written to Kahane. That same day, in a letter to the printer himself, he presented a somewhat different picture of the project. Here he said that "Ezra Pound has some idea that he might translate Homer for you. What about the economic side? Do you suppose you could pay him a regular small income while he was doing it? He couldn't work otherwise."⁵⁹ Pound was finally pacified, and he did look up Kahane during his visit to Paris in May.

F 34. TLS. 1 1.

[Cap Brun, Toulon] 13.4.33 [i.e., post 17 April 1933]

Dear Ezra,

There is no mystery as to the person who wants a translation of Homer. He is a printer called Jack Kahane of 338 rue St Honoré – Clark's old business.⁶⁰ He has done a good deal of de Luxe printing, is I think to be trusted commercially and has a passion for the Greek classics. I have no doubt that he might do some of your other re-prints if you asked him. He wants me to do the ELEKTRA but I don't think I shall. Go and see him when you are in Paris. He'd certainly do a very fine edition of the ODYSSEY if you did it but how much money there would be in it I can't say. I doubt if he would commission the CANTOS. He is a quite commercial person who makes a certain amount of money by fine printing of antiques.

I did not take the Homer proposition seriously, though he was serious enough, otherwise I should have written earlier and with more detail. It was his admiration for your powers of verse rhythm that gave him the idea and I suppose he thinks he could sell Homer in a very expensive edition to George V and President Roosevelt as he has done with other preposterously costly books.

As I said in my last: look in on us on your way up to Paris. It will take you an hour longer but we can discuss things better and save hours of letter writing which personally I detest.

Yrs FMF

F 35. TL (copy). 1 1. Cornell.

[Cap Brun, Toulon] May 1, 1933

Dear Ezra:

I have written Kahane. Did you say in one of your letters that the English publication of the Cantos was fixed up? I have a vague idea that you did but can't find the letter.

Yours,

P 36. TCS.

[Rapallo, p.m. 2 May 1933]

Dear F/

Thanks fer writing to Keh[i.e., Kahane]// Yes/ Faber has contracted for XXX Cantos / for an anthology of active (mostly murkn) potes// and SAYS he wants to do a vol. about 400 pages of my licherary crikizism[i.e., *Make It New*], nex sprung.

Has brought out my ABC of Economics.

WOT I now want is an american pubr/ for the ABC, and gorblime/ fer my Jefferson/ book.[61] probably the only "seller" I have ever written and which wd/ open up pubk/ for the Cantos, once it were got thru the blasted wood of some am pubrs/ noddle.

(I did that in Feb.)

E

P 37. TLS. 3 11.

[Rapallo] 20 Giugn or th 21 st. [1933]

Deah Fordie

I saw yr/ Mr Whatshisname [i.e., Kahane] the printer in Parigi, and we yawped fer Two hours and I don't think he has either capital or connections / affable and if one had 40 years in which to edderkate him . . . . but if one were young enough to take on that job he wd. NOT listen because of one's youth.

He had just done a editionette of Mr Milton's Lycidas or some pome begining

The Lollops of the slop

or Shelley's ode to the skyrocket or something of that nature/

Wop all ye slollops, sloll ye wollywollops

Ye bloppups of the hills and woppy groves

or in short that sort of thing and he said it was YOUR idea not his in the first place. Anyhow I said I wd. return and then the vanity of such action came upon me.

The Trib. lies this a/m/ in saying that the Ministry of Edderkashun has asked me etc. I spose it refers to events that occurred in the spring.[62]

Paris rather improved / Cocteau whom I suspect you have never appreciated enuFFF has done new play and is doing two and makes trouvailles, and has done THE mos' magnif phonograph records// french as a language and NOT as a buggarin mouth full of soup sech as the n/r/f/ etc pronounce it.

Brancus' been ill and a bit low/ Leger, [Hilaire] Hiler; Ernst all in good shape.

BBC probably broadcastin my Cavalcanti muzik.[63]

Faber publishin' me about as fast as the traffick will bear but the god damn amurikun pubrs/ hangin off.

Cantos XXVIII to 39 ready. haven't been in folio. I mean folio goes to 27/

small vols. to XXX (Faber doing Brit. ed. in autumn). 31 to 34, have been in maggerzeens. anyhow eleven ready fer a folio and will be a couple more before a de luxite printer begins to want 'em.

AS usual, pubrs/ continue to want naughtyboyography. IF I expressed my opinion of 20% of the shits I have encountered the bk/ wd. be too libelous to print. and what intelligence I have encountered, I have already mentioned in my articles on this thet an tother.

However I spose they yearn to hear that Ellen Terry was also present / or other world shakin events in the life of the cheenyus'.

Periodicals are duller these las' two months than EVER in the history of printin' // gor damn the bastuds ov editors ennyhow.

Faber, by the way has got out Eliot's castrated edtn/ of my short pomes fer 3/6 so cantinental buyers can get 'em if the book shops permit.[64]

They cd/ have done the coll"cted MY collected (as Liveright Personae) fer about I shd. think the same price . . . . mah !!!

I hope to hell by NOW Farrar has remitted you the items mentioned in yrs/ of the whatever / mine of the whichever/ Farrers of the whoever / etc/ und so weiter.
   It is too god damn wettt to play tennis / hence this deluge of egocentric, centripital verbosity, upon thine defenceless head.
   What are we comin to? the SPECTATOR has asked me to do another obit for pore ole Arold.[65] I axd/ what had happened to 'em. Present edtr/ declines responsibility for the past and says he has never read a line of Gosse. N. Eng. Weekly was lively for about a year/ now dragging. Cockburn's private press service "The Week" occasionaly has a spark.[66] Also pays guinea a page for real NOOZ.
   ave yew seen it?
   Good young man. Was Times correspondent 3 years and then told 'em to go TO.

Cummings in Paris / you might review his EIMI, at any rate wangle a copy from Covici. The Kumrad ⟨Cumminkzs⟩ is I think much more mellow than in ages past.

y ever E

& regards to Janice

During these years Pound was above all absorbed in economics, and a steady stream of articles on the subject was sent from Rapallo to magazines in various countries. His involvement with economic and political reforms is also reflected in books and in the cantos he was writing at this time, published as *Eleven New Cantos XXXI–XLI*. (Ford declined an offer to review his *ABC of Economics*.) His interest in music, together with his organizing zeal, brought about a series of concerts which were given in Rapallo at fairly regular intervals, starting in 1933. With the support of the local authorities he initiated the "Concerti Tigulliani," so called after the bay of Tigullio on which the town is situated. Olga Rudge and the German pianist Gerhart Münch constituted a stable duo of performers/co-organizers. After a summer session, at which they played Mozart sonatas for violin and piano, the first full season began in October. In addition to negotiating with local authorities, performers, and backers, Pound wrote reviews, articles, and program notes to advertise the series. Ford let himself be enlisted in the advertising drive and smuggled the concerts into his notice of *A Draft of XXX Cantos,* which he wrote for the *Week-End Review* (11 November 1933) on the appearance of the English edition in September. For himself Ford wanted a change of scene, and in a note to Dorothy Pound, added to Ford's letter of 8 October, Janice enquired into the possibilities of exchanging houses with somebody in the Pounds' neighborhood for a couple of winter months.

P 38. TLS. 1 1.

[Rapallo, ante 24 September 1933]

Dear Ford

Any glory or noise you can raise re/ the enc/ wd. be welcome.

The Chilesotti stuff is at least as interesting and as good for purpose as was the Fenollosa stuff for me.[67]

Münch excellent.

Re/ the Mozart/ it will be done proper next spring and annually/

One group/ the Six sonatas v/and pyan/ done fer Pcs/ Palatiine in 1778[68]

The Five done at Vienna 1781 and then the developments/ usually before one of the operas/ at least we know a viol/and pyan son/ preceded the Nozze and the Don Giovanni.

chance to HEAR what Moz. meant by a viol/pyan sonata.
date not yet set.

Want pubcty/ tas lever on hotels/// folks gotter eat.

E.P.

vide Chil's section in Encyc. de la Musique & Dictionnair du Conser-
vatoir, – Lavignac & Laurencie[69]

F 36. TLS. 1 1.

TOULON 24.9.33

Dear Ezra,

I wish to goodness I could do something for those concerts – and still
more wish that I could hear them – but I have absolutely no contacts with
any periodical and indeed hardly any contacts with anybody. That suits
me very well for it leaves me time to write hard but it leaves me absolutely
useless for log-rolling. I will however try to get your Faber & Faber
Cantos to review for someone and if I do will slip a note about the concerts into it. Send me another copy of the programme – not the Mozart
one – , will you? I sent the other to someone who might be interested.

In spite of repeated promises Farrer & Rinehart never sent me either a
copy of the Cantos nor yet of the pamphlet – which was stupid because I
might have done some good with the latter. Fabers however say that they
have sent me one, so I may get it – the Cantos I mean.

By the bye – I meant to write to you about your father's pension. In
certain cases of American civil servants living abroad their pay is paid in
dollars at the rate of 25 frs per $. In case his has been affected it is
possible that by applying in the right quarters – say through the Embassy
at Rome – he might get his restored. It is in any case worth trying. I hope
he flourishes.

Yours FMF

P 39. ACS.

[Rapallo] 27 – Sett. [1933]

Thanks. Faber sez he has sent you XXX. Farrar !?! also said he would. –
how vurry amurikun! H.L.P. is O.K. — but as he has no official need of
staying here. I doubt if he can be put on gold standard. — he aint civily
serving now. am sending pamphlet & programs.

If you meet a not yet broke ploot[i.e., plutocrat]. he might hire the
musicians to do Moz[art]. or Chilesotti stuff in Toulon or Nice. ?? Cant
think of any other log.

yr. E.P.

ANY logs I can roll for you?

F 37. TLS. 1 1.

[Cap Brun, Toulon] October 8, 1933

Dear Ezra,

I am duly writing something about the Cantos[70] for an apparently high
brow review in England and I will also slip in a note about the concerts.
As for your kind offer to log roll me I guess I am past log rolling and the
activity would appear too suspect – in the line of 'you scratch my back and
I'll scratch yours'. But if you wanted to please me you would do what you
could to log roll René Béhaine who, in the eyes of Léon Daudet and
myself and other worthy people passes for the greatest living novelist in
the world – who also has been writing one masterpiece for upwards of
twenty years and who, heaven help us, is quite as unpopular as either you
or I.[71] If you think you could do anything effective I will have his books
sent to you.

Both Janice and I are very glad that your father can get along. Do give
him and your mother from time to time the assurance that we do not
forget them. We should have sent them some green corn this year but
owing to the drought the corn was a complete failure.

Yours, FMF

P 40. TCS.

[Rapallo, p.m. 11 October 1933]

Be/haine / be/jabers. I'll roll him if I can read him/ me conscience
permits not other. AND you by persistent settin on goose/eggs have
occasionally hatched a swan/ but more often a one legged duck. However, I'll try to read the blighter/ and if I can read will tootle.

Thanks for intentions// Tell J[anice]/ we dont know anybody going to
frawnce/ Buntin izza goin to th canary isles/ but that wont serve. Might
swap with Münch IF he had a Toulon engagement/ otherwise he wunt
be spendin car fare. (this wild guess anyhow . . .) Activ/ Anth/ due out
this week. Civil review of you by that (??) Bechofer in N.E.W.[72] Holroyd
Reece is at Mas St Gabriel, St Mathiieu, Grasse. Albatross has just
amalgamated with Tauchnitz/ I have explained carefull why he ought
to be poisoned, I mean explained TO him.[73]

But mebbe you cd/ manage him/ He seemed worried by my tellin his
step/daughter I intended to assassinate him. I explained WHY/ but he
is **VERY** resilient. I doubt if grief wd/ sink very deep. I spose ole Duck-

bill [i.e., Duckworth] still pubs/ you in Eng/[74] With stamps at 7 cents/
post cards/ etc.

ever E
E.P.

F 38. TLS. 1 1.

TOULON 28.10; 33

Dear Ezra,

I got the review of the CANTOS complete with blurb of the concerts
off duly[75] last week. It would be better if I had not had to wriggle the
subject around to get the concerts in – there would have been fewer personalities and more about the CANTOS . . . Mais tu l'as voulu, Geo[r]ges
Dandin! One day I will really write something au fond about them.

Your reply about Béhaine reminds me of a day twenty odd years ago
when I went round to No2 The Pines, Putney and told Mr Theodore
Watts Dunton that a remarkable poet had risen in the West, asking him to
log-roll said R.P. He replied: "My dear Fordie you are always umumum
discovering these remarkable geniuses in umumumsnuffleum remote
snuffle deserts. They're never any good I don't suppose I shall be able to
read the umsnuffleum barbaric yawps but I'll ask young Hake andumumum
Caine and umumum the other young of the um Circle and we'll see the
result."[76] And you did, in the ETHENAEUM . . . Eheu fugaces Pontifex,
Putnibus . . Plus ça change plus c'est la même chose . . . Gweil angau na
gwyllyth . . . Eppur – but no, not that . . . . Displicuit nasus suus . . . Eripuit
caelo fulmen sceptrumque tyrannis . . . Ex ungue olenem . . . Io non so
lettere . . . . Neque semper arcum tendit Apollo . . . Sine ira et studio . . . .
Atque ego . . . But no! Atque mihi eruditio quaedam![77]

Yours FMF

P 41. TC.

[Rapallo] 3 Nov. [1933]

Dowbtless yr/ reeward will be great upstairs and by the law of averages
you DO discover 97 ducks to every swan and a half. I dont blame
Watsie[i.e., Watts-Dunton]/ and I dont remember bein revd/ in the
Ethenaeum/ IF that's wot you imp/to mean/ply.

And I will/ as per mine of whenever/ try to read the d/m bustud. I
mean ME myself . . . but I never did like NOVELS just as such. an krrist
you have spieled about a whale of a lot of books that never cast any
illumination on the waste of a questionable world. And the dif/ of
temperameng/ some likes FAX and some falls fer Märchen. mebbe
thet's th difference between one arf en the tother. ///
& thanks fer boomin the concs.

MEDITERRANEAN REVERIE

By Ford Madox Ford

[. . .]⁷⁸

[. . .] at times [Mr. Pound] throws down the pen, grasps any tool, from chisel to sword, and springs, ululating, into any bally-hooly that may be going on anywhere. With these activities he keeps his muscles keyed up. Very likely without them he could not support the strain of his pursuit of the intangible. These, his minor passions, have been innumerable and boundless in scope. Always writing poetry, from the age of ten, he has been by turns professor of the Romance languages, cattle hand in liners, Cook's guide to Spain, founder of movements in London. He has taken chunks of rock, hit them with hammers and produced eggs or golden birds *à la* Brancusi; he has hammered tennis balls with rackets and become champion of Southern countries; he has taken *fleurets* and *épées de combat* and challenged with them admirers of Milton; he has hammered, tickled and blasted pianos, bassoons, spinets and ophicleid[e]s and has produced operas that have been broadcast by the B.B.C. He has been at once the last survivor of Murger's *Vie de Bohème,*⁷⁹ censor of world morals and Professor of Economics for the Province of Genoa.

These activities would be bad for his work if he pursued them *en amateur.* But not a bit of it. He has acquired his fantastic erudition by really being in turn all these things. He was professional Professor of the Romance Languages, professional cattle hand, professional sculptor, duellist, bassoonist and composer of operas. Yesterday he was Professor of Economics at Rapallo. To-day, to my relief, he is head impresario of his Ligurian Academe. His Mozart week rivalled that of Salzburg, and he is at the moment organising concerts of chamber music that should make all proper men desire to go to the Gran Sala Del Municipio di Rapallo. It gives me at least a feeling of, let us say, *Sehnsucht* to think that, if I could exchange the sunlight in which I am sitting for that other sunlight, I could this very afternoon listen to this programme of Ezra's Concoction:

[Quotes program.]

I wonder where in London I could hear the Purcell, or where in Paris the Debussy. Or, in either, such players! And all the while Ezra pursues the writing of his cantos on his fifth floor over the Mediterranean.

Nor is it to be imagined that all his other activities are merely devices for passing the time, getting rid of uric acid or emulating the wasp. The war put an end to his remarkable activities in London of the '13s and '14s. Without that, London might well to-day be the literary, plastic and musical centre of at least Anglo-Saxondom. As it was, the spirit passed to West Eighth Street between Fifth and Sixth,⁸⁰ and from there spread throughout the United States, so that the whole American approach to the Arts resembles to-day very nearly that of the exciting times that we witnessed round Holland and Church Streets when Vorticistes and Cubists and Imagistes and Futurists and the morning stars and Mr. Wyndham Lewis (Percy) and Signor Marinetti sang all together in their glory. . . . *Tempi Passati! Tempi Passati!*

I do not mean that that gay, iconoclastic spirit passed entirely to transatlantic *parages*. Of the contributors to the remarkable, spontaneous tribute to the cantos and their writer that sprang up last year at their first publication in the United States, six at least of the fifteen are European by birth—Hugh Walpole, Francesco Monotti, Paul Morand, James Joyce, Basil Bunting and another; and two more, T.S. Eliot and H.D., have become British subjects, the Old World having thus the majority, the seven dyed in the wool—and Anglo-Saxon—sons of Old Glory being Ernest Hemingway, Elizabeth Madox Roberts, John Peale Bishop, Archibald MacLeish, Allen Tate, Edmund Wilson and William Carlos Williams. So this Poet's Progress has not wanted for observers either in the New or the Old Worlds. And the tributes were as remarkable to his activities as to the cantos themselves. Mr. Walpole says that Ezra stirs both his appetite for beauty and his creative zest; Mr. Hemingway that any poet in this century or in the last ten years of the preceding century who can honestly say that he has not been influenced by or learned greatly from the work of Ezra Pound deserves to be pitied rather than rebuked; Mr. Joyce that "but for him I should still probably be the unknown drudge that he discovered"—and so on through the whole gamut of admiration or gratitude. . . .

The reason is that Mr. Pound has a genius for words that no one—not excluding Shakespeare in England or Heine in Germany—has ever in modern times much surpassed. Almost any line of his: *"Here we are picking the first fern-leaves"*, *"You who lean from amber lattices upon the cobalt night"*, *"And dawn comes, like a silver-sandalled Pavlova"*, *"Kung walked by the silver temple and into the dynastic grove"*—any line of his, in a hundred moods—*"Sleep thou no more, I see the star upleaping that hath the dawn in keeping"*—without context or support, any such line is like the trumpet-call awakening of a good novel. Mr. Pound has, of course, learned a great deal from the novelists—perhaps more from Flaubert than from any other individual, though obviously the Romance and Italian poets of before fifteen hundred and seventeenth-century English—and the Yellow Press and railway time-tables—have all played their parts with his rhythms. So that the range of tones and rhythms of his lyre-bassoon-ukulele-kettledrum-klaxon verse music is almost incredible, and he can turn on this or that stop with the ease and certainty of the consummate organist who plays the double toccata of Bach and at the same time fourteen games of chess at once. I do not recall anyone—not even Pierre Vidal—who ever had the rhythmic virtuosity of the poet of Rapallo—or, indeed, his scholarship, erudition in fantastic human instances and invention.

The 'XXX Cantos' make up part of an immense epic history of the world as it centres round the Mediterranean. It is also the divine comedy of the twentieth century. It differs from most other epics in the fact that it is interesting. Mr. Pound has learnt what there is to know of form from his long apprenticeship to novelists, and the result is a permanent advance of the poetic art. That is what Mr. Hemingway means when he says that the modern poet who has not learned from Mr. Pound is to be pitied. The day is over for the solemn individual who augustly specialised in nothing but archaic verbiage, sham mediaevalism, florists' catalogues and the habits of birds—all things that no human being can much care about. Mr. Pound's words are singularly alive, his mediaevalism is infinitely modern, his subjects infallibly chosen; but his great characteristic is his power to awaken and to hold the interest—a power that is in part the result of training but much more that of his native gift of words—his genius in the strictest sense of the term.

He uses his erudition with extreme boldness, and because Artemis, Sigismund Malatesta, Poggio[81]—and Picasso—all equally live for him, so they and their times and the times between live in his pages. Obviously in so immense a work there will be inequalities. Here and there half a page or half a canto will be given up to humorousnesses that might well have delighted us when we were in the fourth form—and to devote a whole canto of his inferno to human excrement and natural processes is to be prodigal of the inessential. That is no doubt a relic of Americanism. You must have some unpleasantnesses in a hell for financiers, and, for a son of Philadelphia, defective plumbing may well have a hypnotising dreadfulness. I mention these characteristics so that, should, say, the keeperess of the public lavatories in Charing Cross Station be induced by these lines to purchase a copy of 'XXX Cantos' she may not upbraid me. Other adults may well support with equanimity Mr. Pound's boisterousnesses.

Boisterousness—which is also vitality—is, of course, necessary to getting Mr. Pound through his labours. No person of correctitude of views or nicety of expression could have compassed them. In any case here is a work of vast scope, extending from the heights of Olympus to the bottom of the Cloaca Maxima, and one of which our age may well be proud. Banks may break, sterling sink into bottomless pits, and great financial figures know disgrace, and yet the Age need not hang its head. But an Age that does not produce at least one huge, vital and Jovianly laughing epic must stand for ever shamed in the endless ranks of her sisters. From that Mr. Pound's great work may well save us. There seems to be very little else that will.

P 42. TLS. 2 11.

[Rapallo] 16 Nov. XII [1933]

DeeUH Fordie /

It shuure iz th gran' WAZZ drumm with tripple trimmings. An thanks infiniment fer the concert boost. The Pri[n]cess de Polignac[82] sat thru the second show after 9 hours train trip from Rome and no dinner . . . . That might pass fer a record. She is now among the "sostenitori". We have also bought a Steinway pyanny and will give it to the town, after which we will possibly procede toward the amortization of the third foot of the instrument, now aerially suspended over my credit.

The Podesta SEZ "Thet hall iz ter be a tempio d'arte, and nothing is to be played in it unless EZ SEZ it IZ muzik.

(Boccherini chucked out because it wdnt. hold up after J.S.B[ach]. in th rehearsals.)

(Incidentally Elgar's foist woidz on being presented to the lady who had paid for most of Strawinsky's first works, and who at the age of 17 scandalized her family by buying a Manet for 500 francs, were: "Hyperion won." (in hoarse whisper).[83]
which she now tells to illustrate the meaning of aht in Hengland.)

///

Now as to HELL, you god damn ignorant pseudo catholic, have you ever read what authorities have said on the subject, and is there anything ⟨in my hell⟩ save the signs of modern progress in contraceptives, that aint found in the most catholic of mediaeval sermons.

The reason this age is such mass of snot IS purrcisely because the idea of mental ROT has been mislaid. ⟨Protestant shallows.⟩

All they can smell is sewer. The idea that Jum Douglas of the Sunday Morning Stool,[84] and 99 percent of Brit pubcation STINKS . . . has been eliminated from ang/shaxon imagination.

DECOMPOSITION . . . . god damn it. Them cantos ARE London after the war . . . the nearest thing to the exact word attainable . . .

lyric, I admit, and greater force is in Canto XXXVIII. where is FACTS[,] where facts is what there aint nothing else BUT.

THAT IS THE STATE of ENGLISH MIND in 1919. MIND in England of the post war epotch.

Get a photo of Beaverbrooks moog ef yew doant beeleev it.

Saluti. & saluti to lady —

EZ

There are very few letters extant from 1934; evidently few were exchanged, to judge from Pound's complaint about the lack of communication. From his base in Paris Ford seems to have reported on the state of affairs in the French literary world. Ford and Janice had come to Paris early in the year for a three-month spell in the capital. With his most recent memoirs, *It Was the Nightingale,* on the market and feeling a bit uncertain of where to go next, he was angling for a publisher for his *A History of Our Own Times* (never to find one) and for the book on Provence he was planning. In the middle of March he went to London, where he was reminded of Pound's old dislike of the sound of the church bells. (His postcard was forwarded from Rapallo to Rome.)

It seems that while Ford was becoming increasingly uncertain of his reputation and perhaps even of his ability to live up to his own expectations, Pound more and more often was taking the opportunity to insist on Ford's significance as a man of letters. He achieved results when advising the editor of *Esquire* to get for his magazine "ole Ford (Madox, Oxmad, Hueffer Madox Ford Herman Karl Georg Xtn / J / M / Ford."[85] He wrote with affection and concern of his friend in a letter to Iris Barry: "Give my luvv to Ford. I understand I have crucified him or something/ gord know how or when . . . or in whose fervid imagination. A nobl/ figure / and one of the few people who ever have done any real WORK / for which he has had all too little wreathes, mhyrrh, frankin cense."[86]

In his *ABC of Reading,* which appeared in the spring, Pound advocates ways to study and to learn how to handle the form of the novel, in terms that are decidedly Fordian. We recognize the Impressionist insistence on "rendering"—rather than "telling"; Ford's talk of *progression d'effet* turns up as "construction" and "lead[ing] up to an effect." Pound stresses the risks, to the poet, of distancing oneself from "the living language." Ford would also have approved of the hammering home of the idea of "poetry as concentration."[87]

P 43. TLS. 2 ll.

[Rapallo] 11 March [1934]

Dear Ford

I protest against the decline of epistolary correspondence, which iz or wuz onct one of the amenities/

admit it is a luxury when one uses eyetalyan postal stamps on blooey dollar.

BUT still . . . yew can use frog stamps that cost nothing.

Am deelighted with nooz from Paris, but they aint yet got the worst frogs/

I do hope Bill's friend Tardieu'[88] will git nibbled but mebbe he'és too downy.

I think I sent you a card re/ the Bill Young.[89] The fun being that hiz muzik upsets all the gordam tex books. Printed it five years befo yr/ friend Purcell. ⟨wuz born.⟩ AND it is some nice muzik.

Blow all ye/ bloogle horns.

I trust my new text book "ABC of Reading" will chee/uh you. Fer onct something of mine has went straight from desk to printer.

AN I fink wot you have regarded as the right doctrine since 19 when-ever, will be found thaaar to yewer sazisfaxshun.

Cantos 31/41 con[t]racted for N.Y. and London (Farrar and Faber) And a monnymental tombstone (9 essays without vermiform appendix) also combined[i.e., *Make It New*]. Faber's man a measuring or castin' it orf.

I trust even the econ/ problum will soon have attained a imagery sufficiently sensuous to penetrate yr/ catholic carcass.

NO more novels possible until novelists dissociate real dilemmas from false dilemmas/ Means of distribution are KNOWN, just as effective for distributin as are modern factories for Production.
   Do you GIT that?
   No more peeople from infancy like us, allus bothered about vile lucre. It has got as far as the U.S.Senate/ AND the Central Conservate Committee in Lunnon. And a Flood of simple books like McNair Wilson's last.[90]

You can hook it up to middle ages/ when yr/ ole Mama Ecclesia still dissociated economic right and wrong.

all of this sproutin from my startin to write you about Bill Young. 3 sonatas today/ and seven more (fer 3 fiddles, bang/box and cello) on Sardy the 31.st.

Ole Whittaker seems to appreciate local efforks.

Wocher doing / anyhow ??

I think I sent you program/ The Wechmann and Reincken,[91] not so dusty either. But the Young is our trump card/ and the Bach finale pyanny concerto you know.

Have asked the Savona Cantori to come and sing Janequin. They say they are interested.

If you dont want ter come over here/ wot price staging a real concert in Toulon or CanNES?

   and so forth

                                                                            E

F 39. TCS.

                                                            [London] 6.4.34

   We are here for some days or weeks. Walked through Church Walk yesterday. I hear you are coming here. If that's true look us up. The bells of St Mary Abbotts ring as loudly as ever.
                                                            Yrs. FMF.

Contacts
1935-1939

RAPALLO, PARIS, NEW YORK, OLIVET

From the mid-thirties till the outbreak of the war, Pound was hectically occupied with matters that he regarded as desperately urgent: monetary reforms and renewed attention to the American constitution and the great American founders and statesmen—Jefferson, John Adams, Martin Van Buren. He lent his support to the New Italy, to Mussolini, to those aspects of Fascism that seemed useful to him. He was a man with a mission: to help save Europe and his own country by making their leaders see which way they ought to go. He wrote to senators, congressmen, and other important people. Twice he addressed President Roosevelt; he was convinced that Roosevelt would steer the United States into the next war, if it came. Believing himself to be well informed about the matters he engaged himself in, he did not doubt that he was in the right. As Noel Stock suggests, many of Pound's "errors" were unquestionably due to "simple ignorance; the ignorance of a man now imprisoned inside his own dreams of a better world."[1] Certainly his missionary zeal, coupled with ignorance and arrogance, led to disastrous errors of heart and mind. He was not consistent in his sympathies for Fascism and the Axis powers. He was faced with the dilemma of distinguishing the personal-individual from the theoretical-general in his attacks on "usury" and on what he regarded as the negative aspects of Christianity. Speaking his mind in his letters, he reveals his hatred and disgust even in friendly messages to an old companion like Ford. Pound the educator placed at the disposal of whoever wished to educate himself textbooks and other material; in these years he brought out *Polite Essays, Guide to Kulchur,* and several other books and pamphlets.

He was not always pleased with his old friends: both Joyce and Hemingway did wrong, he thought, in disregarding economic issues in their work. Joyce, who saw him in 1934 during one of his visits to Paris, believed he was mad and asked Hemingway to join him for dinner with Pound. Hemingway characterized Pound's conversation during the meal as very erratic.[2]

In spite of his obsessive preoccupation with economics and politics Pound also found time for purely literary pursuits. In 1937 he published another group of cantos, *The Fifth Decad of Cantos,* which express the same concerns as his journalism of the period; the "Usura" canto had appeared the year before. His interest in music did not abate. Largely thanks to his efforts, a Vivaldi revival was brought about.

Ford's concerns with economic matters were of a much more personal and immediate kind. He was desperately short of money and looked to America as the place where his "future" was. Despite its machine-culture and disregard of good food and decent living, America—or rather, Americans—appealed to him. He spent the winter of 1934–35 in New York; at Christmas he and Janice were Theodore Dreiser's guests at Mount Kisco. In March they went south to visit the Tates, and in their company Ford attended a Writers' Conference in Baton Rouge. He was invited to speak at the conference, and he was listened to, although no doubt with difficulty: a heart condition and other handicaps prevented a clear and audible delivery.

The visit to the South entered into his on-going literary project: to present a personal, nonacademic history of his beloved Provence and its culture. This was to be no less than his "message to the world."[3] *Provence,* the first installment of a projected trilogy, came out in March 1935; he was collecting material for the next volume, *Great Trade Route.* (There was no third volume.) It was his ambition to show that the culture of his preference, the humane, pastoral, joyous kind, was to be found in seemingly disparate parts of the world. This venture called for extensive traveling, which was rewarding but tiring for a man of Ford's failing health.

There are no Pound-Ford letters extant from 1935. Although Ford was establishing closer ties with other Americans and was even contemplating living in the United States for part of the year, he had not forgotten his friend in Rapallo. He made, or thought he had made, arrangements with Paul Palmer, editor of the *American Mercury,* to include essays on Pound and Dreiser among a series of "Portraits" he was writing for this magazine. The editor did not really want an essay on Pound; he claimed that Pound—as well as Dreiser—had insulted him. When we next find Ford writing to Pound in September 1936, we hear echoes of this conflict.

F 40. TL. 2 11.

> TRY TO MEMORISE THE FACT WILL YOU
> THAT, AS I HAVE ALREADY TOLD YOU
> C/O GUARANTY TRUST 4 PLACE DE LA
> CONCORDE PARIS FRANCE WILL ALWAYS
> FIND US WHILST NO OTHER ADDRESS IS
> C   E   R   T   A   I   N

VILLA PAUL, CHEMIN DE LA CALADE   T O U L O N VAR
6 Sept. '36

Dear Ezra,
On the occasion of your want of generosity ref; Béhaine I swore on
the bones of St Gengulphus, some of which are handy in the Cathedral
here, that I would never write to you again. I herewith break my vow. I
cabled you because one of my intrigues to get you a settled job in U.S.A.
appeared to be maturing – said Palmer having undertaken to print any
one I told him to, and I thought I had better go to Rapallo and censor
anything you wrote him . . . But, as you expect when I have got so far, I
desisted when I got a letter from Palmer a cable saying that he would
rather die than print anything that you wrote or even to print your name in
his magazine. He said you had insulted him in a manner no human being
could be expected to stand and, as he is a very mild and forgiving person,
I guess you <u>must</u> have done something to him. I daresay I could have
overpersuaded <u>him</u> – and indeed I very nearly did – because in matters
literary he will <u>do</u> pretty well what I tell him; though I don't do it any
more because I am tired of being kicked in the face by people I get printed.
But then the Capitalist behind the Machine sailed in and swore that <u>he</u>
would rather die than let a word of yours appear in his periodical. And he
wouldn't quit.
   As for Palmer, he has the merit of thinking me the greatest writer that
ever put pen to paper and he gives me as much space as I want or if he
cuts me does it with reverence and skill . . . So you can make what you like
of his maternity. The only fly in the jam is that his proprietor does not give
him enough to let him pay too well; nevertheless we have lived for the
last year on him, but it's unfortunately now coming to an end owing to
alterations in the format and staff of the paper. For the rest we have been
in your country, my country, Portugal, Spain, Monte Carlo, Geneva and
have in consequence enlarged our minds and I have written a book that is
practically one long philippic against your ancestral city and the Keystone
State in general . . . Nothing you ever wrote was quite so wounding – because I know how to do it and as a rule something about my subject . . . I
got hold of some publicity for Penna that pointed out that she was the
only State in the World who had never felt the Crisis; that she led the
Universe in the production of rubber pants and linoleum that outbeauted
the famous rugs of Khorassan; and led the U.S.A. in the production of
underpants in shoddy, whilst, round her coal dumps can be seen standing
more men thrown out of work by improved machinery than anywhere in
the created universe.
   So, having renié'd mes dieux by writing on public affairs I feel myself
sufficiently a pariah to re-open a correspondence with You.
   Not that I have anything in particular to say. My collected poems are

being published in September by the Oxford University Press. I wish they
had been selected ones because there's an awful lot of bilge among them.
But they insisted on all or none . . . and then when they read them were so
appalled that they tried to get out of publishing them at all. They don't
like you to mention the Deity except in devotional verse and, when you
insist, remind you tearfully that they were the original publishers of Roger
Bacon's treatise on gunpowder and Dr Watts's Little Hymns.[4] So I insisted on their carrying out the contract – not that I particularly yen to
mention the Deity but that I believe that publishers should be as sadisti-
cally punished as possible . . . and they were and continue to be pained . . .
what between pain at letting the letters G O D come out of their formes
and the thought of the dishonour that would attach to them if it appeared
in litigation that they had refused to carry out a contract. So after a delay
of a year they really appear to be going to bring them out. Their youngest
and newest director,[5] it appears, is my second greatest admirer in the
world and foisted me on them before their eyes were clear of sleep . . . . But
it's been a wearisome transaction.

I have also arranged for my collected edition, the TIETJENS books in
one volume and all my work past and to come with Allen and Unwin of
London.[6] That is satisfactory in a way; there is very little money in it and
what there is goes entirely to Stella – so it does not help us much. Indeed
things are pretty low here and likely to remain so. We are having to give
up this place and go and live in one room in Paris. It's impossible to make
a living outside New York, one's agents are always so incompetent and
we'd both die if we had to live in U.S.A. for good.

I don't suppose you're any better circumstanced. No one is that one
knows. We shall beat the buggers yet – but not soon . . . . Oh, looking
through this – when I said "censor what you wrote Palmer" I meant see
that you wrote Esq after his name on envelopes and the like – not interfere
with your style and content . . . Indeed I'd asked him to subsidise you as
poet, not prosateur; but I was afraid your epistolary-lapidary manner in an
initial letter might make him believe that you were not a poet.

Janice sends her respects: she's engaged in painting a series of all the
cavalry battles of the Civil War – yours – in a neo-pointilliste manner.
She'd switch over to the Spanish war, I think, only they do not appear to
have any cavalry. We hear the guns from Barcelona here on a still day
with the wind in the right direction; the rest of the air is filled with practice
for the resisting of your crowd when you come to annex the Riviera
française . . . 'Cela vous donne une fière idée,' as Maubougon used to say,
bowing., 'de l'homme!'

And so Yechi dachi[7]. . . I must write to the Oxford people again.

Yours[8]

P 44. TLS. 2 11.

310 San Gregorio Venezia
11 Sett anno XIV [1936]

My dear ole Freiherr von Grumpus ZU und VON Bieberstein
I rejoice unduly that you are to receive the dubious honour of bein printed by the vendors of Palgrave-Cohen's "GOLDEN bidet"[9]
at any rate a feat for any madOX to be printed by the asses of Oxon.

And Faber just climbing onto bandwagon by saying they are about to reprint my statement on subject (dated 1913) in "Polecat Essays". but I'll believe it when I see proofs, galley etc.

As fer Noo YUKK, place seems to be teeming with small animals whom I have never heard of, all claiming inestimable honour of having been insulted. Only insult is that which we daily spread to three millyum umpty hundred thousand and ump chinamen and inhabitants of Irtsitk, namely being unaware of their individual sorrows, cognomens stati civili ed incivili etc. waaaaal.

And as fer yr/ frawg. as you and he never sublitted any opusculi for eye-over how the hell was one to know it wasn't another Gladys Bum Sterns, or Walpol or woofle, or Mrs A Mary F. etc. or a Tate or something.[10]

waaaal, I am glad to hear you are goin strong and esp. the KOlected nuvvels. cause I was trying to catch you a peruser down in Siena, but cd. n't say where or how the woiks wuz to had.

Trouble with Punsylvany is with the world. Blokes with a few brains too god damn stubborn to read Gesell, Doug[las]. Por[11] and yr/ deevoted the undersigned. Distribution is effected by little pieces of paper. waal we got a bank act here, and purr-chasing powYer bein' pumped into the workin man. Four millyum more got a rise this week. etc. And the jolly ole jolly roman empire. wot means civilization. superceding a pink bank pimp like Eden. and that suet headed swine Baldwin, who is afraid of ideas. For shit, stewed and unadulterated the heads of the brit. govt. is the 100% at this momeng.

Whereas mr Badoglio has just said the bright word about money.

Waaal I have just knocked off three more Cantos on a patch of hizzery wot the woild needz to be told and have a fourth nearly set up. and this time it is Siena. and to hell wiff the saboteurs, expecially the bastids in licherary commerce.

Thanks, nacherly fer yr. Quixotics with the Palmerworm. what is it? and when did I tread on its ego. ???
Is it Matilda's ex husband?

Thank the lady for greetins. I dont unnerstand about cavalry. the "keep it from degeneratin into a vulhgah brawl" point of view ?? or wottoh?

Ca vous donne une fière idée du Blum? I heard the blighter drool last time I wuzzin Paris. But wotter baht Bastid, Chaux and the Milhaud idee?[12] anything ever PRINTED in that bankrotted frog hole? frogs on the bank !!
    waaal I heer a nice noo 4 tet by mr Buttok or Bartok this week. with a bunch of 4 magyrs wot can tickle the catgut. wot elsz? Mr Buttok hiz 5 th.
    enuff & more than you want fer one morning.

ever EZ

Scribbling a few remarks on a clipping (from a French magazine?) Ford reminded Pound of a disagreement they had had back in 1922 à propos of the animal imagery in what was then Canto VIII. The clipping featured two photos, one representing a doe, the other a lynx. Lynxes, so the photo proved, do *not* have long, bushy tails, no more than does do. This was in reply to Pound's friendly reminder of services rendered by the essay on the Prose Tradition. On the front of a set of proofs of *Polite Essays,* in which the piece on Mr. Hueffer was reprinted, Pound had signaled out to Ford certain important pages, among them page 50 where we read: "The revolution of the word began so far as it affected the men who were of my age in London in 1908, with the LONE whimper of Ford Madox Hueffer."

Pound's Christmas greetings this year reached Ford and Janice—via Paris—at their (very modest) Fifth Avenue address. As usual he offered advice on ways to get published.

F 41. ALS (clipping). 1 1.

[Paris] 6.11.36

Thanks for proofs of P.E. Pray find on rev. evidence of fact that I don't forget . . . either old, unhappy things or anything else!
I observe you are being printed by Camb[ridge]. U.P. Oxford for mine!
My Colld. P's have just appeared chez eux in N.Y. — for wh. place we leave immediately, thus not having time to say more than that I'm in "substantial agreement" with most of yr dicta — except for "whimper"! . . . and monosyllables.[13] Did you ever realise that monosyllables = 9% in Latin: 36% in Fr.: 67% in Eng. Hence both Imagisme & Prose impossible in last language! Because mono's retard thought.
Jechi Dachy — wh. means: may the Devil be on yr. side.

F.M.F.

4 Place de la Concorde will <u>always</u> find me.

See within[14]

[On reverse of clipping, with guidelines to two photos representing, resp., a doe and a lynx:]

Observe long, bushy tail!

F.M.F.

one ditto to match

P 45. TLS. 1 1.

Merry XXXmas   [Rapallo, December] 1936

Me deah Fordie
these Globe blokes seem vurry nice peepul.[15] ⟨apply etc/⟩[16] At any
rate they have pd/ me fer three articles and I have only sent 'em two.

They wd. print real stuff like yr/ "Women and Men" for example that the
higher paying mags/ wd. refuse.
One don't have to stand on head and be funny (as per Esquire)

I shd/ be glad if you can come in on it/ They have practical non literary
aim/ and possibly will raise rate before long. unless they bust.
they call emselves TRAVEL/ romance, adventure woild interest (thazz
me, the last one)

They'd ask you but I only got yr/ Paris address, so this is quicker route.

yrs EZ
EP

use my name s.v.p

F 42. ALS. 1 1.

[New York, late December 1936 or early January 1937]
Happy '37 — & eke 8, 9, '40, '41 et in saeculo saeculorum!

F.M.F.

Will get in touch with that mag. – Thanks!

Both Pound and Ford, each in his corner, were feeling increasingly isolated. It seemed to Ford, so he wrote to Allen Tate, that the Tates were
the only real friends left, that is, "people one can talk to without having
to explain every second word."[17] Some friends found it difficult to communicate with him. Even Caroline Gordon Tate thought she could not

quite reach him. She wrote to Stella Bowen after his death: "These last few years have been very hard for [Ford]. There was only his work—he had got to the point where it was impossible to communicate with him. He and Janice seemed to inhabit a closed world, a sphere which rolled here and there, from France to New York and back again, but never changed inside."[18]

The Tates brought about a contact which was to be very important for Ford during his last few years. In 1936 they had attended a writers' conference at Olivet College in Michigan. The dedicated president of the college, Joseph Brewer, wanted to engage Ford as speaker at the next conference and was even making plans to create a chair of comparative literature for him. The appointment for the academic year 1937–38 was settled during the Christmas holidays of 1936. Ford was to be writer and critic in residence. He was to start by taking part in the writers' conference in the summer of 1937. The happy plans came to include some summer months spent in the company of the Tates, mostly at their house Benfolly in Tennessee.

Robert Lowell, the last in the distinguished series of prominent American writers who befriended Ford and received homage or tutelage from him, had met him in Boston in March the same year. While there were people who in those days found Ford "a rather messy old thing,"[19] Lowell's immediate admiration and appreciation testify to the attraction that Ford still held for such as shared his deep commitment to literature and his basic views of what made life worth living. Uninvited and unheeding of the Tates' polite refusal of still another house guest, young Lowell came down and pitched his tent in their garden for what turned out to be a three-month stay. He has told the story of this summer with an attractively ironical perspective of himself and his hosts and fellow guests.[20]

Just as young Pound had been spending the Christmas of 1913 in an English country cottage in the company of two other "Kreators," so apprentice Lowell was now in the midst of intense literary and artistic creativity. Ford was dictating to Janice's sister-in-law and to Lowell chapter after chapter of his literary history, *The March of Literature,* which was to be the last work he completed.

At the end of May it became known that John Crowe Ransom, close friend and associate of the Tates, was leaving his professorship at Vanderbilt University as a result of the university's failure to recognize his significance as poet and teacher. A committee of writers established itself to protest in the form of a dinner and a statement against Vanderbilt's neglect. Ford helped by sending out a letter requesting support for the statement, which was to be read at the dinner.

Ford sent this letter (typed by a secretary) to Pound, adding on the reverse a personal handwritten message. Pound answered the letter on the very day it reached him. (The envelope of Ford's letter bears three post-marks, the last one being "Rapallo 8.6.37.") Pound sent one private reply and one intended for the eyes of the committee. They are characteristically angry, honest, and sincere.

F 43. TLS (aman.) and AL. 1 1. Envelope.

> Address cable   FORD
> Route 6, Clarksville, Tennessee, U.S.A.
> May 30, 1937

Dear Ezra,

I am writing on behalf of a committee of writers which has constituted itself to celebrate the twenty-fifth anniversary of John Crowe Ransom's Professoriat at Vanderbilt, this coinciding with his departure from that University.

I do not need to describe his achievements as a poet and a critic, as I am sure they are known to you. Mr. Ransom is leaving Vanderbilt to go as a special professor of Poetry to a smaller college where he will have leisure for his own work. As this means a relative cessation of his peda-gogic labours, it seems to be an appropriate time to congratulate him on his work of that sort in the past.

His teaching has had remarkable effects on the culture of this country with reverberations even across the Atlantic.

We are preparing to hold a dinner in his honour on the tenth of June. The following message will be read at that dinner:

> On this twenty-fifth anniversary of his holding a chair of English literature at the University of Vanderbilt, Nashville, Tennessee, we, the undersigned, offer our congratulations to John Crowe Ransom for his distinguished services to our Art.

If you could see your way to adding your signature to the above message, would you be good enough to authorize us, by cable collect, to attach your name to it? If you are unable to send telegrams collect, we shall be pleased to reimburse you.

If you happen to know of anyone who would care to add their names to yours for this purpose, the addition of that name to the telegram will be sufficient.

The state of Poetry in the world at the present moment is so precarious that anything that can give additional strength and confidence to a dis-tinguished teacher of the art, who is also one of its best known prac-titioners, cannot but be of benefit to Literature as a whole and every-

where. I feel, therefore, the less hesitation in asking you to take this
trouble:

Yours very sincerely, F.M.F.

[Autogr. personal message:]

Please do what is asked for within. Ransom's departure has been forced
by a very base University intrigue & he shd. be supported.

I saw yr. letter to Poetry at Chicago the other day... or rather Zabell[21]
read it just before I lectured there. !!!!!!!

Wd. you accept The Eliot Norton lectureship if offered. I sounded a
number of people at Harvard last week & am fairly certain it cd. be
worked . . . . Answer this.

P 46. TLS. 1 1. Enclosure.

[Rapallo] 8 June [1937]

Dear Ford/
        PRIVATE.
    I take it Zabel is sheer SHIT and will do nothing to maintain decent
critical standards.

I take it that Haaaavud is still softer shit and that the YuppyYup Snortin'
lectureships will NOT be offered me.

I have told whats his name[22] that I wd/ come over to lecture IF it can be
arranged in season that wont merely kill me off and thereby satisfy the
shittery generally.

Of course I wd. lecture Eliot Norton IF it pays the transport and don't
occur in rheumatic and bronchitic season.

/The enc/ is as good as I can do for Ransom who has, sfar as I know
always opposed better stuff than his own/
    at least that gang of southern morons has allus been in opposition to
the undersigned SO FAR AS I KNOW / and you can bet yr/ shirt none
of 'em wd. give a stale railway buffet sandwich for support to ole Ez.
    which apart from bein personal, is also a POSITION, a artistic or
whatever, intellexshul POsition. and has to be took into account.

yrs E.P.

P 47. TLS. 3 11. Enclosed with *P 46.*

[Rapallo] 8 June [1937]

Dear Ford

I am perfectly ready to join you and the Ransom committee in congratu-
lating Ransom on whatever he has been able to do in difficult circumstances, by not affronting the most foul of those circumstances, such as the
unprotested existence of Nic Butler at the head of the nation's official
academy.[23]

I know some of Ransom's work, but have had no indication whatever
that he has pursued other than a narrow and local policy in ignorance,
neglect or even in open opposition to any endeavour to induce the U.S.
authors, as such, to accept or even face general standards of criticism or
to lift their work up to a level where it can meet the work of Europeans
and Asiatics on even terms, that is without inflated admiration on the
grounds that some poor simp of an American has written a poem that will
stand comparison with other American poems.

I know of no endeavour on Ransom's part to lift the general level of
American awareness to that of the better nuclei in Europe.

I do believe him to be an honest workman in a land teeming with
blithering fake and tolerators of such utter filth as the American university
system, the American publishing system, the American touts for Utilities,
the Atlantic Monthly, and the degraded apes who support this slop.

I know of no case wherein Ransom and his clique have openly faced
the issues considered vital by the better authors outside America.

I disagree with yr/ paragraph on the state of poetry. But I do not expect
a sectional group in America to take cognizance of good poetry outside
their own geographic area. As for example the activities of Mr Kitasono's
group in Tokio.[24]

If the committee has sufficient virility to read these pages, I am perfectly
willing to sign a statement to the effect that Ransom is a distinguished
operator, and that his intentions have been laudable "to a degree", that is
sincere and upright as far as they go.

I don't honestly know of anyone in Europe who knows enough about
Ransom to sign the congratulations intelligently.

I know of no man in America more qualified than Ransom to be a
professor of poetry, though I cd/ name three outside University circles
who understand it at least as well.

If his friends want mere soft soap and flattery, this wont please 'em. If
they are capable of grasping the fact that I mean what I say, namely AS
MUCH as I say, instead of less, they or perhaps he will take this note as a
respectable support of their message to him.

ever Ezra Pound

When Ford wrote next, he had settled in at Olivet College for the fall term. Now he reopened the issue of bringing Pound to America, for lectures or, better still, to occupy some chair established for imaginative writers. In Chicago? or Boston? We don't have Pound's immediate reply to these suggestions, if there was one. He had sent his most recent decad of cantos, inscribed "To Good ole Fordie still pluggin' at windmills. E. P. 1 Lug XV."[25] Ford as usual insisted on a personal meeting to discuss measures for the improvement of education in the United States. Spending the winter months in Paris he was prepared at least to meet Pound halfway. Ford was, however, both unwell—after another heart attack—and in straitened financial circumstances.

F 44. TLS. 2 11.

[Olivet, Mich.] 23.8.37

Dear Ezra,

We have now gotten something like a permanent address in this country. At any rate they have created for me here a Chair of Comparative Literature which I purpose occupying for some time to come – though we shall run away from the climate at mid-winter till Spring . . . to Paris or Toulon.

I never got the long and serious letter you said you had addressed me – mainly I suppose because we have been incessantly on the move all over the South And Middle West and West as far as Colorado . . . . God, what a State! . . There are, scattered about this Continent, now, a number of smallish and one or two State, Universities that are turning their attentions to fostering creative Lit. rather than pedagogy and I have been visiting several of them and cheering on the good work [.] Even Harvard contemplates something of the sort, though naturally they will spoil the idea before they get through . . . . As it at present stands the plan is to create a number of chairs for imaginative writers who won't do much lecturing but sit about and be Influences: they are also giving scholarships for imaginative writers – though how long states like Illinois and Colorado and Louisiana – not to mention Massachusetts – are going to continue footing the bills no one can be really certain . . . . . probably for three or four years unless the Movement could make itself formidable in some unknown way.

The point is: Would you care to occupy some such chair – in Chicago, say, or Boston, to mention only cities where I and people of good will have a certain pull? . . Chicago particularly might be made attractive if you could bring yourself to view it as such. It is at least a big city with all sorts of people – some of them quite supportable.

None of them pay much more than just a living wage for the frugally inclined . . . But the financial inducements would not anywhere be a great attraction. As far as we are concerned we can just live here on the payment and have plenty of time to do one's own work . . . . But I don't want to try to make the idea too attractive. You would find here troops of immensely admiring students and professors too . . . but you'd find also a great number of not very attractive people who might be able to bother you a[d]ministratively.

Think it over, will you and if you are at all inclined towards such an idea I will go more fully into the matter. This is quite an old college, dating from the early 1800's and the Faculty are all quite sympathetic and agreeable – but it is buried in the heart of the country about a hundred miles from Detroit and rather farther from Chicago, so it might not suit your urbanities.

I am writing a History of Literature – nothing less. If you can get hold of it read my attack on publishers in the Sept Forum.²⁶

For ever in haste F.M.F.

P 48. TLS. 1 1.

[Rapallo] 1 Nov [1937]

Dear Ford

I sent you my Fifth decad (Cantos) to your god damn Paris bank/ and after they have forwarded it to 14 addresses it has come back.

I am trying the present route, as yr/ letter from Choctaw Camp aint in me files.

The bloody bother of posting packets is ENUFF, without having to repeat it. but seeinz itz yew I will remail the book if you want it and if you HAVE an address.

As to nuvvles/ lemme recomend ole Wyndham[Lewis]'s "Revenge for Love" and E.C. Large's "Sugar from [i.e., in] the Air".

both ought to be bukk of monf club meat.

But I pose the shitten shepherds will have bugrocratic reasons against it/ however fer somfink to rread.

Waaal bless yuh an th winter comin on, and the redskins ragin round the block house!

yrz EZ

EP–

F 45. TLS. 1 1.

[Olivet, Mich.] Nov. 13, 1937

Dear Ezra,

I am sorry about the Odyssey of your cantos and sorrier still not to get them. We move about such a lot. And after all it is hardly my fault or even the bank's if you mislay the address I give you.

As things are at present we expect to leave these climes by the Lafayette on the 4th December and to be in Paris for some little time, returning here on the first of April.

As I'm writing a history of the world's literature from Confucius to Gertrude, not to mention Joyce and as I'm involved in certain measures for changing the incidence of cultural education in this realm I sort of feel that we ought to get together and discuss these high matters. The attempts to change the ⟨said⟩ educational incidence here are much more widespread than you have any idea though I don't [have time][27] to write about them.

I am getting rather stiff in the joints and the worse from traveling. But we shall probably be in Toulon early in the new year. Could you possibly come along there for a day or two? Or, if you could find us some really cheap lodgings and if you can protect us from all possible assaults of Kerensky[28] we might come and spend a week or so at Rapallo. I think this is the point at which you ought seriously to consider taking a hand in things. Don't answer this until you hear that we have arrived in Paris and then answer to 31 Rue de Seine 6. Of course if you happen to be in Paris it would be all the better. But whether you come to Toulon or we to Rapallo is simply a matter of which of us is the harder up.

Our love to Dorothy.

Yours, F.M.F.

P.S. I enclose a copy of a lecture delivered by Janice at various cultural centers in this place.

F 46. TLS. 1 1.

31 rue de Seine   P a r i s   VI   1.i.38

Dear Ezra above the above festal date our quite permanent if troglodytic address.[29] But it is not a good place to which to address mail when we are away because the people are hopelessly negligent about forwarding letters. When we are away the Guara[n]thy Trust (4 Place de la Concorde) is better.

We shall probably however be here for some time now – that rather depending on you. I think we ought really seriously to make an attempt to meet. This Olivet experiment is extremely meritorious – I having indeed a chief hand in it – and in other ways the moment is crucial, if only because I shan't last for ever and the arrow that flies nocturnally has had two or three shots at me lately. The real, immediate point is: Which mountain is to go to the other – and that being mainly financial. We can't quite af-ford to come to Rapallo but must if there were no other way. Or could you come here and stay as extendedly as you like with us? The point about that is that you would probably be extremely uncomfortable. Both Janice and I dislike modern comforts and live here like the poorer sort of peasants in old and mouldering rooms without water laid on or <u>central Heizung</u>? Or: Could we meet half way – say at Marseilles and stop a night or so at an hotel modeste.

Anyhow, sketch your ideas or preferences by return and we will try to work our necessities in somehow. We have of course tangles of dates. I don't want to leave here because of the libraries. Janice who sold a good many things at Detroit wants to have an exhibition here – towards March – so we should somehow have to fit that in. But we'll do our best if you will define your position. So do so.

In the meanwhile Prosit acht und dreitsig.

Yours F.M.F.

P 49. TLS. 2 11.

[Rapallo, ? 7 January] [1938]

biff in a eye plus ONE or the Seventh/[30]

My deah ole Freiherr von Bluggerwitzkoff, late baron of the Sunk Ports etc/[31]

I on the contrary not only loathe all forms of discomfort, but consider it a waste of time and jeopard of my delicate health to purr/form by manual labour offices wich can be did as well and more expeditiously by a stuvv or a ornry piece of plumbing.

Also as per ENC// I certainly can NOT leave Rapallo fer some time as PURcell / whereof am I the most active begetter/ ⟨vide ENC.⟩[32]

You on the udder hand might rake in a tidy tip by presenting yr/ opinyms of the FIRST (in a century) purrformance of the 12 ⟨Purc. sonats⟩ to Yawpers[i.e., Harper's], Scrubbers [i.e., Scribner's] or some other cesspull.

I have just reSponded to a western edtr/ by a narticle entituld "Reorganize yr/ DEAD universities" (una FUSSItes).[33]

I can go on beating the drum on THAT line/ with ref/ to the HNBL Freiherr WHEN his pograum is a li'l more CLEAR//

For the histery ov letters and BETTERS, he shd/ nacherly follow my ABC of the subject/ plus my later D/E/F/ on the orient[34] and further correlations/

Re/ the NUVVL/ I wd/ not venture to add one YOTT or one quota to the knowledge already possessed by the Hnbl/ Freiherr, which same HAZ allus been my fount and origin, and in fackk nursemaid to the subjekk/ and I aint never changed it.

WOT else?

I reship the Fifth Decad/ with evidence of its let me voyage. (sep/ cov/ racc/[35]) to day.

AS to LIE% berries, there are in various places/ but I reCOGnize the use of the Bib/ Nat of Paris, bad as its ketterlogue iz
⟨not of cauce that you are likely to read anything in it.⟩
and so forth/

Glucklichen (or S as the case may be) LAUF.

                                                                    ever Ez P.

Having received the go-ahead from President Brewer to negotiate with Pound, Ford began an all-out campaign to get him to Olivet College for a permanent or temporary engagement.[36] A genuine concern for educational standards and a more selfish wish to secure the company of a lively and amusing fellow-fighter combined to make his efforts persistent and energetic. He resorted to friendly "blackmail" in impressing on Pound how much he, Ford, had done for him. Pound was more than willing to keep up his booming of every Ford venture, but insistence on a certain minimum of physical comforts and a general distrust of the American academic world were serious obstacles to any plans for a visit to the United States. Involvement with the Rapallo concerts prevented a personal reunion with Ford. Perhaps he was also less anxious to meet Ford these days? Their main concerns had diverged in the mid-1930s. Ford, who was decidedly against all dictatorships, who was *for* Zionism, and who protested against anti-Semitism, could have no sympathy for Pound's admiration of Mussolini and the Fascist ideologies. He had unequivocally taken his stand *for* the legal government of Spain and had expressed these views in reply to a questionnaire sent to a number of writers, asking: *"Are you for, or against, the legal Government and the People of Republican Spain? Are you for, or against, Franco and Fascism?"* Pound's answer, which was couched in abusive language, evaded the issue and was placed among those who were "Neutral?"[37] Ford had offered to write articles on the fate of German Jewish refugees, and he informed his agent that he did not wish to be published by a Nazi publisher. He expressed readiness to sign a manifesto against Nazism.[38]

F 47. TLS. 2 11.

                                        31 rue de seine [Paris] vi 17.2.37 [i.e., 38][39]

Dear Bertran de Struwwelpeter y Bergerac,
    I was taken seriously ill with heart trouble shortly after getting your last and am not much better now, but just able to write.
    This is the point on which I wish you would focus your opinion. Both

Janice and I spend a large portion of our very occupied days – from time
to time – in trying to get you permanent writing jobs with editors – and
are always put off with the information that you have long since tried to
blackmail all the editors in question and that they'll be damned to Hell
etc. . . . . . Under my contract with one of them I wrote an article booming
the Cantos: he refused to print it: I have lost my contract which I could
ill afford to! . . . having to take myself to the FORUM.

A point however has arrived at which through me perfectly firm admirers of yours are ready to offer you a permanent contract – to fill a job
I'm filling myself and if it's good enough for me it's damn good enough
for you, concealed son of the authoress of John Halifax Gentleman[40]
though you be. It means of course going to America: but that would give
you an opportunity of getting rid of the cobwebs from your blackmailing
instruments.

In short, you are invited to stroll for eight months of a year – or several
years – about the philosophers' groves of Olivet. I personally give a couple
of lectures a week to classes because I like lecturing. You would not have
to if you did not want to. You would be conferring obligation if you talked
to any youth or youths you thought intelligent. There the duties would –
or could – stop. The real point is that you would have complete leisure to
write whilst earning a living wage. They pay me slightly less than a living
wage but would pay you more and with your greater skill in expenditure
and ability to eat bleeding beef you would of yourself it draw very well.
(French idiom: too tired to think of English for same). They also pay
boat fares from Europe and back.

The point about Olivet is that here is a college of old establishment that
under its new management has for profes[s]ors exclusively practitioners of
the arts. Li[t]erature is looked after by me; music by a pretty sensible
orchestra conductor who has several composers writing music for his
orchestra to work out. (You would have his orchestra at your disposal.
There is also a pretty good library and they get me all the books I want)
Painting by a rather indifferent painter – though for all I know you might
think him pretty good . . . and so on. The point is that the aim of these
people is not to turn out youthful genius but to get into the heads of the
general public what the arts are about. The music students for instance try
out any passages that the composers want to experiment with – one of
them is pretty good – and in that way the pupils get some idea of forms,
orchestration and so on. You may of course jeer at this or try some other
form of blackmail but observe that that would be rather more unprofitable
than even your normal unprofitalia because you are offered a complete
finger in the pie, so that if you don't accept the offer . . . I shan't finish the
sentence because I am tired of finishing sentences. But if you did choose
to go to Olivet you would have a working, model educational machine to

play with . . . A man said to me the other day that he did not care for your CANTOS because of their umer [i.e., humor] – or rather that he detested the umer of your CANTOS so much that he never opened them for fear of coming on some of it. "But", he added, "no-one can deny that Ezra is the greatest Educator in the world." You will I suppose refuse the offer and throw bâtons in its roues when occasion serves. That would be a pity because it is difficult to get good teachers for the place and your example would probably bring them . . . and the enterprise is a good thing because the eccentric Principal, Brewer, who once humorously sub-edited – or rather literary-edited the SPECTATOR for three weeks and then was summarily retired because my influence on him was too great and who is also one of the best clog-dancers in the world, is quite impressionable and youngish and ready to learn.

Of course I know that one cannot expect a man of your age to change his habits or renier his material gods. But you have arrived at an age when few men save themselves unless they do change their habits and travel a little.

There are two other points about Olivet. It ought to continue because it is perfectly ready to become a refuge for good writers who are down on their end-bones, which in itself is valuable. AND then, you have no idea how extraordinarily many prostrate admirers you have in the U.S. And if you add the people who are avidly curious about you, you would arrive at a pretty good figure . . . . It is one of my normal worries thinking about your material prospects and I can assure you of this that if you did go to the U.S. you could, if you would lecture or radio or something, make enough in a few months without going out of the Detroit district to keep you for the rest of your life in comfort.

Still I know all this is beating the wind. The main point is that I should like to see you. I don't take myself to be an educational panjandrum and would like to talk the subject over with you. We have now added to the palatialness of this apartment, kitchens, baths, eau, gaz, électricité, open wood fires and most of the things demanded by the Victorians. So you could safely come here and we'd welcome you after March 4th when Janice's exhibition opens. Or, would it suit you to meet us at Bandol which is a regular Mediterranean Coney Island, complete with plages, gramophones. I could get as far as there and there is there a man, a painter, whom Janice wants to see . . . equally after March 4th, but before the 23d when our boat sails. I am not quite certain that we can do even this – but if you can fall in with it we will try. Bandol is the next station but two or three before Marseilles.

F.M.F.

P 50. TCS.

[Rapallo, 21 February 1938]

Dear Fordie

Vurry sorry you have been ill. Does Olivet USE my text books? Will
the clog-dancer [i.e., Joseph Brewer] communicate with me direct and
ANSWER a few civil questions? Will he GET a printing press/ LINO or
monotype/ I.E. practical and not fancy hand arty machine for the
DISTRIBUTION of knowledge and ideas?

No use discussing details viva voce unless or until fundamentals can be
got on paper.

you git well.   yrz deevotedly EZ

21 Feb

and dont think I dont appreciate yr/ noble efforks on my behalve. am
perfectly willing to ASSIST Olivet, but not to lay down life for a pig in a
poke./

F 48. TLS. 1 1.

31 rue de seine   p a r i s vi   9.3.38

Dear God, Father Divine . . . . .

I know that Your awful face must be veiled to the lesser mackerel
nuzzling between Your toes in the ooze. Indeed this lesser mackerel knows
also how it turns Your divine stomach to have to communicate with lesser
ones at all. But in this case it would be a convenience if Your Divinity
would communicate direct to this 1.m. the nature of Its exactions. Should
Your Godhead write to the tops of Olivet – and sure Its communication
should only be with tops – the message would only be forwarded to this
lesser mackerel to decide on – except on the financial requisitions which
will have to be referred to the Trustees. But for all other purposes this
1.m. here may be regarded as tops too and thus time will be saved and
confusion avoided. And your petitioner shall ever pray . . . . . .

F.M.F.

P 51. TCS.

[Rapallo, 11 March 1938]

very well then/ let me put my question in the form: Will YOU answer
my questions about the beanery?

You haven't answered those in my preceding letter or on preceding card?
if Olivet refers enquiries to YOU that means more circumlocution? or
what does it mean?

Have you a catalog of the joint? Any notes on the present curriculum?

11 Marzo

yr E.P.

DO they use my text books?

F 49. TLS. 1 1.

31 rue de seine [Paris] vi 16.3.38

Dear Ezra,

Do exercise a little imagination and try to understand the situation. I am an <u>extremely</u> sick man and your incomprehensible scrawls are a torture to me – to read and to have to answer. Get the waiter at your hotel to write your letters for you; he will at least write comprehensible dog-English. Your 1892 O Henry stuff is wearisomely incomprehensible by now.

The situation is this: I am offering to give up my job at Olivet to you because you have been making noises about Universities for a long time and it would give you a chance really to do something. I have already answered your question about a press. They have already a press at Olivet. They print a paper. They would no doubt do any necessary scholastic printing you needed. But they probably would not print Mussolini-Douglas propaganda for you. They might. But it would be up to you to persuade them. They do not, as I have already told you use your books as text books because "They" are I and I do not approve of the use of text books. At the same time I constantly recommend my classes to read your books. You understand I do not approve of making any reading compulsory. If a boy tells me he does not like Vergil I tell him to find something he does like and then read it with attention. That gives results that satisfy me. If you wanted to revert to text books you could

With regard to salary etc. Olivet pays me $125 a month, say 1500 a year. They would pay me more if I wanted it but their endowment is not very big and as I find it quite possible to live on that sum there and have plenty of time to do my own work I do not think fit to do so. In addition, last year, I made about another $1,200 by lecturing in the neighbourhood. I could have made a great deal more but I am pretty feeble these days. (They also pay my round trip fares to Europe). Ref all this: You will probably want more than that salary. You can take either one of two courses: Either write direct to Joseph Brewer, President Olivet College, Mich. and tell him how much you want or write to me and I will do my best to get it for you. All I am empowered to offer you is the $1,500 and round trip fare as above. It would be better in any case to let me know what you are asking because I shall probably have to explain to them

⟨the Trustees⟩ why you want so much. For myself I should certainly think you would be wise to ask more. You will probably be let in for extra expenses as not at first knowing your way about – and, anyhow, you should ask more on principle.

We expect to leave here today week for N.Y. going on to Olivet after I have lectured at N.Y. university, on the 5th August.[41] If you want to ask any more questions do so before we leave here. But try to understand. Disciplinary and other matters in the English section are entirely in my hands and the faculty consult me as to the other branches that interest me – i.e. Music, painting, history. There are other departments – several science branches, municipal law and other things that I am vague about because they are no affair of mine. The number of students at the moment is 305 – the capacity of the college; the number of the faculty 45. The system is tutorial, each teacher having so many students to boss for study and discipline – that not applying to me and not to apply to you unless you wanted it to. I teach what I want to – i.e. comparative literature from the beginning of time to the moment of speaking. No one interferes with me in the slightest degree. Nor would they with you. I don't know just what they would do if you tried to introduce your politics into your teaching – nothing at all probably unless you were too loudly communist in which case the local farmers would shoot you.

Please understand: I am not a confidence trickster trying to induce you into some disastrous folly. I am <u>not</u> trying to persuade you to take the job. You would probably turn that pleasant place into a disastrous sort of hell. But it is my duty to say that there the place is for you and the College authorities want you because they admire you as a poet and teacher. Nor is it part of a sinister conspiracy on my part to rob you of your claim to be the greatest discoverer of literary talent the world has ever seen. I don't care a damn: I wish to God I had never "discovered" anyone . . . . The only conspiracy I am in is to get you the Charles Eliot Norton professorship at [*crossout:* Boston] Harvard to which Olivet would be a stepping stone. The snag as to that is that the Professor ought to be an Englishman – but I have tried to persuade the Boston authorities that you are English enough.

I do not know if I have any Olivet prospectuses. If I find any I will send them on.

Please again: If you want to ask any more questions get someone to put them into comprehensible English.

F.M.F.

P 52. TLS. 1 1.

[Rapallo] 18 March [1938]

Dear Ford

THANKS for a CLEAR statement, and a few lucid answers. I am very sorry you are ill/

1. I do NOT want your job.

2. If Olivet wants me to do 1500 dollars worth of work or even less in my own way, I am ready to talk. BUT It wd/ mean ⟨their⟩ doing something DIFFERENT from what is done in other colleges.

I do NOT propose to go into any sort of YOKE, whether devised by the Prex of Olivet or by YOU.

I do NOT suspect you of plotting and am not to be confused with our dear friend mr LEWIS (of London, vorticist)

Of course ALL american colleges think they are ON the map. I won't wrangle about that.

I could PUT Olivet on some parts of the map where it isn't. I can offer QUALIFIED students something not on other collegiate menus. BUT I shd/ do it in my own way.

and without committing suicide (physically)

As to their press/ WILL they START by reprinting the necessary parts of John Adams and Jefferson?

The lousy and stinking book trade is NOT doing this. How the hell people think there can be any clear American history (and/or study of american WRITING) while Adams and Jeff are unobtainable, is a MYSTERY.

y E

F 50. TLS. 1 1.

——c/o Professor Richard Cox
130 Morningside Drive, New York City
<u>till April 5th</u>
afterwards
Olivet College, Michigan

[Paris, c. 20 March 1938]

Dear Ezra;

I take it that I may take it from your letter that you would be willing to accept $1,500 per university year from Olivet, though you do not say so implicitly. I think myself you ought to ask for more.

It is not a case of your getting me out of a job – or not any longer for I am so weak that it is unlikely that I shall be able to get through this half year there, though I am going to have a try.

Ref. printing. I doubt whether Olivet would want to go into publishing

though they might very well print lectures of yours. Shall I ask New York
University Press if they would do what you want? I am lecturing there and
shall be seeing the Press people about a project of my own. In strict
confidence I am told that they intend to ask me to take a professoriate
there on the lines of the Olivet one. I should not accept but shall suggest
that they write to you. Please write me, as above, the letter to reach me
preferably before I leave Cox's what exactly it is you want printed;
whether the N.Y.U.P. would be agreeable to you for that purpose and
whether you would accept the New York Professorship for the year after
next. I understand that N.Y.U. is seriously thinking of following the
example of Olivet and handing its literary teaching entirely over to writers.
But do not talk about this please or the project – there is of course a violent opposition – might be bitched.

As soon as I get to Olivet I will ask them to write formally to you about
their job, so you should hear about the middle of April

Yours F.M.F.

P 53. TLS. 2 11.

[Rapallo] 22 March [1938]

Dear ole Fordie

ONCE you git an idea in yr/ head it is difficult to deracinate it.

Let me put it in yet another form. I do not want YOUR job. I do not
want the JOB you have got/ whether you keep it or not. I will not go [to]
Olivet and teach.

I am ready to do WORK, in my own way, that wd/ probably teach 'em
more and give 'em more kudos/ I could do more or less ⟨of it⟩ and be
paid in proportion to what I do.

//

N.Y. job not so bad: but doubt if they wd/ pay $ 5000, and I cert will
not accept less from a big beanery. I mean I wont take a third class salary
in relation to the usual Proferror's pay.

//

I Imagine N.Y. Uv. is violently subversive and OPPOSED to all the
sanities on which the republic (our geelorious) was founded and functioned till the overthrow of man by shit hell and the bankers.

It is a shitten outrage that Johnnie Adams' letters are out of print.

Only the irresponsible triviality of the whole universitaire set up can be
blamed for lack of available edtns/ of Adams/ Jefferson etc.

I will naturally work with ANY press or pubr/ who isn't tired to quick
profits on shit.

AND there are continually arising occasions in which some pubr shd/ be in position to DO what I tell him/ and also to know after 25 years of my picking the real stuff, that I do NOT recommend crap/ and that even such lice as Tauchnitz Albatross have had finally to print what I have picked

may hell rot the lot of 'em and god damn their progeny.

Usury has never endowed a press/ It is time someone burnt the stock exchange and set up a linotype on the ruins. At any rate a Rothschild has been arrested/[42] but I am afraid they wont kill him//
   toting money to Skoda for the usual Paris and London pimps.

By the way as you are in N.Y. who is <u>William</u> <u>Mahl</u>/
   american dramatist.[43]

All study of old music and oriental study revolutionized by microphoto processes.
   Know anything about <u>Chas. Rush of Yale?</u>[44]

Waaal naow dont you go gettin weak and pindlin/ and lets hope they give you a chobb in noo yok.

I can always PRINT anything I write in Italian/ after all why wait for the backward nations.
   I don't spose N.Y. univ. wd/ publish anything more progressive than Lenin's reminiscences of Hobson ???[45]
   Such a conservative country/ no place for contemporary ideas whatever/ esp/ when orthologic.

                                                            ever Ez. P.

   In *The March of Literature,* which Ford was finishing in the early summer, he quoted liberally from the numerous authors included. Pound's bad temper flared up when he learned that Ford's editor might have preferred other translations than his own for extracts of Chinese texts, that is, those done by Arthur David Waley. Ford managed to pacify him by appealing to his interest in music and by suggesting new ways to pick up a few bucks.

F 51. TLS (aman.). 1 1.

                                          [Olivet, Mich.] June 21, 1938

Ezra Pound, Esq.
Via Marsala 12, Apt. 5
Rapallo, Prov.
Genova, Italy

Dear Ezra:

I have been quoting rather freely from your CATHAY and HOW TO READ in my book, and my publisher insists that I obtain your formal permission to use these quotations. Perhaps you would be good enough to send me this as early as you can so as to foil him, because what he really wants is to have me quote Waley instead, he being Waley's publisher.

Yours, F.M.F.
FORD MADOX FORD

P 54. TL. 2 11. [?]. P's retained carbon. Yale.

[Rapallo? post 21 June 1938]

Dear Ford

WHO is yr/ publisher and why shouldn't he pay me for all extracts and the usual fee for co[m]plete poems?

Even old Yeats [*crossout:* god damn thieves] pubrs/ have paid up.

Of course if you want to Quote Waley ??!!!

The first duty of a civilized people is to feed its best writer[.] Publishers / even the Oxford Press finally pay, but usually weep copiously first.

I have for years made NO exceptions to anthologists or cutters of complete poems.

A few lines are usually enough to illustrate a critical point.

Why dont Oliv grove send me that CATALOG/?

cordially yrs.

To make it formal/ F.M.Ford authorized is hereby

to quote extracts of prose not more than 17 lines in le[n]gth and of poems, no quote being more than one fifth of any one poem, and no prose extract to be on same page with another.

Prose quotes totalling about 22 pages, shd. be paid for by publishers/

Anthology fee for complete poems 25 dollars per poem/ U.S. and Five guineas for British rights.

No exceptions to this rule have been made (for Yeats, Eliot or any smaller or bulkier collectors)[.] I cant start now. And all publishers are rolling in money and have no reason to exist unless they feed the authors they have to print (however unwillingly).

F 52. TLS (aman.). 2 11.

[New York] November 10, 1938

Dear Ezra:

If they havn't already paid you, the Dial Press owe you $25 for quotations in my book. I had quoted a great deal more from CATHAY and your educational works but they cut the quotations out and there would appear to be no legal means here of forcing a publisher to print books as their writers write them. It, of course, spoils the book because I meant it to show without saying it in so many words that for the last twenty-five years or so, you and I have supported in our different ways almost the entire burden of the aesthetics of literature in this world. To say so has its invidious sides. To prove it by quotations is convincing. However, we must go on supporting the Muses on a little thin oatmeal. One or two ways have lately occured to me by which you might make some money. But only one of them is in my mind at the present: a young commercial dramatist who has written a quite imbecile play about the Troubadors has approached me to provide incidental music for his work. I daresay I could do it but I have a great many other things on hand and don't feel much inclined to. I don't know whether you would do it. The play is frankly absurd but it seems to be going to be put on by Katharine Cornell in an elaborate way and should mean a good deal of money for everybody concerned. But there are so many uncertainties in this sort of thing that I don't take my young friend too seriously. If, however, it really materializes, I will send you a wire and you could signify in the same way whether on general lines you would accept the job.

Yrs F.M.F.

P.S. The address of the Dial Press is
432 Fourth Avenue, New York City

P 55. TL. 2 11. [?]. P's retained carbon. Yale.

[Rapallo?] 29 Nov [1938]

Dear Fordissimus

Delighted to hear that somebody owes me something specific, as apart from the general concept of the woild owink me a living.

Thanks also for suggestion that I cd/ horn in on a dud play with "incidentals"/ I cant quite see it unless a LARGE sum of money were involved. The authentic 12 th century (if the buggars dont mean the 14th and the light guitar claptrap) wd/ be lost in a whirl of saxophones.

Or possibly not if rightly done/ But unless a singer were sent over here to be KILLED and reborn I dont see how the authentic wd/ have a chance of reaching the stage (and presumably being disliked in a land of soft shit and crooners)

A man who COULD do something wd/ be Serly
  Tibor Serly 212 Central Park South
who cd/ also conduct their bleedin orchestra and at least GET
what he wanted DONE. A mere treatise on excellence from me here wd/
be powerless to break the neck of the god damned ZINGER.
  Serly could set some of the authentic Troubadour melodies to an
orchestral syncopation that might have a chance in de teYater. He once
meant to set my Pere Noe/[46] Nobody in Gnu Yok will know Villon from
Bertrand de B/
  Also the A la vi jalous/[47] cd/ take orchestral underworks. Possibly
Tib/ has a copy.

I understand the patrons of Dutch and Rotschildian banking calling
'emselves the LEFT have completely eliminated my nayme and woiks
from Manhattan and points west/ and that no one dares mention the
constitution or the national founders in view of Kennerley etc/ and
Gollancz or whoever represents that fish in amurikun waters.[48]
  However / if you have got as far as the Col[lege]/ of the Cit[y]. of
N.Y. that is one up.
  Waaal; if young Jas/ aint sent you KULCH or Ez' Guide to Culture
send a line to Nude Erections/ Norfuck, Conn.[49]

You understand Serly is COMPETENT/ no question of his having to
mouse round for lacunae in training etc/ / has conducted whole concert
of his own stuff with Budapest philharmonic/ been chosen fer their fest at
Szeged etc/ as well as knowing how good my Villon is.
  and so forth/ more power to yr. helBOW and more stuff in yr/ purse.

Always interested in promising young men and women and eager to get
outlets for his own work, Pound was enthusiastic about Ronald Duncan
and his new magazine *Townsman*. Pound was a contributor from the start.
One of his pieces was a "rectification" of a point in literary history: he
wished to put on record *who* had been the important theorist in prewar
London. In his article, "This Hulme Business," published in the issue for
January 1939, he wrote:

Among the infinite stinks of a fœtid era is that arising from the difficulty of
not being able to do a man justice without committing some sort of inflation.
I attempted to do Hulme justice in the last pages of Ripostes (a.d. 1910).
  Without malice toward T. E. H. it now seems advisable to correct a distortion
which can be found even in portly works of reference. The critical LIGHT
during the years immediately pre-war in London shone not from Hulme but
from Ford (Madox etc.) in so far as it fell on writing at all.
  To avoid mere argument or expression of opinion, let me put it as datum
pour servir. I used to see Ford in the afternoons and Yeats at his Monday

evening, Yeats being what Ford called a "gargoyle, a great poet but a gargoyle," meaning by gargoyle a man with peculiar or gothic opinions about
writing.

The "image" does exist in the early Yeats, syntactical simplicity is in the
pages of "The Wind Among the Reeds." Ford knew about WRITING. The
general tendency of British criticism at the time was toward utter petrifaction
or vitrification, and Henry Newbolt was as good an example of the best
ACCEPTED criteria as can be unearthed.[50] [. . .]

The EVENT of 1909–10 was Ford Madox (Hueffer) Ford's "English Review," and no greater condemnation of the utter filth of the whole social
system of that time can be dug up than the fact of that review's passing
out of his hands. [. . .]

This was the same assessment that Pound had impressed upon a writer
who was working on a book about T. E. Hulme: "The man who did the
work for English writing was Ford Madox Hueffer (now Ford)." He had
also complained to William Carlos Williams of the "American time lag"
and the snobbish neglect of writers like Williams himself which dominated
American universities. "And," he wrote, "bloody distortion and misrepre-
sentation of London LIFE 1908 to 1914. Hell, Yeats for symbolism /
Hueffer for CLARITY / [. . .] The main injustice is to Ford / 2nd is
to you."[51]

Ford felt that the Dial Press had ruined his book *The March of Literature*
by removing a lot of the extracts he regarded as essential. (One reviewer
thought that it was Pound's influence that damaged the book, in promulgat-
ing "enormous and paradoxical views."[52])

P 56. TLS. 1 1.

[Rapallo] 20 Dec [1938]

Deah Fordie
MERRYrrysmass annaRappy noo yeah.

ThereZa kid named Duncan ⟨Ron. not Isidore⟩ got first chance to do a
magerzine of some use, I mean in ten years this is about the first chance
I see of a new young mag/ doing any good.

You will probably hear from him. He wd/ like a poEM. In desolate
moment so far as young are concerned, I mean the young doing so little,
Dunc/ is out for SHORT stuff. Printing eggspenses wont run to your
usual 3000 woids to turn round in.

I think he intends to unearth your oriGinal preface to yr/ poEMS/
also might do something about yr/ pet cockerel BEEhaine if the bloke
really is any use.

I've a note on Crevel due in next Criterion, but mainly about something else/ as I was interrupted.

//

You might putt in alik of work educating ole Georgie Dillion, ov Harriet's ex/.[53] Bloke seems to mean well.

If you'll pass on the enc/ to yr/ pubrs/ we might git you whatever its called a notice in Broletto.[54]

yrz EP

I don't think they have spotted up anything yet. but havent time to go thru files

P 57. TLS. 1 1.

[Rapallo] 17 Jan [1939]

Dear Fordie

Whether yr/ BUK wuz spoiled or not by the stinginess of yr/ pubrs/ Broletto wd/ git a review of it done by one of the few peepul in this country capable of understanding it.

I might even review it myself, though "we" prefer Brol/ reviews to be done by autochthones.

Whachabaht lichery life in Gnu Yuk? And when are the hebes going to reply by attacking aryan sons of bitches like all financiers ??

This line of reply seems singularly neglected by our semitic friends. Morgan wasn't a jew/ nor was Kreuger nor Mellon, yet they stank nearly as high as Sasoon or Rotschild.

Why will NO jew carry the scrap onto a proper field?

enquirin/ly yrn az usual Ez P/

EP

Ford's last year was filled with almost constant ill health; nevertheless he worked hard and made plans for new books and publishing ventures, such as a projected revival of the *Transatlantic Review.* The summer months of 1938 spent at Olivet College were to be his last extended stay there; at the June commencement he was honored with a Litt. D. degree. He no doubt looked upon Olivet as a *point de repli* which would have served well—if only the climate and the food hadn't been so damaging to his health and general well-being! Apart from a brief return in the spring of 1939, Ford's educational "experiment" at Olivet was over.

Robie Macauley, a former Olivet student, has given us a picture of Ford as teacher. The view of Ford as one for whom all literary works were "contemporaneous" touches an essential feature of Ford as historian and champion of Literature. "He succeeded," Macauley writes, "in giving the impression [. . .] that, though he had just missed meeting Marlowe in London, he knew all about him and was very much excited by the young man's work."[55] Ford was at his best as tutor and as an adviser-critic in the art of writing; up till the very end he took it upon himself to go through masses of manuscripts from budding young writers. He was less successful as a lecturer; for one thing, he had difficulty making himself heard by a fair-sized audience. It was all in line with his temperament and his philosophy of life to disdain the use of a microphone.

Ford's power of initiative was indeed far from exhausted. In January 1939 he started organizing a literary society with the aim of providing the stimulus and support that American authors sorely needed. The Society of the Friends of William Carlos Williams, founded in February, was, Ford said, modeled on the Académie Goncourt.[56] This was Ford's last contribution to the creation of a literary "group." During his long career he had always managed, for longer or shorter periods, to enter into or to gather around himself some sort of literary fellowship. He announced the founding of the Society in a circular letter. He sent it, with an autograph greeting, to Pound. This is the last letter we have from Ford in the correspondence which accompanies the thirty-year relationship between the two. It is quite fitting that it should be concerned with the promotion of fellow writers and the cause of Literature. That the meetings were to be complemented with dinners made the project no less Fordian!

Pound did not commit himself as to membership, but he clearly approved of the idea. He was actually supposed to attend one of the monthly meetings in New York, one which was in honor of E. E. Cummings, presumably on 2 May; when the occasion came, he was, however, too tired to attend.[57] His replies to the circular show that his mind was buzzing with thoughts and ideas. American university education and the general state of affairs in his home country were topics which made him boil over. He did not mince words.

F 53. TLS (aman.). 1 1. Circular letter with autograph note and signature.

[New York, January 1939]

de la part de F.M.F.

It is proposed to found a society to be called the Friends of William Carlos Williams. Its purpose is to assure Mr. Williams and the public of the great esteem in which he is held by his brothers of the pen, an esteem which is withheld from him in any reasonable measure by both the public, the Trade and the very press itself. Its purpose then is to remove a blot from the scutcheon of both branches of Anglo-Saxandom.

Explicitly, it is proposed that the Friends should dine together on the first Tuesday of each month and that at such dinners the topics of conversation shall be within loose bounds the works of Mr. Williams and by implication those of any of our brothers of the pen whose want of recognition by press, trade and public is similarly if in differing degree soiling to our shield. In that way under the aegis of the name of Dr. Carlos Williams a considerable public service might result. For a quarter of a century now Mr. Williams has been acknowledged by all the keener intellects of Anglo-Saxandom as standing on a level with themselves. Will you not then make the public gesture of acknowledging yourself to be amongst his admirers and champions? If you agree will you please signify at your early convenience to

> Paul Leake
> Honorary Secretary
> The Friends of William
> Carlos Williams

There are no fees. The dinners will be Dutch Treats.

P 58. TLS. 1 1. Initials typed. Enclosure.

[Rapallo] 31 Jan [1939]

Dear Fordie

Friends of ole Bull is a good idea (I spose yours) for a country so lousily LOW that everything is run on personality and Baruch's[58] deputy F.D.R. is worked on sentiment/ idea CAN be inserted in his kidney BY being nice to his Ersatz crook offspring.

(e. grat.)
//
A "sort of" Academie Goncourt COULD be used as prod. to the useless Institoot of Letters. (whereto, as item for the Friends of Yam Carlos, you can say I nominated the said Yam Carlos with in 24 hours of my own admission. BUT the sap headed nominatin kummytee did NOT putt his name with Walt Disney's when it came to the annual recommendations.)

THAT body IF seriously criticized/ Murry Butler strangled and Canby educated or drowned COULD be useful, at least in getting certain things reprinted.

There are 1700 perverteries called colleges/ ⟨in the U.S.⟩ quite enough to assure publication of EVERYTHING needed IF the endowments were properly set and used.

It is a rabbit headed country/ ⟨probably⟩ mongrelized past redemption but a bit of coherence might be obtained as it were by stealth and in defiance of Wall St Trotsk and Mr Rothschild's local agents

over.[59]

The really damned foetid and buggy ignorance of 76% of things vital,
as slewed thru the univs/ is such that even the eeeeeelite friends of the
somewhat borné Bill have probably never heard of J.A's proposal for a
soc/ to ascertain the language.[60]
I wonder what Ers[a]tz, if any, ever resulted.

deevotedly yrs/EZ

with flowers in current Townsman. That kid Duncan is ⟨making⟩ the best
bet for a magazine since the Little Review demised and/or the transatlantic desisted.

please transmit enclosure.

Enclosed with *P 58*. TLS. 1 1.

[Rapallo] 31 Jan [1939]

Sec/ Soc/ friends Bill Williams
interim note
If you people really want to get RESULTS, either about circulating
Bill's work or getting recognition for ANY new work having any merit
whatsoever; you shd/ I think consider the extremely PERSONAL cur-
rents in the American sink.

There is NO use in ideological propaganda, meaning strife FOR any
valid criteria in letters, while you have the controll posts filled by old
cheese;

you MUST, if you want RESULTS, remove the purely personal stinks[,]
the individual and incarnate CLOGS, which have names, front names and
addresses. Williams will probably NEVER be recognized till you kill off
Wm Lyon Phelps; and possibly the venerable Cross.[61] People like this who
are never heard of outside their own districts, and of whom I shd/ be
utterly unconscious save for private information from the U.S.

VAST sums are spent professedly on literature or to encourage it, in the
U.S. but they are BLOCKED by the sheer ignorance and idiocy of these
old gorillas, who have never READ anything contemporary, and get their
ideas from the London weeklies, the OLD weeklies, Times Lit/ Shup etc.

things beyond the IMAGINATION, and that are only forced on one's
attention by concrete cases of FACT.

---

to the friends of BILL for their private consideration.

E.P.

Pound had been thinking of returning to America, but presumably only
for intermittent stays.[62] Behind this lay no doubt an urge to help set things

straight in American economy and education. His negotiations with Ford and Joseph Brewer about an engagement at Olivet may have been half-hearted on his side, but they met with great response at the Olivet end. He could afford, literally, to be rather choosy these days about what assignments to take on. Olivet may have seemed too uncomfortable, too modest and out of the way, and too reluctant to promote his monetary-reform interests for Pound to accept the offer of a post there.

At the end of 1938, having spent some time in London—where Lewis painted his portrait—he decided to visit the United States. His aim was to try to influence American leaders by his arguments for economic and political reform and in doing so help prevent the war. He was willing to act as adviser on a fairly regular basis.

On 13 April he left by boat for America, arriving in New York a week later. He had not been back since 1911. Before debarking he gave an interview in which he held the bankers and the munitions interests responsible for the threats of war; he praised Mussolini and referred favorably to Cummings. His most important destination was Washington, D.C., and he stayed there for a fortnight. The highest placed politician he managed to meet was the Secretary of Agriculture, Henry A. Wallace. By early May he was back in New York, disappointed by his failure to obtain any results in the nation's capital.

The reunion that Ford had wished for for so long took place in May. Pound had evidently been in no hurry to look him up, but then the main purpose of his visit lay outside Ford's sphere of immediate interests. They probably saw each other in New York more than once. Ford had been forewarned by William Carlos Williams, who had happened to meet Pound in Washington: Pound had seemed "very mild and depressed and fearful."[63] Pound was indeed not in the best of moods. The fact that he had made his transatlantic crossing in a first-class suite on board an Italian liner evidently became a sore point with him. According to Janice Biala he was irritated because he thought Ford suspected him of being "in Mussolini's pay."[64] (Twenty years later he returned to the subject, explaining that he had booked second-class accommodation but had been offered the suite for $160 because the ship was empty.) Ford and Janice tried to revive his spirits by leading him onto other topics than economics and politics. "Lechery" was one such topic, according to Williams, who has given us a glimpse of the interplay between Ford and Pound those May days in New York.[65] Pound was supposed to come by to 10 Fifth Avenue on 25 May to say goodbye—Ford and Janice were leaving for France on 30 May—but he didn't show up.

After a few days in New York, Pound had gone to Cambridge, Massachusetts, where he was invited to read from his own work in Harvard's Sever Hall. On 17 May he recorded some of his poems for the Harvard Vocarium Series. From Cambridge he sent a note to Ford, the last one.

Ford had managed to find money for a literary prize to be awarded by the Society of the Friends of William Carlos Williams.

P 59. ALS. 1 1.

[Cambridge, Mass.] 16 May [1939]

Dear Fordie.

———

Jury of Friends W.C.W.
my vote iz that it consist of
    Ford M Ford
    Marianne Moor[e]
    W.C. Williams

yr Ez. Pound

In some respects he was the same old Ezra: he could still play a decent game of tennis (he defeated his Cambridge host); his way of dressing was casual; he did a lot of talking. At the commencement festivities on 12 June at his alma mater, Hamilton College, he was awarded an honorary degree of Doctor of Letters. At the alumni lunch afterward he created a minor scandal by heckling another honored guest who was giving the main speech. The topic was democracy vs. dictatorship.

Shortly after the Hamilton event he returned to Italy, his main mission having failed. He may have been in Siena when word reached him of the death of his old friend Ford.

Ford and Janice had planned to spend three to four months in midyear in France, on the Normandy coast. French cooking, he believed, could better than any medicine bring him back to health. He fell ill on board the ship going over, and they went no further than Honfleur. He suffered from uremia. On 24 June he was brought to a Catholic clinic in Deauville, and he, died there two days later. His heart had failed. Two friends joined Janice for the funeral, and he was buried in the Deauville cemetery.

It is a striking coincidence, somewhat prophetic, that in a poem written almost twenty years before his death, Ford had, sentimentally and self-pityingly, visualized the lonely death of a poet dying abroad: "We read: You have died at a distance, / And that's all: that is all! But it's queer / That that should be all! You dying so lonely, / The news not striking any ear / With any insistence. [. . .]" The poem ended: "Heaven knows, you may well prove immortal / Having consummately earned / Your Immortality!"[66]

On 10 July Pound wrote from Siena to Stella Bowen, telling her of the obituary he had written of Ford. A week later he communicated with President Brewer concerning Brewer's plans for a volume of memorial tributes.[67] Janice told Pound that Ford had asked her to consult him any time she needed advice. "He was so glad to see you in New York," she continued. "Whenever anyone criticized you in the last few years for your political opinions—Ford always said that you had carried the aesthetic burden of English letters for the last 30 years entirely by yourself."[68]

Pound also wrote to Violet Hunt encouraging her to deposit her Ford material at the Olivet College Library: "They think no end of F. M. H. (F.) out there. It is the one place where any papers, or a set of Fordie's books would be really preserved and used and done honour to."[69]

Pound's obituary of Ford appeared in the August issue of the *Nineteenth Century and After*. This is one of his most important published statements on Ford. In early August he wrote to Wyndham Lewis reminding him of what Ford had been up against and what he had achieved:

> I have burried pore ole Fordie in (of all places) "the XIXth Century and After" / only hole left. And an inadequate oration as they had room for "under 1500" and by the day after the day etc/ an I think you cd make a beau geste and putt a penny on the ole man's other eye. No one else will.
>
> Kussed as he wuz in some ways / when you think of Galsworthy's England etc/ etc/ and fer ten years before we arruv I spose he had NO one else to take the punishment from the frumpers// wuz again the "mortisme" of our venbl. friend the Possum, and in short virtuous as these things go in a world of Gosses, Royal Acc/ etc. He did NOT regard prose as mere syntax.[70]

FORD MADOX (HUEFFER) FORD; OBIT

THERE passed from us this June a very gallant combatant for those things of the mind and of letters which have been in our time too little prized. There passed a man who took in his time more punishment of one sort and another than I have seen meted to anyone else. For the ten years before I got to England there would seem to have been no one but Ford who held that French clarity and simplicity in the writing of English verse and prose were of immense importance as in contrast to the use of a stilted traditional dialect, a 'language of verse' unused in the actual talk of the people, even of 'the best people,' for the expression of reality and emotion.

In 1908 London was full of 'gargoyles,' of poets, that is, with high reputation, most of whose work has gone since into the discard. At that time, and in the few years preceding, there appeared without notice various fasciculæ which one can still, surprisingly, read, and they were not designed for mouthing, for the 'rolling out' of 'ohs.' They weren't what people were looking for as the prolongation of Victoria's glory. They weren't, that is, 'intense' in the then sense of the word.

The justification or programme of such writing was finally (about 1913) set down in one of the best essays (preface) that Ford ever wrote.

It advocated the prose value of verse-writing, and it, along with his verse, had more in it for my generation than all the retchings (most worthily) after 'quantity' (*i.e.,* quantitative metric) of the late Laureate Robert Bridges or the useful, but monotonous, in their day unduly neglected, as more recently unduly touted, metrical labours of G. Manley Hopkins.

I have put it down as personal debt to my forerunners that I have had five, and only five, useful criticisms of my writing in my lifetime, one from Yeats, one from Bridges, one from Thomas Hardy, a recent one from a Roman Archbishop[71] and one from Ford, and that last the most vital, or at any rate on par with Hardy's.

That Ford was almost an *halluciné* few of his intimates can doubt. He felt until it paralysed his efficient action, he saw quite distinctly the Venus immortal crossing the tram tracks. He inveighed against Yeats' lack of emotion as, for him, proved by Yeats' so great competence in making literary use of emotion.

And he felt the errors of contemporary style to the point of rolling (physically, and if you look at it as mere superficial snob, ridiculously) on the floor of his temporary quarters in Giessen when my third volume displayed me trapped, fly-papered, gummed and strapped down in a jejune provincial effort to learn, *mehercule,* the stilted language that then passed for 'good English' in the arthritic milieu that held control of the respected British critical circles, Newbolt, the backwash of Lionel Johnson, Fred Manning, the Quarterlies and the rest of 'em.

And that roll saved me at least two years, perhaps more. It sent me back to my own proper effort, namely, toward using the living tongue (with younger men after me), though none of us has found a more natural language than Ford did.

This is a dimension of poetry. It is, magari, an Homeric dimension, for of Homer there are at least two dimensions apart from the surge and thunder. Apart from narrative sense and the main constructive, there is this to be said of Homer, that never can you read half a page without finding melodic invention, still fresh, and that you can hear the actual voices, as of the old men speaking in the course of the phrases.

It is for this latter quality that Ford's poetry is of high importance, both in itself and for its effect on all the best subsequent work of his time. Let no young snob forget this.

I propose to bury him in the order of merits as I think he himself understood them, first for an actual example in the writing of poetry; secondly, for those same merits more fully shown in his prose, and thirdly, for the critical acumen which was implicit in his finding these merits.

As to his prose, you can apply to it a good deal that he wrote in praise of Hudson (rightly) and of Conrad, I think with a bias toward generosity that in parts defeats its critical applicability. It lay so natural on the page that one didn't notice it. I read an historical novel at sea in 1906 without noting the name of the author. A scene at Henry VIIIth's court stayed depicted in my memory and I found years later that Ford had written it [i.e., *The Fifth Queen*].

I wanted for private purposes to make a note on a point raised in Ancient Lights; I thought it would go on the back of an envelope,[72] and found to my young surprise that I couldn't make the note in fewer words than those on Ford's actual page. That set me thinking, *mehercule*. I did not in those days care about prose. If 'prose' meant anything to me, it meant Tacitus (as seen by Mackail), a damned dangerous model for a young man in those days or these days in England, though I don't regret it; one never knows enough about anything. Start with Tacitus and be cured by Flaubert *via* Ford, or start with Ford or Maupassant and be girt up by Tacitus, after fifty it is *kif kif*, all one. But a man is a pig not to be grateful to both sides.

Until the arrival of such 'uncomfortables' as Wyndham Lewis, the distressful D. H. Lawrence, D. Goldring, G[ilbert]. Cannan, etc., I think Ford had no one to play with. The elder generation loathed him, or at any rate such cross-section of it as I encountered. He disturbed 'em, he took Dagon by the beard, publicly. And he founded the greatest Little Review or pre-Little Review of our time. From 1908 to 1910 he gathered into one fasciculus the work of Hardy, H. James, Hudson, Conrad, C. Graham, Anatole France, the great old-stagers, the most competent of that wholly unpleasant decade, Bennett, Wells, and, I think, even Galsworthy.

And he got all the first-rate and high second-raters of my own decade, W. Lewis, D. H. Lawrence (made by Ford, dug out of a board school in Croydon), Cannan, Walpole, etc. (Eliot was not yet on the scene).

The inner story of that review and the treatment of Ford by its obtainers is a blot on London's history that time will not remove, though, of course, it will become invisible in the perspective of years.

As critic he was perhaps wrecked by his wholly unpolitic generosity. In fact, if he merits an epithet above all others, it would be 'The Unpolitic.' Despite all his own interests, despite all the hard-boiled and half-baked vanities of all the various lots of us, he kept on discovering merit with monotonous regularity.

His own best prose was probably lost, as isolated chapters in unachieved and too-quickly-issued novels. He persisted in discovering capacities in similar crannies. In one weekly after another he found and indicated the capacities of Mary, Jenny, Willard, Jemimah, Horatio, etc., despite the fact that they all of 'em loathed each other, and could by no stretch of imagination be erected into a compact troop of Fordites supporting each other and moving on the citadels of publication.

And that career I saw him drag through three countries. He took up the fight for free letters in Paris, he took it up again in New York, where I saw him a fortnight before his death, still talking of meritorious novels, still pitching the tale of unknown men who had written the *histoire morale contemporaine* truthfully and without trumpets, told this or that phase of America as seen from the farm or the boiler-works, as he had before wanted young England to see young England from London, from Sussex.

And of all the durable pages he wrote (for despite the fluff, despite the

apparently aimless meander of many of 'em, he did write durable pages)
there is nothing that more registers the fact of our day than the two portraits
in the, alas, never-finished *Women and Men* (Three Mountains Press, 1923),
Meary Walker and 'T.'

                                                        EZRA POUND.

A Friendship in Retrospect
1939-1972

Ford's death marked yet another stage in Pound's growing isolation. Now he could almost count the "surviving members of the human race" on his ten fingers. Soon he began asking for news of his old friends ("Have you had any news of Duncan or Eliot or anyone?") and complaining of lack of information of what was going on in the United States.[1]

As Pound entered the limbo of World War II, Ford did not disappear completely out of his ken. Addressing his Italian readers, Pound drew their attention to worthwhile writers that were unknown to them, Ford and W. H. Hudson, among them. "One who really understood the question of clear expression," he wrote, "was Ford Madox Ford." None of the speeches he broadcast over Rome Radio during the war seems to have been devoted to Ford, but "ole Fordie" is part of the frame of reference for his remarks on literary and other topics. There is Ford referring to some of Hardy's writing as "that 'sort of small town paper journalese,' " or talking about the decline of the feudal system. While stating his unfamiliarity with Germany, Pound also referred to those summer days in 1911 when "Ole Ford toted me 'round about Hessen Darmstadt [. . .] , tellin' me what a fine country was Germany." "Then," Pound added laconically, "he wrote *When Blood is their Argument*."[2]

In the New Directions volume, *Homage to Ford Madox Ford,* assembled by Joseph Brewer, Pound's obituary of Ford appeared together with tributes by old associates from Imagist days, like Aldington and Fletcher, and by American friends of later years, such as the Tates and Katherine Anne Porter, with William Carlos Williams straddling two eras.

After Pound's world had collapsed with the fall of Fascism in Europe and he was entering upon his years of containment and rehabilitation at St. Elizabeths Hospital in Washington, D.C., he was in greater need than ever of finding out who had survived and of renewing old bonds and creating new ones. From Gallinger Municipal Hospital—three days after the doctors had declared him "insane and mentally unfit for trial"—he greeted the Cummings with a "God bless the survivers." And from St. Elizabeths, in a pencilled, irregular scrawl, came: "Who the hell lives in this hemisphere?" "I like getting letters" was his simple and naked message from the lunatics' ward. He asked Stella Bowen to write him "ABOUT People not about ideas."[3]

Ford was often in his thoughts, the memory slightly saddened by a twinge of bad conscience, for "Old Fordie saw more than we gave him credit for." He regretted not having been able to attend the meeting of the Society of the Friends of William Carlos Williams: "still regret fatigue that prevented my gettin' to top floor in '39. [. . .] [it] was [the] day [I] was unable to git round to pore Fordie's. fer reunion of Doc. Wms satelites."[4] The neglect of Ford, also by Pound himself, was a topic he returned to: "I did Fordie as much justice as any one (or almost any one) did – but still not enough," he wrote to Williams. Ford "knew more than any of us." In another letter to Williams (probably written about a fortnight later), he repeated: "Fordie knew more about writing than any of 'them' or of 'us'." He recommended Ford's works to old and new readers alike. "How 'bout ole Fordie? didja learn anyfink from 'im?" he asked of Williams. He singled out the Tietjens series as especially worthwhile and interesting for their relationship to Ford's life and his image of himself.[5] He encouraged Ronald Duncan to "dig up UNEARTH Fordie's collected p[oe]ms/ and On Heaven and NOTE the validity of F's language as distinct from candied dialects, book talk, etc." He referred to the time when "Ford started his purge. 1902–'12."[6]

He was eager for reading material. "One day," Charles Norman writes, "[Pound] occupied himself by drawing up a list of books 'chosen by Ezra Pound, from the estate of the late Miss May Sinclair.' There were 173 items, of which he named thirty-four by Miss Sinclair, seventeen by himself, two by Yeats, one by Joyce, one by Eliot, one by D. H. Lawrence, and nine by Ford Madox Ford, plus several Ford had done in collaboration with Conrad and Violet Hunt."[7] He was rereading—or reading—Ford these first few months at St. Elizabeths. He told a visitor, the poet Charles Olson, of this beneficent experience: "Ford, I happened on a novel of his, and it did me more good than anything has, to restore me, except Katherine."[8] Olson came to see him several times—each visit lasted about twenty minutes—and made notes of their conversation. Often Pound touched on the subject of Ford the important and neglected writer. Pound advised him to read Some Do Not; the second volume, No More Parades, wasn't so good as the first, Pound said, adding, "but I had forgotten what a fine novelist he was." From another visit Olson reported: "On Ford [Pound] is bothered by some sense of guilt, apparently at either not having fought for him as a writer or for having attacked him, though he insisted—'no backbiting.' Something in the Ford matter is bothering him. He again said SO LET IT BE [i.e., Some Do Not] is fine, the second volume, [Olson's blank for No More Parades], not so good. But he kept reiterating: He knew how to write." Pound had been reading South Lodge by Douglas Goldring, and Olson noticed again the sense of guilt: "Except for Goldring he feels he said as much as anyone for Fordy." Goldring's book recalled the happy brotherhood of prewar London: " 'It was the high period of my life. . . .['] (or something like that, a sort of apology for his sentimentality about it, as he is reading it)."

Olson encouraged Pound to set down "his feelings on Ford," and Pound acknowledged Ford's salutary influence on himself and on later writers. He spoke once more of the Giessen experience when Ford "saved" his literary career. After having been criticized by Ford for not writing "Anglese," Pound had tried in his new book, *Canzoni,* to write in "Oxfordese." The result we know: "F rolled on the floor, with his hands over his head trying to teach me how to speak for myself." He recognized Ford's role as teacher. From a later (1948) conversation Olson reports: "[Pound] speaks as though he found himself like retarded when he began. Apropos Ford (F. M.), he said to me once: 'From the intellectual centre, 30 yrs start of me.' " And at another time: "Ford knew, when I was still sucking at Swinburne." "Ford was the one contemporary & he was ignored," Pound declared.

Pound saw the role of the aging Ford as preeminently that of a teacher; Confucius had said that "after a man is 60 he is no longer active, but influences the action of younger men." Olson testified: "I told [Pound] the story of how I was impelled to write to Ford the night before he was leaving for Europe. How much it had meant to us younger men to have him in N.Y. Pointing out that only he and Bill Williams were there for us among Pound's generation. I did not realize at the time I said it that it was a sort of comment on Pound being in Rapallo, exile."

It was time to revive Ford, Pound thought; he was "a thousand times more alive" than some living writers who were being celebrated. In all this praise, there are only a couple of echoes of past criticisms and misunderstandings: Ford "didn't know what to keep off the page. He saw the danger, but . . . ." An afterthought: "Maybe Fordie did not understand me as he said he didn't. Now I know the guck over here I guess he didn't." Olson sent his poem, "Auctour," which pays homage to Ford, as part of a letter to Pound. Pound acknowledged a promised visit, and perhaps also the tribute to Ford, with an "OK."

There was more than one book by Ford that Pound had not seen before. He reproached Williams for failing to mention "Fordie's li'l buk," *The English Novel;* "buzzard never mentioned it to me / how he spected me to see it [in] woptaly gornoze."[9] He also read *Henry for Hugh* for the first time. It was "irritatin' an meritorious – as usual," he told Stella Bowen.[10] He recommended for her perusal *The Simple Life Limited* and *Mr. Fleight;* he also referred to *Great Trade Route.* Dorothy Pound wrote to her husband's former teacher, J. D. Ibbotson: "We have so much enjoyed F. M. Ford's 'Great Trade Route.' "[11]

Pound was trying to cheer up Stella, who was dying of cancer, and his compassionate and gentle letters to her during the summer and fall of 1947 (she died on 30 October) reveal his deep affection and loyalty. His own troubles, he wrote, were nothing compared to hers. He was out of the "snake-pit" and could have a chair "when put out on lawn under surveillance." In his last letter to her he summed up several of Ford's characteristics: "yes. yr. F. a prubblum. – knew more than any – see how good Goldring is, when obeyin F's formula." Goldring's biography of Ford, *The Last Pre-Raphaelite,* published in 1948, evidently called forth some very negative assessments of Ford; his "untruthfulness" was being attacked. Pound commented: "the old walrus hd/ his pts. and .·. they kuss him."[12] Even Wyndham Lewis, never an admirer of Ford, came to his defense: the reviewers ought to have spoken of Ford *the critic.*

Olga Rudge's re-translation of the Rapallo "interview" was published in 1947, and the same year Canto LXXIV appeared in print, with its nostalgic passage on friends cherished and lost. At night, in the Disciplinary Training Center outside Pisa, Pound had typed the first draft of such lines as the following, about his companions Ford, Yeats, and Joyce:

> Lordly men are to earth o'ergiven
> these the companions:
> Fordie that wrote of giants[13]
> and William who dreamed of nobility
> and Jim the comedian singing:
> "Blarrney castle me darlin'
> you're nothing now but a STOWne"
> (Canto LXXIV, pp. 432f.)

In Canto LXXX, similarly: "Orage, Fordie, Crevel too quickly taken" (p. 510). In the same canto Ford is presented as a link to the nineteenth-century English tradition; there is an allusion to the Swinburne anecdote he used to tell, about his grandfather rescuing drunk poets: "'Tyke 'im up ter the bawth' (meaning Swinburne)"; and to a memorable visit to a grand old lady-novelist:

> which is what I suppose he, Fordie, wanted me to be able to picture
> when he took me to Miss Braddon's
> (I mean the setting) at Richmond
> (Canto LXXX, p. 508)

Ford and Yeats are juxtaposed in Canto LXXXII:

> and for all that old Ford's conversation was better,
> consisting in *res* non *verba,*
> despite William's anecdotes, in that Fordie
> never dented an idea for a phrase's sake
> and had more humanitas [. . .]
> (Canto LXXXII, p. 525)

In *Thrones de los Cantares XCVI–CIX,* begun in the early 1950s, Ford is quoted as a giver of sound advice: "And as Ford said: get a dictionary / and learn the meaning of words" (Canto XCVIII, p. 689). This is echoed in Canto C: "and Fordie: / 'A DICtionary / and learn the meaning of words!" (p. 719) In Canto CIV Ford is mentioned as one of the dead companions. In the same canto Pound alludes to the neglect of Ford: "Les Douze unconscious of Fordie" (p. 741). There is also a reference to Ford's ousting from the *English Review* and to the "French" phase of his life: "Mond killed the English Review / and Ford went to Paris (an interval)" (Canto CIV, p. 744).

In the last two decades of his life, while he was still at St. Elizabeths Hospital and after his release and return to Italy in 1958, Pound came back several times in letters and interviews to the subject of Ford. He was anxious to put Ford permanently on the map, for the intrinsic value of his writings and above all for services rendered to the literary community, especially to Pound himself. (Wyndham Lewis, for one, thought that Pound was overdoing his boosting of Ford.) In his correspondence with Patricia Hutchins concerning the work which was to be her *Ezra Pound's Kensington,* there are naturally many references to Ford, to his work as editor and to his helpfulness to younger writers. Pound emphasized: "[. . .] don't forget that Ford and Orage are the two men who keep getting LARGER as the time passes."[14]

Among the numerous visitors who came to St. Elizabeths in the 1950s, there are several who later published Pound's comments and answers in articles and books. In his remarks on Ford he tended to come back, again and again, to the same expressions of praise, gratitude, and regret. Denis Goacher, an English poet and BBC actor, who visited Pound in 1954, broached the topic of the literary milieu in England before 1914. This brought Pound onto the significance of his meeting Ford early in his career. He talked about his coming to London in order to "learn" from Yeats, and staying on to learn also from Ford; about how he "plugged" up Campden Hill to get his daily dose of instruction, and how he and Fordie "groaned" at each other from 1910 on for almost thirty years. He mentioned a novel by Ford that he was reading, or rather reading *at.* Of Ford's nonfiction works he commented on *The English Novel* and *The March of Literature;* the latter was "a gentle meander, and a great gift to the young." There was a question of a reputed hostility between Ford and Yeats. Pound explained: "There was the matter of 'visions.' There is no doubt whatever that Ford, from time to time, used to have visions without any effort at all: this was a little humiliating to dear Yeats, who spent a lifetime trying to have visions: he did have some, I think, but he would keep trying to have more than nature allowed him."[15]

In "A Wreath for Ezra Pound: 1885–1972" Donald Pearce reports from a talk he had with Pound before he was released from St. Elizabeths.[16] Pound was very pleased to talk about Ford. Once again he attested to Ford's knowing more about writing than anyone else. "Just his presence in a room could sometimes make people feel uncomfortable," Pound said. "I remember an instance of this happening when Yeats was giving a lecture once on something or other he thought he knew a little about, Irish poetry maybe, or maybe it was Irish theater, and Fordie came into the hall and seated himself—a 'large pink object' Yeats later described him—in the only seat that was left, which was in the front row right under the lecturer's eyes, and his presence there caused the lecturer such discomfort that before long he was talking nonsense. Well, Yeats was infuriated . . ." On Ford's fiction Pound told the visitor: "The trouble with Fordie was that he couldn't see Venus crossin' the tram tracks."[17] Wyndham Lewis' fiction was much more "important" than Ford's, he thought, explaining that Lewis "had the more entertaining intelligence of the two."

Of all records of Pound's views at about this time, Donald Hall's interview (done in 1960) is probably the most significant.[18] Pound was encouraged to restate the four useful hints he had received in his formative years. He willingly summed them up once more: they were from Bridges, Hardy, Ford, and Yeats (the last name was supplied after a little prodding from the interviewer). The hint received from Ford was formulated as "the *freshness* of language." Pound reformulated an assertion he had made earlier about Ford's wholesome influence on Yeats: "As far as the change in Yeats goes, I think that Ford Madox Ford might have some credit. Yeats never would have taken advice from Ford, but I think that Fordie helped him, via me, in trying to get towards a natural way of writing." Ford's own writings, however, had appeared "too loose" then, but, he added, "he led the fight against tertiary archaisms." (The interviewer's hints on "criticism or cutting" failed to remind Pound of Ford's detailed comments on "Eighth Canto.") While Ford could and did help Pound find "a simple and natural language," Pound, Lewis and the rest of *les jeunes* became Ford's allies in a hitherto lonely struggle: "He was definitely in opposition to the dialect, let us say, of Lionel Johnson and Oxford." The interviewer asked Pound who had been the most stimulating of all the artists, literary and other, that he had known during the first two-three decades after he came to Europe. Pound's answer is revealing, for it helps to explain his ability to appreciate and use certain qualities in people, while disregarding other aspects of their personalities. It also suggests some of the impersonal quality of his relationship to friends and acquaintances throughout the years. Pound:

> I saw most of Ford and Gaudier, I suppose, I should think that the people that I have written about were the most important to me. There isn't much revision to make there.

I may have limited my work, and limited the interest in it, by concentrating on the particular intelligence, instead of looking at the complete character and personality of my friends. Wyndham Lewis always claimed that I never *saw* people because I never noticed how wicked they were, what S.O.B's. they were. I wasn't the least interested in the vices of my friends, but in the intelligence.

Discussion and disagreement were necessary to Pound's development. At least in retrospect, he saw himself as having consciously put fuel onto the fires of Yeats and Ford: "I made my life in London by going to see Ford in the afternoons and Yeats in the evenings. By mentioning one to the other one could always start a discussion. That was the exercise. I went to study with Yeats and found that Ford disagreed with him. So then I kept on disagreeing with *them* for twenty years." "The fun of an intellectual friendship," he maintained, "is that you diverge on something or other and agree on a few points." (This was apropos of Eliot.)

We witness what may have been Pound's last semipublic confrontation with the memory of his friend Ford Madox Ford in Michael Reck's description of a scene in October 1967: Reck, the English poet Peter Russell, Allen Ginsberg, Olga Rudge, and Pound were dining out in Venice; the visitors were trying to draw Pound out of his gloom and silence. He seemed to come to life for a brief moment when Russell handed him a copy of Ford's *It Was the Nightingale:* " 'Yes, yes,' said Pound. His eyes lit up, and he riffled through the pages with a pleased, almost excited smile. Then he put the book down and was again silent."[19]

Close to sixty years earlier Pound had come to Europe to learn, seeking out one Master, and being led to another, who also became a lifelong friend. Now it was his turn to be called upon to act the Master. Receiving the blessing of his American visitor, Ginsberg, he gave his in return, "for whatever it's worth." Pound was a tired and disappointed man who had been humbled by life; even so, he was aware of the *virtù* of the literary tradition and of his own role in passing it on to a new generation. His main regret was that he himself had not done better.

They were all gone now: Yeats, Ford, Joyce, Lewis, Cummings, Williams, and Eliot. Two days after his eighty-seventh birthday Ezra Pound joined these lordly men.

Notes

INTRODUCTION

1 *The Selected Letters of Ezra Pound 1907–1941,* ed. D. D. Paige, London: Faber and Faber, 1971, and New York: New Directions, 1971, pp. 24–25 and 338. Hereafter the abbreviation, P *Letters,* will be used.

2 *Letters of Ford Madox Ford,* ed. Richard M. Ludwig, Princeton, N.J.: Princeton University Press, 1965, p. 29. Hereafter the abbreviation, F *Letters,* will be used.

3 David Dow Harvey, *Ford Madox Ford 1873–1939: A Bibliography of Works and Criticism,* Princeton, N.J.: Princeton University Press, 1962, items F23 and D296, respectively. Hereafter the abbreviation, Harvey, with item designation will be used.

4 Robie Macauley, "The Dean in Exile: Notes on Ford Madox Ford as Teacher," *Shenandoah,* 4, No. 1 (Spring 1953), 43–48; quotation on p. 48.

5 *Pound/Joyce: The Letters of Ezra Pound to James Joyce, with Pound's Essays on Joyce,* ed. Forrest Read, New York: New Directions, 1967; London: Faber and Faber, 1969, p. 272.

6 Ford Madox Ford, *The March of Literature from Confucius' Day to Our Own,* New York: Dial Press, 1938; London: Allen and Unwin, 1939, p. vi.

7 *Pound/Joyce,* p. 197.

8 David Garnett, *The Golden Echo,* New York: Harcourt, Brace and Company, 1954, p. 38.

9 Harvey D344.

10 Joseph Blotner, *Faulkner: A Biography,* London: Chatto & Windus, 1974, II, p. 1426.

11 P *Letters,* p. 221.

12 Harvey D94.

13 F *Letters,* pp. 54, 55, and "Impressionism—Some Speculations," in *Critical Writings of Ford Madox Ford,* ed. Frank MacShane, Lincoln: University of Nebraska Press, 1964, p. 141, respectively. ("Impressionism—Some Speculations" first appeared in *Poetry,* 2, No. 5 [August 1913], 177–87.)

14 "The Approach to Paris," *The New Age,* 13, No. 23 (2 October 1913), 662–64 (quotation on p. 662) and *Literary Essays,* ed. T. S. Eliot, London: Faber and Faber; New York: New Directions, 1968, p. 362 (hereafter abbreviated *LE*), respectively.

15 Harriet Monroe, *A Poet's Life: Seventy Years in a Changing World,* New York: Macmillan, 1938, p. 267n.

16 F *Letters,* p. 87.

17 P *Letters,* p. 213.

18 *"Ezra Pound Speaking": Radio Speeches of World War II,* ed. Leonard W. Doob, Westport, Connecticut: Greenwood Press, 1978, p. 138.

19 P *Letters*, p. 267.
20 Letters by Pound and Ford which are reproduced in this book are referred to by the following abbreviations: *P 1, P 2, F 1, F 2*, etc. For copies of D. D. Paige's transcripts of Pound's letters the abbreviation, Paige, is used.
21 Harvey E472.
22 P *Letters*, p. 322.

C H A P T E R   O N E

1 Ford Madox Ford, *Portraits from Life: Memories and Criticisms*, Boston, New York: Houghton Mifflin Company, 1937, p. 74.
2 F *Letters*, p. 40.
3 Quoted in Douglas Goldring, *South Lodge: Reminiscences of Violet Hunt, Ford Madox Ford and the English Review Circle*, London: Constable & Co. Ltd., 1943, p. 24.
4 *South Lodge*, p. 15.
5 *The Golden Echo*, p. 129.
6 *Portraits from Life*, p. 71.
7 "An Autobiographical Outline (Written for Louis Untermeyer)," *Paris Review*, 28 (Summer-Fall 1962), 18–21; quotation on p. 19. Pound is referring to the verdict of those who caused his dismissal from his post at Wabash College, Crawfordsville, Indiana.
8 *The Selected Letters of William Carlos Williams*, ed. John C. Thirlwall, New York: McDowell, Obolensky, 1957, p. 6.
9 "Hilda's Book" appeared in print in 1979 as an appendix to Hilda Doolittle's *End to Torment: A Memoir of Ezra Pound*, ed. Norman Holmes Pearson and Michael King, New York: New Directions, 1979. TMs at Harvard.
10 "How I Began," *T. P.'s Weekly*, 21, No. 552 (6 June 1913), 707.
11 Unless otherwise indicated all quotations from Pound's letters to his parents refer to the carbons of Paige's transcripts at Yale.
12 Quoted in Patricia Hutchins, *Ezra Pound's Kensington: An Exploration 1885–1913*, London: Faber and Faber, 1965; Chicago: Henry Regnery Company, 1965, p. 57.
13 Note dated January 1937 and submitted to Harriet Monroe's reminiscences, *A Poet's Life*, p. 267.
14 ALS at Cornell.
15 6 April [1909]; TL at Cornell.
16 P *Letters*, p. 7.
17 The check is in the Humanities Research Center at the University of Texas at Austin. I thank Research Librarian Ellen S. Dunlap for making this document known to me.
18 AMs at Cornell.
19 *Ezra Pound's Kensington*, p. 71.
20 Describing his life at 10 Church Walk to Patricia Hutchins in 1957 (see *Ezra Pound's Kensington*, p. 69), Pound evidently confused the profes-

sional painter William Henry Hunt (1790–1864) with Violet Hunt's father, Alfred Hunt (1830–96); Alfred Hunt had given up an academic career in order to devote himself to art. Pound may also have had in mind the Pre-Raphaelite painter William Holman Hunt (1827–1910), who figured in Ford's flora of anecdotes.

21 Copied from a carbon of Paige's transcript.

22 11 February 1910. Ford evidently read aloud to him from his manuscript; cf. F to James B. Pinker, 30 March 1910; F *Letters.*

23 22 March 1910. Lady Low was a London hostess.

24 "Ford Madox Ford When He Was Hueffer," *South Atlantic Quarterly,* 57, No. 2 (Spring 1958), 236–53; quotation on p. 249.

25 "Book Chat," *Punch,* 141 (16 August 1911), 122–23; quotation on p. 122. This was not the first time Pound was spoofed in *Punch;* see the issue for 23 June 1909.

26 29 August 1911.

27 ALS at Humanities Research Center, University of Texas at Austin.

28 Quoted in *Pound/Joyce,* p. 285.

29 The postcard is among the recently acquired Katharine Lamb papers at Cornell. Camilla B. Haase kindly drew my attention to it.

30 P to Isabel W. Pound, 21 February 1912; P to Homer L. Pound, 14 March 1912.

31 P *Letters,* p. 10.

32 Reprinted in *LE;* quotation on p. 12.

33 Quoted from *Selected Poems. Ford Madox Ford,* ed. Basil Bunting, Cambridge, Mass.: Pym-Randall Press, 1971.

34 Quotations on pp. 123, 125, and 126 of the January 1913 issue of *Poetry.*

35 P *Letters,* p. 11.

36 P *Letters,* p. 23.

37 P *Letters,* pp. 20, 21, respectively.

38 In *Ladies Whose Bright Eyes.*

39 P *Letters,* p. 37.

40 Reprinted as in *LE.*

41 Poems quoted from in this essay are Christina Rossetti's "At Home," "Somewhere or Other," and "A Pause of Thought" and Ford's "Finchley Road," "Views," and "The Three-Ten."

42 Pound's note: "or at any rate a canzone."

43 Casella, a musician of Florence or of Pistoia and a personal friend of Dante. He is said to have set some of his verses to music. Cf. *Purgatorio,* II. Casella's name occurs in Pound's "ur-Cantos" (1917): it is time for the poet to "leave" Casella, who represents lyricism.

44 *Atalanta in Calydon,* a drama in the classical Greek form by Swinburne.

45 Both letters are at the University of Chicago Library and are printed here with the permission of the library. I thank Mary E. Janzen Wilson, MSS Research Specialist, for her help in my locating these letters. Part of Ford's letter is quoted in Ellen Williams, *Harriet Monroe and the Poetry Renaissance: The First Ten Years of Poetry, 1912–22,* Urbana: University of Illinois Press, 1977, pp. 81f.

46 P *Letters*, p. 28.
47 P to William Carlos Williams, 19 December 1913; P *Letters*.
48 P to H. L. Mencken, 3 October 1914; P *Letters*. Ford kept up his associa-
    tion with Imagists Flint and Aldington; he was never close to the two
    Americans, Amy Lowell and Eliot.
49 "Mr. James Joyce and the Modern Stage. A Play and Some Considera-
    tions," *Drama*, 6, No. 21 (February 1916), 122–32; reprinted in *Pound/
    Joyce*, pp. 49–56.
50 *Pound/Joyce*, p. 44.
51 " 'Dubliners' and Mr James Joyce," *The Egoist*, 1, No. 14 (15 July 1914),
    267; reprinted in *LE*. Quotation on pp. 401f.

C H A P T E R   T W O

1 "Literary Portraits [. . .] ," *Outlook*, 34 (4 July 1914), 15–16; quotation
   on p. 16.
2 "The Poet's Eye," *New Freewoman*, 1, No. 7 (15 September 1913), 126–27;
   quotations on p. 127.
3 July 1915; quoted in Ellen Williams, *Harriet Monroe and the Poetry Renaissance*, p. 127.
4 "A Retrospect"; reprinted in *LE*. Quotation on p. 14.
5 P *Letters*, p. 137.
6 "Affirmations . . . VI. Analysis of This Decade," *The New Age*, 16, No. 15
   (11 February 1915), 409–11; reprinted in *Gaudier-Brzeska*. Quotation on
   p. 115 of this work.
7 9 November 1914; P *Letters*, pp. 46f.
8 P *Letters*, pp. 61, 63, respectively.
9 Quoted from *Personæ*, New York: New Directions, 1949; London: Faber
   and Faber, 1952.
10 P *Letters*, p. 145.
11 F *Letters*, p. 101.
12 "Thus to Revisit . . . V. Combien je regrette . . . ," *The Dial*, 69, No. 3
    (September 1920), 239–46; quotation on p. 240.
13 F *Letters*, p. 101.
14 Among the poets who figure in Ford's review are the elegists Meleager of
    Gadara (fl. *c.* 60 B.C.) and Sextus Aurelius Propertius (b. *c.* 50 B.C.);
    the Chinese Li-Po (Rihaku) (701–62); and the troubadours Bertran de
    Born, Lord of Altafort (1140–1215), Guillem de Cabestanh (fl. *c.* 1200),
    and Sordello di Mantovana (1180?–1253?). Laurent Tailhade (1854–1919)
    was one of the French poets Pound had introduced to English readers be-
    fore the war in his "Approach to Paris" series in *The New Age*.
15 F *Letters*, p. 106.
16 *Thus to Revisit: Some Reminiscences*, London: Chapman & Hall, 1921,
    p. 208.
17 J. C. Squire was literary editor of the *New Statesman*. The *Athenaeum* was
    founded in 1828 and was later incorporated in the *New Statesman*. In a

review in the *Athenaeum* Edith Sitwell's work had been favorably compared to Flint's poems.

18 Longhand marginalia probably refer to the words "and I had intended it [. . .] something."

19 *Mr. Croyd,* also entitled *The Wheels of the Plough,* and later *That Same Poor Man;* this novel was never published.

20 F *Letters* prints "knowing" for "honouring."

21 Ford imitates Pound's handwriting by shaping a few words in long, forceful, uncurved lines, with the help of a broad pen. The "ideograph" is made with the same pen.

22 Ford obviously could express himself in several other languages than his native English. True to character he does not care about correctness and precision; he freely invents words which at least faintly resemble genuine ones. This outburst in a mixture of genuine and "approximate" Dutch seems to refer to the chaos of premoving and to the mental make-up of poets.

23 Ford remembered the British novelist and essayist H. M. Tomlinson as the man who had never heard of Conrad. —R. B. Cunninghame Graham, noted British writer, traveler, and politician. —Wilfrid Scawen Blunt, venerated British poet and publicist. —George Stevenson, British novelist. —Mary Butts was one of the many British writers that Pound boosted.

24 Gr. νὺξ γὰρ 'ἔρχεται ("Night is coming").

25 *Instigations* was published in April 1920. Associating to papal bulls, Pound may have had "encyclicals" in mind.

26 Jean-Pierre Rousselot (1846–1924), French professor of experimental phonetics; formerly a priest.

27 "A Few Don'ts by an Imagiste," *Poetry,* 1, No. 6 (March 1913), 200–06.

28 B. W. Willett was one of the directors of John Lane The Bodley Head Limited.

29 Like John O'Leary (1830–1907), immortalized in Yeats's poem "September 1913," Blunt was an Irish nationalist.

30 "The Island of Paris" letters ran in *The Dial* in the fall of 1920, to be followed by the "Paris Letter" series in 1921–23.

31 Rodker's Ovid Press published *Hugh Selwyn Mauberley.*

32 John Lane had published Pound's memoir of Gaudier-Brzeska; he had also brought out several books by Ford, among them, *The Good Soldier.*

33 F *Letters* erroneously gives the date as "[September, 1920]."

34 In the August 1920 issue H. G. Wells vehemently denied that he had ever "lectured" Ford on how to write, as Ford had claimed in his *Dial* article for July. The August issue of the *English Review* also printed a letter from Ethel Colburn Mayne protesting against Ford's assertion about her influence in the *Yellow Book.*

35 Ford is referring to a remark in the "Literary Gossip" column which suggests that although M. de Régnier writes well "he would hardly pass as [morally] respectable" in England. Ford no doubt regarded an article in the same issue (30 July 1920) by Walter Edwin Peck, "More Shelley Letters with corrections of previously published texts: the whole from MSS.," as the typical product of the Pedantic Academic.

36 The offensive remark in the May/June issue suggests that Ford's best work was written ten years earlier.

37 The August installment of the "Thus to Revisit" series in *The Dial*, subtitled "A Lordly Treasure House" and "Mots Justes . . ."

38 Ford's offense consisted in tagging two etceteras onto the name of Wyndham Lewis in the list of authors that he had been asked to treat of in *The Dial*. (Lewis is conspicuously missing from the corresponding passage in the book version.) The "etceteras" might refer to Lewis' habit—according to Ford—of ending his spoken utterances by "And so on" (Ford in *Piccadilly Review* for 13 November 1919).

39 F *Letters*, p. 190.

40 "Hudson: Poet Strayed into Science," *The Little Review*, 7, No. 1 (May-June 1920), 13–17; reprinted in *Selected Prose 1909–1965*, ed. William Cookson, London: Faber and Faber, 1973; New York: New Directions, 1973. Quotations on pp. 402 and 432 respectively.

41 Ford evidently never did a translation of *Du côté de chez Swann*.

42 Scofield Thayer was the editor of the (New York) *Dial*, Gilbert Seldes its managing editor; James Sibley Watson, Jr., was president of the Dial Publishing Co., and John Quinn backed the magazine.

43 Pound altered "Poetry" to "Peotry," perhaps to suggest a "genteel" editorial attitude.

44 The October issue of *The Dial* printed Proust's "Saint-Loup: A Portrait" translated anonymously by Pound (Gallup C597a, *Paideuma* [Fall 1973]).

45 In "The Battle of the Poets" Ford attacked, among other things, a—to him—reprehensible interest in Keats's biography and in the orthography of the Folios. —Gaston–Alexandre–Auguste de Galliffet (1830–1909), French general, who distinguished himself in the battle at Sedan (1870).

46 The passage beginning "One or two minor points" and ending with the words "necessary part)'" is crossed over, probably by Pound himself, in the original letter.

47 In the January 1921 installment in *The Dial* Ford reminisced about Vorticists, Cubists, Imagistes, and other revolutionary artists that he had known.

48 The chronological placing of this letter is uncertain; it might belong *before* Ford's of 10 September 1920.

49 Violet Hunt had engaged the wife of the Bedham carpenter to "spy" on Ford and Stella. Stella was pregnant.

50 Pound answered almost by return of post. Cornell owns an envelope, addressed in his hand to Ford M. Ford Esq, Scammell's Farm, Bedham nr. Fittleworth, Sussex, and postmarked 22 September 1920; the letter is missing.

51 P *Letters*, p. 158.

52 In British World War I soldier's slang, this is the Englishing of *il n'y en a plus + fini*. Elsewhere (*Parade's End*) Ford spelled it "napoo finny."

53 *A House* was published by Harold Monro the following March, but without the projected illustrations.

54 G. D. H. (Douglas) and Margaret Cole, writer-friends. Stella gave birth to a daughter, Esther Julia, on 29 November.

55 Coventry Patmore's early work was collected in *The Angel in the House,* whose subject was married love.

56 Pound shared Ford's high esteem of Théophile Gautier's work. The collection of stories, *Soirées de Médan*—taking its title from Zola's Villa Médan—included writings by Zola and his friends.

57 Henry Seidel Canby added a *Literary Review* to the *New York Evening Post,* whose literary editor he was. Later, as editor of the *Saturday Review of Literature,* Canby was to be the object of Pound's unmitigated scorn. His association with the National Institute of Arts and Letters did not improve his image in Pound's eyes.—Pound's recommendation of Ford may have accompanied a contribution of his own (Letter to the Editor, published in the *N.Y. Evening Post* for 4 December 1920). Ford's "Two Americans—Henry James and Stephen Crane" appeared there the following March.

58 Letter from the editor of *The Dial.*

59 Pound wrote to Harriet Monroe in October suggesting that she publish "A House"; it appeared in the March 1921 issue of *Poetry.*

60 In presenting his Hamletesque dilemma, Pound seems to allude to the magazine *Time and Tide* ("in the teeth of time"); Margaret Rhondda (1883–1958), industrialist and author, was its editor.

61 Editor of the *English Review,* which evidently remained closed to Pound.

C H A P T E R   T H R E E

1 Interview quoted by Noel Stock, *The Life of Ezra Pound,* London: Routledge & Kegan Paul, 1970; New York: Pantheon, 1970, pp. 235f.

2 Flint's "epistle" is the very letter whose existence Christopher Middleton conjectures in his article "Documents on Imagism from the Papers of F. S. Flint," *The Review,* 15 (April 1965), 35–51. It is possible that the invitation for a proposed meeting between Pound and Flint to discuss the project is to be found on a typescript re *Imagisme* that Flint had submitted to Pound for his comments. Middleton suggests 1913 as the likely date of this draft; my surmise would date it to the end of 1920.

3 *Drawn from Life,* London: Collins, 1941, p. 80.

4 The *Dial* articles correspond largely to the following chapters of the book: July 1920 installment = Part II. Prosateurs. I Credentials. II Puiser dans le vide ...; August 1920 installment = III The Lordly Treasure-House. IV Mots Justes ...; September 1920 installment = V Combien je regrette ... VI Coda ...; January 1921 installment = Part III. The Battle of the Poets. I "Thoughts Before Battle." II.

5 Quotations from *Thus to Revisit* refer to pp. 153, 159, 167, 168, 201, and 206, respectively.

6 10 February 1921; Chicago UL.

7 P *Letters,* p. 166.

8 Quoted in Charles Norman, *Ezra Pound,* revised ed., London: Macdonald & Co., 1969, p. 253.

9 P *Letters*, p. 169.

10 P *Letters*, p. 169; Paige's ellipsis.

11 Ford may have commented on Cantos V–VII.—Hardy's house in Dorchester was called Max Gate. Pound thanked him for valuable suggestions re "Homage to Sextus Propertius" in a letter of 31 March 1921 (quoted in Patricia Hutchins, "Ezra Pound and Thomas Hardy," *Southern Review*, 4 [N.S.], No. 1 [January 1968], 90–104).

12 Ford had once (1913) reviewed *The Second-Class Passenger* by Perceval Gibbon (1879–1919). Pound may have had a nonce-word *numino* (from It. *nume* "divinity") in mind when associating to the great historian.— Possibly the American writer Ferdinand Reyher (b. 1891), author of *The Man, the Tiger, and the Snake* (1921) and *David Farragut, Sailor* (1953).

13 Constantin Guys (1805–92), Dutch-born French artist.—Francis Picabia, French painter and writer.

14 Cf. Pound's affectionate form of address, "DEER old Bean," in his letter of 26 May.

15 Pound envisages his role as exiled adviser in terms of Dante's "philosophical family" (*Divina Commedia*, I, 4, 132) and Manente Farinata, thirteenth-century Ghibelline savior-heretic. By the reference to the *chanson de geste* named for the illustrious cemetery at Arles, he may be seeing himself in the role of the hero Guillaume who manages to rally support for a threatened cause.

16 Pound's French poem appeared (10 July 1921) in a magazine published by Picabia; see Donald Gallup, *A Bibliography of Ezra Pound*, second impression, corrected, London: Rupert Hart-Davis, 1969, item C623.

17 W. C. Blum (pseudonym for James Sibley Watson, Jr.) reviewed *Thus to Revisit* in the issue for December.

18 "Indeed, almost everybody I have ever come across has lectured me—from Mr. Holman Hunt to Mr. Pound" (*Thus to Revisit*, p. 45).

19 The historical Colonel (Thomas) Blood (1618?–80) was a notorious but evidently charming Irish adventurer, whose most audacious feat was the attempt to steal the Crown Jewels.

20 *The Heart of the Country* was never published in the U.S.A. *Women & Men* appeared in Paris in 1923; Ford had earlier referred to the projected book as "Men and Women."

21 "Parisian Literature," *New York Evening Post Literary Review*, 1, No. 49 (13 August 1921), 7.

22 Bernard Van Dieren's book on Epstein was published by John Lane in 1920. The book that Pound proposed to write on Brancusi, Lewis, Picabia, and Picasso was never written.

23 Stella was in London the first week of October.

24 Thus Ronald Bush (*The Genesis of Ezra Pound's Cantos*, Princeton, N.J.: Princeton University Press, 1976, p. 239) accepts Myles Slatin's assertion that Pound had not referred to this canto before its appearance in print.

25 Victor Llona, Peruvian-born writer, living in Paris. In 1926 the Paris publisher Simon Kra brought out a French translation of *Romance*, a novel that Ford and Conrad had collaborated on.

26 Written between 21 and 27 March, which was the day when Pound left for Italy.

27 In the summer of 1919 the Pounds, with Eliot for a companion part of the time, went hiking in southwestern France; they started and ended at Excideuil, to the south of Eleanor of Aquitaine's Poitiers.

28 ðonne onwæcneð eft winelēas guma,
gesihð him biforan fealwe wǣgas,
baþian brimfuglas, brǣdan feþra
("then the friendless man wakes up / and sees in front
of him the yellow waves, / the seabirds bathing, spreading
their feathers [wings]") from *The Wanderer*, 11. 45–47.

29 "The Seventh Canto" contains a few phrases quoted mosaiclike from the opening of Flaubert's story, "Un Cœur simple."

30 Pound seems to be referring to the documentary-biographical quality of Flaubert's work.—Grégoire de Feinaigle (1765–1820) and Francisco Amoros (1769–1848) inspire the pseudoscientific pursuits of Bouvard and Pécuchet, the main characters of the book which bears their names.

31 "James Joyce et Pécuchet," *Mercure de France*, 156, No. 575 (1 June 1922), 307–20. Among writers descending from Flaubert, Pound mentions Ford: " [. . .] Hueffer, en Angleterre, écrit une prose lucide [. . .] " (quoted in *Pound/Joyce*, p. 202).

32 Fr. slang for "shoddy."

33 This may be an instance of advice adopted: in the canto as printed in *The Dial*, and in later appearances, there is no "receding wave." In Ford's letter of 21 March there is no reference to such a phrase, nor does he in that letter comment on the word "splay." This suggests that he either enclosed a sheet of further criticisms, which has been lost, or that he commented on the canto in a second, no longer extant, letter.

34 *A Portrait of the Artist as a Young Man* was translated by Mme. Ludmilla Bloch-Savitsky and appeared as *Dedalus* in 1924.

35 P *Letters*, p. 178.

36 Cf. Ford's poem "The Great View." Quotations from Pound's article refer to pp. 144, 145, and 146.

37 *It Was the Nightingale*, London: William Heinemann Ltd., 1934, p. 275.

38 P *Letters*, p. 183.

39 F *Letters*, p. 47.

40 These drafts were evidently never put into final, publishable form. Although late 1923 is a possible date for the early notes, the beginning of 1924 seems more likely: in the section on Ford, Pound refers to the novel *Some Do Not*, which appeared in April 1924, after partial publication in the *Transatlantic Review* from January 1924 on; and at the conclusion of these notes on the series, Pound quotes from—but does not name—a review of a book published in 1924 (D. B. Wyndham Lewis' *At the Sign of the Blue Moon*, reviewed by Ronald A. Knox). In these notes *in our time* is still untitled, which indicates that Pound drafted them probably not much later than January 1924; this was when Hemingway's book came from the binder's

(see Carlos Baker, *Hemingway: The Writer as Artist,* 3rd ed., Princeton, N.J.: Princeton University Press, 1963, p. 22).—The date of the later notes can be fixed by a reference (Pound's page 5) to Robert McAlmon, who was missing from the series: "In 1926 he is the most formidable proposition 'of the lot.' "

41 Pound is quoting from chapter IV, "Average People." "Mr T.," wealthy bachelor friend of the author, is referring to a hymn whose subject is death, inevitable destiny of us all ("Sweet day [. . .]"). Meary Walker represents the heroism of "average people." One of Ford's favorite parables of the artist was one reportedly derived from a Chinese proverb, "to the effect that it would be hypocrisy to seek for the person of the Sacred Emperor in a low tea-house" (*Thus to Revisit,* p. 179). The point of Ford's parable is that this is exactly what can happen, as in the case of Henri Gaudier-Brzeska.

42 F *Letters,* p. 147.

43 [November?] 1922; Paige conjectures August.

44 P to HLP, 12 September 1923.

45 P *Letters,* p. 186.

46 After the scandal caused by their serialization of *Ulysses,* Margaret Anderson and Jane Heap—the ones "possessed by the evil spirit"—moved to Paris, where they brought out the last numbers of the magazine (1924–29).

47 *The Letters of Wyndham Lewis,* ed. W. K. Rose, London: Methuen & Co. Ltd, 1963, p. 137.

48 For details of Ford's involvement with the project I have consulted Bernard J. Poli's account in *Ford Madox Ford and the Transatlantic Review,* Syracuse, N.Y.: Syracuse University Press, 1967.

49 *It Was the Nightingale,* p. 274.

50 Quoted in Donald Gallup, *T. S. Eliot & Ezra Pound: Collaborators in Letters,* New Haven: Henry W. Wenning/C. A. Stonehill, Inc., 1970, p. 30.

51 P *Letters,* p. 190.

52 Probably Stéphane Joseph Vincent Lauzanne (b. 1874), author of "Sa Majesté la Presse, Choses vues," *Les Oeuvres libres,* 32 (Février 1924), 251–88.

53 Poli had to rely on copies of Paige's transcripts of this material, which explains errors in his rendering and interpretation. It has not been possible to establish with certainty the writing-and-sending history of these two letters and Pound's notes in response to them. Pound wrote his replies in the margins of Ford's first letter and at the end of his later note.

54 For Robert E. Rodes, see *It Was the Nightingale,* p. 331.

55 This note was written on a small leaf of onionskin paper. If sent as a separate letter, it can be assigned to the period between Ford's reception of Pound's Assisi letter and Ford's departure for the U.S.A., which took place *c.* 31 May.

56 Cf. William Carlos Williams' poem "Last Words of My Grandmother," published in the March issue of the *Transatlantic Review;* the dying old woman's last words are:

> What are all those
> fuzzy looking things out there?
> Trees? Well, I'm
> tired of them.

57 Among those "approved" are the less well-known Swiss writer Charles-Albert Cingria and the American Kennon Jewett. British contributors who apparently did not make the mark were: A. E. Coppard, Catherine Wells, Ethel Colburn Mayne, and "R. Edison Page" (according to Mizener a pseudonym for Ford himself). Poli surmises that "Bill Exe" is William Carlos Williams.

58 Possibly John St. Loe Strachey (1860–1927), editor and proprietor of the *Spectator*. The "Strachey female" may be his daughter, Amabel Williams-Ellis, literary editor.

59 Editorial, *Transatlantic Review*, 2, No. 6 (December 1924), 682–86; quotation on p. 684.

C H A P T E R   F O U R

1 See letter from Pound to William Bird, 13 June 1925; copy of Paige's transcript at Yale. The proof copy is now on deposit at the Washington University Library, St. Louis, Missouri. I owe this information to Sondra J. Stang.

2 Letter to A. P. Saunders, 25 January 1925; Hamilton.

3 Letter to HLP, 28 November 1925.

4 A typescript of the article was sent to Donald Friede in 1926. I am indebted to Donald Gallup, who owns the typescript, for bringing it to my attention and for allowing me to publish excerpts from it.

5 Letters to IWP and HLP, 21 and 24 January 1927, respectively.

6 Possibly Stella Beatrice (Mrs. Patrick) Campbell. The famous actress lived in Kensington Square. Or was the Beautiful Lady Florence Farr?

7 Mary Johnston (1870–1936), popular American novelist; John Erskine, American scholar and novelist, author of *The Private Life of Helen of Troy* (1925).

8 Owner and manager of a lecture tour bureau.

9 21 April 1927; copy of Paige's transcript at Yale.

10 3 April and 1 May 1927, respectively.

11 Thomas Bucklin Wells was editor of the magazine.

12 Robert Chanler, American artist.

13 Gennaro Favai, Venetian painter.

14 4 October 1927; Chicago UL.

15 Letter to Stella Bowen, 13 November 1927; Cornell (transcript).

16 TMs (carbon); Cornell.

17 Quoted from *Buckshee*, Cambridge, Mass.: Pym-Randall Press, 1966.

18 Quoted in Charles Norman, *Ezra Pound*, p. 303.

19 The present rendering differs slightly from the letter as printed in F *Letters*.

20 Presumably "Publishers, Pamphlets, and Other Things," *Contempo*, 1, No. 9 (15 September 1931), 1, 2.

21 Here, as elsewhere, Ford treats history somewhat cavalierly. Pound first appeared in the *English Review* in June 1909 with "Sestina: Altaforte." "Ballad of the Goodly Fere" was printed in the October issue. Some of the details of Pound's early life had been told in his *Indiscretions* (1923).

22 This translation is in places only tentative, to some extent owing to the difficulty of reading some of the autograph corrections in the original (Italian) typescript; the essay's character of a draft accounts for most of the uncertainties.

23 The Pre-Raphaelite painter Ford Madox Brown (1821–93) was Ford's grandfather. "The young Rossettis" (Olive, Arthur, and Helen) were his cousins; they were the children of his uncle by marriage, William Michael Rossetti, brother of Dante Gabriel and Christina.

24 On Nurse Atterbury and Norman MacColl (1843–1904), editor of the *Athenaeum* for three decades, see *Return to Yesterday*, pp. 78ff. and 178ff., respectively.

25 Dante describes Mahomet, one of the "sowers of Scandal and Schism," horribly cleft from the chin downward, entrails hanging between his legs, "and the wretched sack that makes excrement of what is swallowed" bursting out of his body (quoted from The Modern Library College Edition of *The Divine Comedy*). Pound first typed *"triste"* and then changed it to *"tristo,"* thereby keeping the wording of the original (" [. . .] e 'l *tristo sacco / che merda fa di quel che si trangugia"* (quoted from *La Divina Commedia*, ed. A. Chiari).

26 William Gifford (1756–1826), critic, editor, and translator; staunch adherent to the old school in literature.

27 Cf. Dante's *Vita nuova* (XIX and XX, respectively): *"Donne ch' avete intelletto d'amore, / i' vo' con voi de la mia donna dire"* and *"Amore e 'l cor gentil sono una cosa, / si come il saggio in suo dittare pone"* (quoted from the 1973 edition published by Mursia).

28 Editor of *The New Review;* Pound figured as subeditor.

29 Ford's anecdote features the Catholic writer Hilaire Belloc—not Cunninghame Graham—and "Our Lord" (*Return to Yesterday*, p. 368).

30 American (Liveright) edition, p. 307. Ford reminisces about his visit to New York (in 1906). He says he went down town "on a horse-trolley," the fare for the ride being a dime.

31 Fl. 1260–1300; author of a metrical chronicle from earliest times down to 1272.

32 English statesman (1830–1903).

33 Ovid, *Fasti*, IV, 425–28.

34 Quotations from Crane's "The Open Boat" (inexact) and Aeschylus' *Prometheus*, ll. 89f. ("and laughter of the seas innumerable" [G. Murray]).

35 Cf. letter to Stella Bowen (22 July 1947; Cornell): "I've got shot of Fordie under Chris. Colombo – [. . .] Olga translation of interview I did with him @ that time – after gettin' the wrong thing first. & long hunt." In *Ezra Pound and His World* (London: Thames and Hudson, 1980), Peter Ack-

royd reproduces one of these photos, locating it to Paris *c.* 1923. The second snapshot appears in Mizener's biography, where the place and date are given as Rapallo *c.* 1927. A letter from Ford to Ray Long (8 August 1932; *F Letters*) strongly indicates that the correct place and date are Rapallo, August 1932. Janice Biala corroborates this conclusion (letter to the present editor).

36 A young American who acted as Ford's secretary.

37 Mary Elizabeth Braddon (1837–1915), author of a very popular novel, *Lady Audley's Secret* (1862).

38 Novels by George Davis and Caroline Gordon, respectively.

39 Presumably Lincoln Kirstein, who became sole editor of the *Hound and Horn* after it moved to New York.

40 Cadman (1864–1936) was a popular American cleric, who attacked Mencken's *American Mercury*. For Dr. Parker, see *F 28*. "Canby & Co." were the subject of Pound's letter to the Editor of the column "The Bear Garden," *New York Sun* (16 April 1932).

41 Ford's promotional drive for *A Draft of XXX Cantos*.

42 Pound referred to the *Hound and Horn* as "Bitch and Bugle" and "Bitch and Whiffle."

43 Possibly the *Atlantic Monthly*.

44 Bion (*c.* 150–200 B.C.), Greek pastoral poet; Pound had used his "Adonis" as a model for the metre in *Mauberley*.

45 The "others" were Edmund Wilson, William Carlos Williams, Allen Tate, Elizabeth Madox Roberts, Francesco Monotti, Paul Morand, H. D., John Peale Bishop, and Basil Bunting.

46 Schaunard is the musician-Bohemian in Puccini's opera *La Bohème* (1896); the libretto was based on Henri Murger's novel, *Scènes de la vie de bohème* (1848).

47 At the end of March Pound gave a series of lectures in Milan under the general heading, "An Historic Background for Economics."

48 The "Buckshee" poems were included in *New English Poems: A Miscellany of Contemporary Verse Never Before Published,* put together by Lascelles Abercrombie.

49 Presumably Robert McAlmon who had written several pieces with American subjects, among them, *Village: As It Happened Through a Fifteen Year Period* (1924).

50 *P 34* was enclosed with this letter.

51 *F Letters* erroneously indicates the place of writing as Toulon.

52 Jack Kahane, publisher of the Obelisk Press in Paris; in 1933 he brought out an edition of Milton's "Lycidas."

53 T. E. Lawrence's translation of the *Odyssey* was published in 1935.

54 The Aquila Press (London) had planned to publish Pound's edition of the works of Guido Cavalcanti, but the venture had to be abandoned because the Press went bankrupt. Pound had a volume of Cavalcanti's poems (with some translations and commentary) printed in Genoa in 1932. Part of the book consisted of sheets completed by the Aquila Press.

55 Hugues Salel (*c.* 1504–53), French translator of Homer; Arthur Golding (1536?–1605?), English translator of Ovid's *Metamorphoses.*
56 *A Draft of the Cantos 17–27,* published in September 1928.
57 *ABC of Economics* was published by Faber and Faber on 16 April.
58 E. E. Cummings' *Eimi* appeared on 28 March 1933.—Other Americans mentioned in this letter are: Katherine Anne Porter's husband Eugene Pressly; Walter Lowenfels, poet, playwright, and newspaperman, publisher of the Carrefour press in Paris; and Peter Blume, an American painter.
59 Retained carbon copy at Cornell.
60 Herbert Clarke, British printer in Paris; shortly before his death he had gone into partnership with publisher Kahane.
61 Liveright published an American edition of *Jefferson and/or Mussolini.*
62 Pound may be referring to the lectures he gave in Milan.
63 The plans for a BBC broadcast of Pound's opera *Cavalcanti* were not realized.
64 *Selected Poems.* Edited with an introduction by T. S. Eliot. London: Faber & Gwyer, 1928.
65 Pound reviewed *The Collected Poems of Harold Monro* in the 23 June 1933 issue of the *Spectator.*
66 Claud Cockburn published *The Week,* a privately circulated newsletter.
67 Oscar Chilesotti (1848–1916), Italian musicologist, edited old music for the lute with modern musical notation.
68 The "Princesse Palatine" referred to was Elisabeth Augusta, wife of Prince (Kurfürst) Karl-Theodor of the Palatinate (Pfalz); Mozart dedicated the six sonatas (Köchel 301–306) to her.
69 *Encyclopédie de la musique et Dictionnaire du Conservatoire* (1914), edited by French musicologists Albert Lavignac and Lionel La Laurencie.
70 F *Letters* prints "[you]" for "the Cantos."
71 René Béhaine, author of *Les Nouveaux Venus* (1908), the first of a series of novels entitled *Histoire d'une société.*—Novelist Léon Daudet, son of Alphonse Daudet.
72 In C. E. Bechhofer Roberts' "Some New Novels," *New English Weekly* (5 October 1933), *The Rash Act* is favorably reviewed.
73 John Holroyd-Reece, British publisher; founded the Albatross Continental Library in 1931 and took over control of the Tauchnitz Editions in 1934.
74 *Last Post* was the last book by Ford that Duckworth published (1928).
75 F *Letters* prints "only" for "duly."
76 Walter Theodore Watts-Dunton (1832–1914)—Ford's snuffling "Pontifex Putnibus"—contributed many literary articles to the *Athenaeum.* He was a kind helper to poets, among them, Swinburne, who stayed in his house at Putney. Ford's memory evidently failed him about having managed to have Pound reviewed in the *Athenaeum.*—Possibly Alfred Egmont Hake, author and journalist (d. 1917).—Presumably Sir Thomas Henry Hall Caine (1853–1931), author of numerous popular novels.
77 These Latin, French, Welsh, and Italian quotations and phrases associate to Horace, Galilei, Juvenal, Benjamin Franklin, Pope Julius II, Tacitus, and

Nicolas Poussin. Starting out with a sigh at the passing of time, they consequently end up with the assertion that "I, too, know a thing or two!" The Welsh phrase (*Gwell angau na chywilydd*) means: "Better death than shame."

78 The first paragraph and a half resemble the opening of Ford's "testimony" on *A Draft of XXX Cantos.*

79 Henri Murger (1822–61), author of *Scènes de la vie de bohème.*

80 Ford had got to know several Southern writers who lived in or visited Greenwich Village.

81 Poggio Bracciolini (1380–1459), Italian writer and papal secretary.

82 The Princesse Edmond de Polignac, the former Winnaretta Singer (daughter of the sewing-machine millionaire), was a patroness of the arts. She helped Stravinsky financially in his early career.

83 The incident occurred at a concert given by Yehudi Menuhin in London in the spring of 1933. Hyperion was a famous race horse, who won several races in 1933, among them the Derby.—The Manet painting that young Winnaretta bought (for 2,000 francs) was *La Lecture* (see Michael de Cossart, *The Food of Love: Princesse Edmond de Polignac [1865–1943] and her Salon,* London: Hamish Hamilton, 1978, p. 16).

84 Possibly the James Douglas (1867–1940) who had once written a very negative review of *Blast* in the *Star* for 23 July 1915. The newspaper Pound abuses may be the *Sunday Express,* edited by Douglas 1920–31. This was one of Lord Beaverbrook's papers.

85 Letter to Arnold Gingrich, 26 July [1934]; Berg Coll. NYPL.

86 13 December [1934]; Yale.

87 References to *ABC of Reading,* pp. 74, 90, 185, 36.

88 Probably Jean Tardieu (b. 1903), poet and playwright. "Bill" may be William Bird.

89 William Young, seventeenth-century British composer, whose work was being revived by the Scottish musicologist William Gillies Whittaker (1876–1944).

90 Probably *Promise to Pay* by R. McNair Wilson.

91 Matthias Weckmann (*c.* 1619–74), one of the leading composers of the North German tradition; Jan Adam Reinken (1623–1722), of Dutch descent, composer of organ music.

C H A P T E R   F I V E

1 *The Life of Ezra Pound,* p. 336.

2 See Norman, *Ezra Pound,* p. 322.

3 Letter to Stanton Campbell, 24 August 1938; quoted in Harvey A74.

4 Roger Bacon (1214?–94), philosopher and scientist.—Isaac Watts (1674–1748), author of *Hymns and Spiritual Songs, Divine Songs for Children,* and other volumes of devotional verse.

5 Probably Howard F. Lowry, general editor and manager of the American branch of the OUP.

6 The collected edition, which Ford eagerly hoped for, never materialized.

7 Ford's salutation approximates the Welsh phrase, *Iach ydych chwi* (literally, "you are well"); a colloquial translation might be "cheerio." I owe this information to Bjørn Braaten.

8 The letter is unsigned; it contains an autograph greeting from Janice Biala to Pound's wife and parents.

9 Francis Turner Palgrave's *The Golden Treasury of the Best Songs and Lyrical Poems in the English Language* was for decades the leading anthology.— Pound's rejoicing at the *Collected Poems* was evidently slightly qualified; in a letter to the editors of the *Globe* (3 November 1936; Hamilton) he exclaimed: "Good GAWD/ Madex Ford with Preface by Benet. !! Waaal; thaaar she blows. If a man has weaknesses." Whether the "weaknesses" belong to poet William Rose Benét or to Ford is not clear.

10 Gladys Bronwym Stern (b. 1890), prolific British novelist, and Hugh Seymour Walpole (1884–1941) can be identified as two of these "inferior" writers; the third is possibly the American novelist and illustrator Mrs. Mary Anna [Hallock] Foote (1847–1938).

11 Silvio Gesell (1862–1930), German economist; Odon Por (b. 1883), Hungarian-Italian economist.

12 Paul Bastid (1892–1974), French politician; Alphonse Chaux (b. 1908), French industrialist; Maurice Edgard Milhaud (1899–1974), Swiss-born economist.

13 On Ford's "LONE whimper," see Pound's " 'We Have Had No Battles.' " In his essay on Laurence Binyon's translation of Dante's *Inferno* Pound applauds the translator's frequent use of monosyllables, suggesting that *De Vulgari Eloquentia* may have "put him on the trail."

14 The clipping on which this "letter" was written was folded once, and the illustrations were on the reverse.

15 Pasted onto the notepaper is a piece of paper with the name and address of Globe Magazines, Inc., Saint Paul, Minn. The brothers J. W. G. Dunn, Jr., and James Taylor Dunn were the editors.

16 The words "apply etc/" are typed right above "seem vurry"; it is unclear where they belong.

17 6 September 1936; F *Letters*, p. 258.

18 Quoted in Arthur Mizener, *The Saddest Story: A Biography of Ford Madox Ford*, New York and Cleveland: World Publishing Company, 1971, p. 425.

19 Quoted in Mizener, *The Saddest Story*, p. 437.

20 "Visiting the Tates," *Sewanee Review*, 67, No. 4 (Autumn 1959), 557–59.

21 Morton Dauwen Zabel succeeded Harriet Monroe as editor of *Poetry*.

22 Presumably Lee Keedick.

23 Professor Nicholas Murray Butler was Chancellor of the American Academy of Arts and Letters 1924–28 and its President 1928–41.

24 Kitasono Katue, editor of the Japanese literary magazine *Vou*.

25 Formerly in the Biala Collection at Cornell.

26 Ford's "The Sad State of Publishing" appeared in the August number of *Forum;* the issue for September carried his article on "The Fate of the

Semi-Classic," in which he boomed William Carlos Williams, Edward Dahl-
berg, and E. E. Cummings.

27 Emended as in F *Letters.*

28 "Kerensky" was not just a private code name for Mussolini; Wyndham
Lewis, in *Blasting and Bombardiering* (London: Calder and Boyars Ltd.,
1967, p. 232), writes that "people in London used to discuss Mussolini and
dismiss him as 'the Kerensky of the Italian Revolution' [. . .] ."

29 The rue de Seine address is typed above the date.

30 This somewhat opaque (Cockney?) wordplay seems to translate a "sock"
into the number six. Pound typed "Senenth."

31 Reference to Ford's *The Cinque Ports* (1900).

32 Pound was organizing Purcell concerts for his "muzikfest" in the first week
of February 1938.

33 "Reorganize Your Dead Universities," *Delphian Quarterly,* 21, No. 2 (April
1938), 20–22, 28.

34 *Confucius: Digest of the Analects. Guide to Kulchur* was about to come
out later in 1938.

35 It. *raccomandato,* "special delivery."

36 Cf. my article, "Letters from Ezra Pound to Joseph Brewer," *Paideuma,* 10,
No. 2 (Fall 1981), 369–82.

37 *Authors Take Sides on the Spanish War,* London: Left Review, 1937.

38 Letters to the editors of the *Daily Mail* and the *Daily Telegraph,* ante 6
March 1933 and 13 March 1933, respectively.—Letter to Jenny Bradley,
18 December 1933.—Letter to Albert H. Gross, 7 December 1938. Carbon
copies at Cornell.

39 Cf. Mizener, *The Saddest Story,* p. 599.

40 Dinah Maria Mulock Craik (1826–87), author of *John Halifax, Gentleman*
(1857), a British version of the Horatio Alger story of success.

41 Ford most certainly meant April.

42 Louis de Rothschild was arrested when the Nazis entered Vienna in March
1938.

43 Author of *Two Plays of the Social Comedy* (1935), containing *The Age of
Gold* and *The Great and the Small.*

44 Charles Everett Rush, Associate Librarian at Yale University 1931–38.

45 John Atkinson Hobson (1858–1940), British economist, whose *Imperial-
ism: A Study* (1st edn. 1902) influenced Marxist thinkers. Lenin's *Im-
perialism: The Highest State of Capitalism* was published in 1916.

46 "Pere Noé" is Pound's version of François Villon's "Ballade et Oraison"
("Pere Noé, qui plantastes la vigne").

47 "A la vi, jaloux" occurs in the chorus of Pound's poem "La Regine
Avrillouse." It means, in Pound's drastic translation, "Get out, you blithering cuckold" (quoted in R. Murray Schafer, ed., *Ezra Pound and Music:
The Complete Criticism,* New York: New Directions, 1977; London: Faber
and Faber, 1978, p. 396).

48 Mitchell Kennerley, English-born publisher. Ford had tried to get Victor
Gollancz to bring out an English edition of *A Draft of XXX Cantos.*

49 The New Directions issue of *Guide to Kulchur* (under the title *Culture*)
had just come out. Young James Laughlin had met Pound in 1934.

50 Sir Henry Newbolt (1862–1938), well-established man of letters, was among those who—surprisingly—welcomed the new poetry. Newbolt appears in the "Lordly men are to earth o'ergiven" passage in Canto LXXIV.

51 Letters to Michael Roberts, July 1937; P *Letters;* and William Carlos Williams, 24 January 1937; Yale, respectively.

52 Quoted in Harvey E881.

53 George Dillon was editor of *Poetry* 1937–49.

54 Pound tried to get *The March of Literature* reviewed in *Broletto,* a literary magazine published in Como, Italy.

55 "The Dean in Exile: Notes on Ford Madox Ford as Teacher," p. 44.

56 See letter to Joseph Brewer, 17 February 1939; Cornell (carbon).

57 See letter to E. E. Cummings, 13 November [1946]; Harvard.

58 Bernard Mannes Baruch acted as adviser to several American presidents, among them Franklin D. Roosevelt.

59 Written in longhand in the lower righthand corner of Pound's page one.

60 As a young man John Adams was a member of an informal "sodality" whose purpose was to study law and oratory.

61 William Lyon Phelps (1865–1943) and Wilbur Lucius Cross (1862–1948), American educators.

62 I am particularly indebted to Stock's biography for information about Pound's life and thinking during the late 1930s.

63 F *Letters,* p. 319.

64 Quoted in Norman, *Ezra Pound,* p. 363.

65 See *The Selected Letters of William Carlos Williams,* p. 177.

66 From "Immortality: An Elegy on a Great Poet Dying Abroad," *Chapbook,* 3 (July 1920), 20–24; quoted from Harvey D280.

67 Pound's letter to Stella Bowen is at Cornell; for his letter to Brewer, see my "Letters from Ezra Pound to Joseph Brewer."

68 18 July 1939; Yale.

69 18 October 1939; copied from Paige's transcript (carbon copy at Yale).

70 P *Letters,* p. 323. As printed here a few alterations have been made in agreement with the original letter (Cornell).—"The Possum" was Pound's name for Eliot.

71 Monsignor Pisani; see P *Letters,* p. 278.

72 For this note which was to go "on the back of an envelope," cf. a similar remark in Pound's (1924?) "Inquest" notes.

E P I L O G U E

1 P *Letters,* pp. 328, 348.

2 "A Visiting Card," in *Impact: Essays on Ignorance and the Decline of American Civilization,* ed. Noel Stock, Chicago: Henry Regnery Company, 1960, p. 57.—*"Ezra Pound Speaking": Radio Speeches of World War II,* pp. 8, 55, and 137, respectively.

3 17 December 1945; 4 March [1946]; and p.m. 25 January 1946, respectively; Harvard.—[Ante 25 April 1946] Cornell.

4 Letters to Cummings, 4 March [1946] and 13 November [1946], respectively;
   Harvard.

5 9 Ag [1940s?], 24–5 Ag [1940s?] and 10 Lug [1940s?]; Yale. These letters
   were written at St. Elizabeths. I have tentatively dated them the 1940s,
   rather than the 1950s, because their contents resemble those of other letters
   of the period.

6 4 August 1939; Paige.

7 Norman, *Ezra Pound*, p. 432.—May Sinclair died in 1946, and it seems
   likely that Pound made the list shortly after.

8 *Charles Olson & Ezra Pound: An Encounter at St. Elizabeths*, ed. Catherine
   Seelye, New York: Grossman Publishers, p. 58. Quotations from Olson's
   notes appear here as edited by Seelye (with the omission of her endnote
   numbers), but with a few editorial explanations added. References are made
   to pages 58, 71, 84, 85, 86, 89, 97, 107, 111, and 135.—Katherine Proctor
   visited Pound in the District of Columbia jail.

9 Letter of 16 November [1954?]; Yale. The year is here conjectured on the
   basis of a letter from Pound to Wyndham Lewis, dated 19 November 1954;
   Cornell.

10 Letter of 22 August [1947]; Cornell. The other letters quoted from were
   written on 22 July [1947] and 16 September [1947].

11 16 March 1947; Hamilton.

12 Letter to Wyndham Lewis, 6 April 1948; *The Letters of Wyndham Lewis*,
   p. 441, n.2.

13 Probably a reference to the great literary figures Ford had been writing
   about. In a letter to William Carlos Williams (12 Maggio [1956?]; Yale)
   Pound makes reference to "Fordie's Two Giants," presumably James and
   Conrad, to each of whom Ford devoted a book. In a preliminary announce-
   ment heralding the appearance of the *Transatlantic Review* Ford mentioned
   the "young giants" that he hoped to launch (see Goldring, *South Lodge*,
   p. 145).

14 *Ezra Pound's Kensington*, p. 104.

15 "Pictures of Ezra Pound," *Nimbus*, 3, No. 4 (Winter 1956), 24–32; quoted
   matter on pp. 31, 32. Goacher's "pictures" are a composite of memories
   from his visit and things read.

16 *Shenandoah*, 24, No. 3 (Spring 1973), 3–14; quoted matter on pp. 11, 12.

17 Cf. Pound's obituary of Ford, where he asserts the opposite view.

18 "Ezra Pound: An Interview," *Paris Review*, 28 (Summer/Fall 1962), 22–
   51; quoted matter on pp. 29, 30, 33, 34, 36.—Cf. also Pound's remarks on
   Ford which occur passim in Appendix I of *Confucius to Cummings: An
   Anthology of Poetry*, edited by Ezra Pound and Marcella Spann, New York:
   New Directions, 1964.

19 *Ezra Pound: A Close Up*, New York, etc.: McGraw-Hill Book Company,
   [1967] 1973, pp. 151, 156.

List of Works Quoted

Note: Only works by Pound and Ford are included in this list. Bibliographical information on other works quoted is to be found in the text and the notes.

W O R K S   B Y   P O U N D

ABC of Reading. London: Faber and Faber, 1951. Norfolk, Connecticut: New Directions. New Classics Series No. 30, 1951. First edition: London: Routledge & Sons, 1934.

Active Anthology. Ed. Ezra Pound. London: Faber and Faber, 1933.

"Affirmations . . . VI. Analysis of This Decade." *The New Age,* 16, No. 15 (11 February, 1915), 409–11. Reprinted in *Gaudier-Brzeska.*

"Appunti: 'Return to Yesterday.' Memorie di Ford Madox (Hueffer) Ford" [1931], unpublished; see "Notes: 'Return to Yesterday.' Memoirs of Ford Madox (Hueffer) Ford."

"An Autobiographical Outline (Written for Louis Untermeyer)." *Paris Review,* 28 (Summer-Fall 1962), 18–21.

"Beneath the sagging roof." Section X of *Hugh Selwyn Mauberley.* Reprinted in *Personæ.*

"The Book of the Month. *High Germany.* By Ford Madox Hueffer." *Poetry Review,* 1, No. 3 (March 1912), 133.

The Cantos. Rev. ed., third printing. New York: New Directions, 1972. London: Faber and Faber, 1975.

" 'Dubliners' and Mr James Joyce." *The Egoist,* 1, No. 14 (15 July 1914), 267. Reprinted in *Literary Essays.*

"Editorial Comment. Status Rerum." *Poetry,* 1, No. 4 (January 1913), 123–27.

Ezra Pound and Music: The Complete Criticism. Ed. R. Murray Schafer. London: Faber and Faber, 1977. New York: New Directions, 1977.

"Ezra Pound Speaking": Radio Speeches of World War II. Ed. Leonard W. Doob. Westport, Connecticut: Greenwood Press, 1978.

"Ford Madox Hueffer." *New Freewoman,* 1, No. 13 (15 December 1913), 251.

"Ford Madox (Hueffer) Ford; Obit." *Nineteenth Century and After,* 126, No. 750 (August 1939), 178–81. Reprinted in *Selected Prose 1909–1965.*

Gaudier-Brzeska: A Memoir. New York: New Directions, 1970. First edition: London: John Lane, 1916.

"Harold Monro." *The Criterion,* 11, No. 45 (July 1932), 581–92.

"How I Began." *T. P.'s Weekly,* 21, No. 552 (6 June 1913), 707.

How to Read. London: Desmond Harmsworth, 1931. Reprinted in *Literary Essays.*

"Hudson: Poet Strayed into Science." *The Little Review,* 7, No. 1 (May-June 1920), 13–17. Reprinted in *Selected Prose 1909–1965.*

"Hueffer." *Future,* 2, No. 8 (July 1918), 210.

Hugh Selwyn Mauberley. London: The Ovid Press, 1920. Reprinted in *Personæ.*

Impact: Essays on Ignorance and the Decline of American Civilization. Ed. Noel Stock. Chicago: Henry Regnery Company, 1960.

"[The Inquest]" [1924?], previously unpublished notes.

"The Inquest, and other, in varying degrees neglected, writings" [1926], previously unpublished notes.

"James Joyce et Pécuchet." *Mercure de France,* 156, No. 575 (1 June 1922), 307–20. Reprinted in *Pound/Joyce,* ed. Forrest Read.

Letter to the Editor [signed "Old Glory"]. *Transatlantic Review,* 1, No. 6 (June 1924), 480.

Literary Essays. Ed. T. S. Eliot. New York: New Directions, 1968. First edition: London: Faber and Faber, 1954.

"Madox Ford at Rapallo: A Conversation between Ford Madox Ford and Ezra Pound." *Western Review,* 12, No. 1 (Autumn 1947), 17–18. Reprinted in *Pavannes and Divagations.*

"Mr Hueffer and the Prose Tradition in Verse." *Poetry,* 4, No. 3 (June 1914), 111–20. Reprinted as "The Prose Tradition in Verse" in *Literary Essays.*

"Notes: 'Return to Yesterday.' Memoirs of Ford Madox (Hueffer) Ford," previously unpublished essay. Transl. Brita Lindberg-Seyersted.

"On Criticism in General." *The Criterion,* 1, No. 2 (January 1923), 143–56.

Pavannes and Divagations. Norfolk, Connecticut: New Directions, 1958. London: Peter Owen, 1960.

Personæ: The Collected Shorter Poems of Ezra Pound. New York: New Directions, 1949. London: Faber and Faber, 1952.

Polite Essays. London: Faber and Faber, 1937. Norfolk, Connecticut: New Directions, 1940.

Pound/Joyce. The Letters of Ezra Pound to James Joyce, with Pound's Essays on Joyce. Ed. Forrest Read. New York: New Directions, 1967. London: Faber and Faber, 1969.

"Praefatio, aut tumulus cimicium." Preface to *Active Anthology,* ed. Ezra Pound. Reprinted as "Prefatio Aut Cimicium Tumulus" in *Selected Prose 1909–1965.*

Profile: An Anthology Collected in MCMXXXI. Ed. Ezra Pound. Milan: Giovanni Scheiwiller, 1932.

"A Retrospect." In *Pavannes and Divisions.* New York: Alfred A. Knopf, 1918. Reprinted in *Literary Essays.*

The Selected Letters of Ezra Pound 1907–1941. Ed. D. D. Paige. London: Faber and Faber, 1971. Originally published as *The Letters of Ezra Pound 1907–1941.* New York: Harcourt, Brace and Company, 1950. Paperbook reissue: New York: New Directions, 1971. New Directions Paperbook 317.

Selected Prose 1909–1965. Ed. William Cookson. London: Faber and Faber, 1973. New York: New Directions, 1973.

The Sonnets and Ballate of Guido Cavalcanti. Transl. Ezra Pound. Boston: Small, Maynard and Company, 1912.

"This Hulme Business." *Townsman,* 2, No. 5 (January 1939), 15.

"A Visiting Card." In *Impact: Essays on Ignorance and the Decline of American Civilization,* ed. Noel Stock.

W O R K S   B Y   F O R D

Buckshee. Cambridge, Massachusetts: Pym-Randall Press, 1966.

"Canzone À La Sonata. To E. P." In *High Germany.* London: Duckworth & Co., 1912. Reprinted in *Selected Poems.*

Collected Poems. London: Max Goschen, 1913.

"Communications." *Transatlantic Review,* 1, No. 6 (June 1924), 480.

Critical Writings of Ford Madox Ford. Ed. Frank MacShane. Lincoln: University of Nebraska Press, 1964.

Editorial. *Transatlantic Review,* 2, No. 6 (December 1924), 682–86.

"Editor's Note" [signed D. C.] . In *The Cantos of Ezra Pound: Some Testimonies.* New York: Farrar & Rinehart, 1933.

"Ezra." *New York Herald Tribune Books,* 9 January 1927, Section VII, pp. 1, 6.

"Fleuve Profond." In *New English Poems.* Ed. Lascelles Abercrombie. London: Victor Gollancz, 1931. Reprinted in *Collected Poems,* 1936, and in *Buckshee,* 1966.

"From China to Peru." *Outlook,* 35 (19 June 1915), 800–01.

"From Ford Madox Ford." In *The Cantos of Ezra Pound: Some Testimonies.* New York: Farrar & Rinehart, 1933.

"Immortality: An Elegy on a Great Poet Dying Abroad." *Chapbook,* 3 (July 1920), 20–24. Reprinted in David Dow Harvey, *Ford Madox Ford 1873–1939: A Bibliography of Works and Criticism.* Princeton, N.J.: Princeton University Press, 1962.

"Impressionism—Some Speculations," *Poetry,* 2, No. 5 (August 1913), 177–87. Reprinted in *Critical Writings of Ford Madox Ford.*

Letters of Ford Madox Ford. Ed. Richard M. Ludwig. Princeton, N.J.: Princeton University Press, 1965.

"Literary Portraits—XLIII. Mr. Wyndham Lewis and 'Blast.' " *Outlook,* 34 (4 July 1914), 15–16.

The March of Literature from Confucius' Day to Our Own. New York: The Dial Press, 1938. London: Allen and Unwin, 1939.

"Mediterranean Reverie." *Week-End Review,* 8 (11 November 1933), 495–96.

"The Poet's Eye." *New Freewoman,* 1, No. 7 (15 September 1913), 126–27.

Portraits from Life: Memories and Criticisms. Boston, New York: Houghton Mifflin Company, 1937.

"Pound and 'How to Read.' " *The New Review,* 2, No. 5 (April 1932), 39–45.

Reminiscences 1894–1914: Return to Yesterday. London: Victor Gollancz, 1931. First American edition: *Return to Yesterday.* New York: Horace Liveright, 1932; reprinted 1972 in a paperback edition.

Return to Yesterday, see *Reminiscences 1894–1914: Return to Yesterday.*

Selected Poems. Ed. Basil Bunting. Cambridge, Massachusetts: Pym-Randall Press, 1971.

"Some Expatriates" [1926], previously unpublished essay.

"Thus to Revisit . . . V. Combien je regrette . . ." *The Dial,* 69, No. 3 (September 1920), 239–46.

"Thus to Revisit . . . . . . IV. —New Forms for the Old." *Piccadilly Review* (13 November 1919), p. 6.

Thus to Revisit: Some Reminiscences. London: Chapman & Hall, 1921.

Index